ADVENTURES
IN
ANGLOTOPIA

Other books by Jonathan Thomas

Anglotopia's Dictionary of British English
101 London Travel Tips
101 Budget Britain Travel Tips

Adventures in Anglotopia

The Makings of An Anglophile

By Jonathan Thomas

To My Wife Jackie
The Only One I Love More Than England
Yes, really.

I will not cease from Mental Fight,
Nor shall my Sword sleep in my hand:
Till we have built Jerusalem,
In Englands green & pleasant Land.

Jerusalem - William Blake 1804

Table of Contents

INTRODUCTION

I was standing in front of Buckingham Palace the day before the Royal Wedding (the one for Prince William). It was a surreal moment. I was in my best suit, standing in front of a BBC camera, I was about to be interviewed by a BBC presenter I had seen on TV countless times. I was suitably nervous. This interview was the whole reason I came to cover the Royal Wedding. Running Anglotopia at this stage, I rarely left the basement; that's the joy of running a home-based business. Now, I was in front of the world. It was an opportunity I didn't want to squander.

There was a 'pre-interview' before the actual interview started. Then, *the* question was asked.

"Why are you such an Anglophile?" he asked, or a variation of that. It was a long time ago.

Why, indeed?

It's a question I've thought a lot about. I almost choked when it was my moment to answer; I'm sure I rattled something off quickly that didn't really answer the question. It's a question I've been seeking the answer to ever since I started Anglotopia in a closet in Chicago in 2007. Why do I love Britain so much? Why am I obsessed with a country that is not my own—a place I don't live, a place in which I don't have any immediate physical or familial connection? If I got the phone call tomorrow that I could move to Britain, why would I do it at the drop of a hat?

In almost every interview I've had over the years, I've been asked this question. When we meet Brits in person, they wonder the same thing. It's such a curious thing to them that someone could love their country so much. I get at least one email or online comment every week from someone wondering the same thing. It's a good question, but I've never really had a good answer for it.

When I was pondering what type of book I wanted to write, I settled pretty quickly on answering this one question. Coming up with an answer would not be easy. I would have to peer back deeply into my own past, before and after I started Anglotopia. I would have to find nuggets along a trail that weaved through my entire life and encompassed almost all the trips I've taken to Britain over the last

1

twenty years. At last, I finally have an answer.

The journey starts in a classroom in Indiana in the late '90s. When I walked into my seventh grade geography class and saw the TV, I was thrilled. It was a cold winter day, just a few days before we were supposed to go on Christmas Break. Our minds were already on Christmas, and we had no desire to learn about the geographical issues facing the Indonesian islands. A TV in the room meant one thing: we would be watching a movie that day — what a relief. We could just sit back and watch the movie.

But Mr. Milakovic did things a bit different. Rather than turn the movie on and return to his desk to do whatever it is he would rather be doing, presumably not teaching a bunch of ungrateful white kids about geography and instead planning a canoe trip through the Isle Royale in Lake Superior, he made us earn our movie. We had to fill out a worksheet with questions so specific, it would ensure we had to pay attention to every line in the movie. I'm grateful for this teaching strategy because it forced me to pay attention to the film. And it turned out that the film we watched that day, *The Empire of the Sun*, would become one of my favorite movies – and, consequently, provide the nugget of Anglophilia that I have today.

I knew nothing about the film. It had an alluring title. Mr. Milakovic introduced it to us quickly, telling us that it was a film about a little boy, about our age, surviving a time of war. I had heard of World War II by that point. How could I not even in the woefully inadequate US education system? But I had no idea *The Empire of the Sun* would personalize it, and put it in a context that would lead to a lifelong fascination with World War II and all things British.

I listened to every line in that film with great interest. Class was only forty-five minutes long, so it took us most of the week to get through it all, and I was excited every day to go to school and finish it. During Christmas break, I begged my mum to rent the movie from the video store (this was the late '90s, they still existed) and I watched it again with her.

The Empire of the Sun is a Steven Spielberg directed film (I consider *The Empire of the Sun*, *Schindler's List* and *Saving Private Ryan* to be the perfect unofficial trilogy about World War II) about a little British boy called Jamie (Christian Bale), living in China with his imperialist family, getting caught up in the Japanese invasion of China, and subsequently the greater events of World War II. He gets separated from his parents and lives on his own for a while, before befriending a couple of Americans (John Malkovich and Joe Pantoliano) and ending up in a Japanese Concentration Camp. He's ignorant of the world and, in fact, has a lot of respect for the Japanese and their amazing airplanes. The adults around him struggle to cope with the depredations of war, while he comes of age in a time of suffering with a childlike wonderment at everything happening around him.

It must have been a bizarre world to live in. This boy lives in China, but he might as well have been living in Surrey. Their house was English. Their furnishings were English (with a dash of the Far East). Their food was English. Their car was English. His education was English. Their attitudes were English — post-Victorian Imperialist, to be exact. In the first act of the movie, he only sees glimpses of the country he really lives in and notices things aren't quite right. War is looming.

Jamie has spent his whole life in China, but he's British. Yet, Britain is a foreign place to him.

"I'm English, but I've never been there," he says.

That line spoke to me, and it still speaks to me. For a large part of my childhood and teenage years, I loved England, but I wasn't English, and I'd never been there. Why?

I found, as I was writing this book, that I kept looking for a single event that led to me becoming an Anglophile. But there wasn't a single one. It was the culmination of many events. British culture was everywhere in my childhood, often in the background. It was Roald Dahl books that I loved. It was British TV shows on PBS late at night. It was the classical music I liked. It was the history I devoured. It was popular culture with the Beatles and other British bands who were popular in America. It was Patrick Stewart and Marina Sirtis in *Star Trek: The Next Generation*. I'm an Anglophile because Britain's biggest "soft-power" is its culture, and its, admittedly superior, culture is simply everywhere.

I grew up with Roald Dahl books. They were everywhere in school, and the '90s were the heyday of his books being turned into films. I read all of them. But here's the thing: young me didn't realize they were British. I just really enjoyed the books. I remember reading the description of the teacher's cottage in Mathilda and falling in love with the idea of that. It turns out it was an English cottage in the English countryside. His books were dark and twisted, but as I child, I

3

loved them, which was strange because I had a perfectly fine and well-adjusted childhood. What, exactly, was the attraction of reading about fellow children in horrible situations?

However, by far my favorite Dahl books were the two he wrote about his own life. They were the first autobiographies I ever read. He wrote them for children, and they were a joy to read. I loved hearing about his British childhood before the war. I wanted it. I even liked the idea of his boarding school. These were the days before Harry Potter when all the fans wanted to go to a British boarding school. I liked them before they were cool. I remember being so enraptured by *Boy* that I read it at home, then read it in the car on the way to my family's holiday cottage by a lake in Michigan, then did nothing but read the entire book until I was finished. I don't remember anything from that weekend by the lake other than reading that book. When I got home, I remember begging to go to the bookstore at the now-demolished Century Mall to order the sequel because you couldn't find it locally. These were the days before Amazon. I was so excited when they called to tell me the book had arrived.

When I reread the book last year in preparation for writing this book, I was immediately taken back to the bunk bed in that lakeside cottage, enraptured by Dahl's descriptions of his British childhood. It was like visiting an old friend, and I was surprised at how much I remembered. I was made an Anglophile before I even knew what an Anglophile was.

And that's what I realized writing this book. There was something in my personality that was predisposed to the enjoyment of English and British things. Still, it was stoked by the fact that the British (and its sub-cultures) were and are everywhere in American media, history, and life. You don't really notice them until they're pointed out by the British. Iced tea is a favorite beverage in America, and while the British fundamentally disagree with the concept of iced tea, we got our love of tea from them (even if we'd bastardized it). Our government, while a uniquely American creation, had its roots in the British parliamentary system.

Britishness is subtle and somewhat insidious in American culture. It's a British villain in a blockbuster film. It's a classic British show, airing late at night on PBS. It's in the speeches you hear or read in history class. Disney may have taken *Winnie the Pooh* and turned it into its own thing but *Winnie the Pooh* is fundamentally British.

4

Its creation and genesis could not be more British. And if you grew up in my generation, Pooh was a critical part of that. The same with Peter Rabbit, another British import that we've begun to just think of as American, even though it's British (the less said about the recent Americanized film adaptation, the better).

When you learn American history in school, they do go back in time and cover the colonization of the USA and how society here developed. It's a very British story, one of a brave people setting out across the vast ocean and populating a foreign and dangerous land (and unfortunately, displacing and killing the existing inhabitants, which is another very British way of doing things). America used to have a King. He's a joke to us, the mad king who let America go. But, he was our King until he wasn't. Then history progresses, and America and Britain become best of friends. We fight side by side in World War I and World War II. These seminal events, which are usually portrayed as being a bigger deals for Britain than us, had a huge effect on Anglo-American relations. There were hundreds of thousands of English war brides. They brought a fresh injection of English culture into the background of American life.

You only have to look at how our media goes crazy when there is a major royal event on. Americans love the Royal Family, a family we rejected. We have no real loyalty to them, but we love watching them get married and have babies and do all the things we expect of royalty. When Princess Diana died, it was almost as if we lost one of our own. Her shadow still looms large over American Anglophilia. Whenever I publish anything on Anglotopia about the Royal Family, inevitably Princess Diana will come up in the comments section. Instead of Godwin's Law (the theory that any internet argument will descend into comparison with the Nazis), we have Diana's Law. We even have similar affections for the Queen, and I expect that when the dark day comes when she's no longer with us, America will mourn hand in hand with Britain. Will our affections transfer to Prince Charles? Who knows.

I especially see it now that I have my own children. They're heavily influenced by British soft power. My daughter's favorite show for many years was *Peppa Pig*, a British cartoon. Some American parents have even claimed their children are watching it so much it gave them British accents (I was not so lucky). Disney may have co-opted princesses and princes, but you can bet my little girl loves hearing about the real ones. The books and movies that were popular when I was a child are still as popular today. And now we have Harry Potter, a British cultural juggernaut, though as much as I've tried, I just can't get my kids into Harry Potter. Maybe when they're older.

British foods are more prevalent now than ever. You can find McVitie's digestives in Wal-Mart now. Finding good British tea (as in tea blended and packaged *in* Britain) is not hard to do. You used to have to order it from abroad. Finding good back bacon or English sausages is easy. American cuisine may be a fusion of many different cultures, but the foundational block is British cooking. Heck, roast turkey on Thanksgiving is a British import! Even the very idea of a "Thanksgiving" meal is British, and let's not forget that the first to celebrate were themselves English. America is a land in search of a native culture that has found it in its British roots.

I would revisit *The Empire of the Sun* every few years after that first time, eventually buying it on Blu-ray when its 25th anniversary happened. As I got older, the film became harder to watch. When I first saw the film, I was Jamie's age. So I identified with him and his fascination with the terrible world around him - and making the best of it. But then I grew up. I went to college. Met my wife, Jackie. Got married. Had kids.

Now, when I watch the film, I watch it in horror. I can't imagine the pain and suffering Jamie's parents went through in the film - being separated from their son for *five years*. My god, I don't even like to be away from my kids for a weekend. The thought of missing five whole years of their lives is almost more horrible than the terrible things Jamie witnesses in the film. Your child would be a stranger.

I also learned more about the author of the original book the film is based on, J.G. Ballard, as I got older. The film portrays Jamie's adventures as if he gets through them rather unscathed. He has depredations, but he's British about it. He grows up faster than he normally would - and there's a poignant scene at the end where we throw his suitcase in the water, essentially jettisoning his childhood. But if you delve into Ballard's other literary works, you understand that he was scarred for life by his experiences. Not only that, he gained a perspective on humanity at its worse.

There's even a word for it now: "Ballardian," meaning a picture of a modern world that alienates the people that live within it. I dare you to watch or read *Crash* or the film *High-Rise* and not think that Ballard had lost all hope on humanity being capable of sensibility.

My son is now nine years old, and he's approaching the age of Jamie in the film. I can't imagine ever showing the film to him. I want to shield him from the horrors of the world, and of its capabilities. I know it's an impossible task, but this film means so much to me.

Through it all, and despite his admiration of American culture presented in the film, Jamie never lost his Britishness. He was stoic in the face of adversity. He was interested in what was happening around him. He was resourceful, still willing to learn his Latin in the middle of a war. Jamie embodied some of the things I loved most about Britain. It's strange that I got all of this from a Hollywood film, produced by Americans, based on a British book. Britishness is in the background. It's always there. We only need to look for it. picture of a modern world that alienates the people that live within it. I dare you to watch or read *Crash* or the film *High-Rise* and not think that Ballard had lost all hope on humanity being capable of sensibility.

My son is now nine years old, and he's approaching the age of Jamie in the film. I can't imagine ever showing the film to him. I want to shield him from the horrors of the world, and of its capabilities. I know it's an impossible task, but this film means so much to me.

Through it all, and despite his admiration of American culture presented in the film, Jamie never lost his Britishness. He was stoic in the face of adversity. He was interested in what was happening around him. He was resourceful, still willing to learn his Latin in the middle of a war. Jamie embodied some of the things I loved most about Britain. It's strange that I got all of this from a Hollywood film, produced by Americans, based on a British book. Britishness is in the background. It's always there. We only need to look for it.

THE FIRST TIME

The first time I visited Britain, I hated it. As a lifelong Anglophile whose entire identity had hinged on discovering Britain in person, this was a bit of a problem. I blame TV and movies for this. This was the age of *Notting Hill* and *Mr. Bean*. I expected London to be like what I'd seen on the screen. Even a show I considered to be as factually accurate and real as possible, Rick Steves' *Europe*, failed to prepare me for the "real" London. There was quite a bit of soul-searching on the trip as I coped with having all my fantasies about London crushed by reality.

My first trip to Britain was a graduation present. Well, really a pre-graduation present. I was going to graduate early from high school in January 2002 and the plan was to go with my mother after that. But, British Airway's direct marketing efforts (as in they sent us brochures in the mail) were so good in early 2001, we ended up going early. They had a deal that was too good to be true and we decided to take it. So, in June 2001, the era before 9/11 and before air travel became much worse, I took my first transatlantic flight to London.

I had one problem, though.

I'd come down with a cold the day before we left.

This meant that I flew with a head cold that was made substantially worse by the journey.

I struggle to sleep on planes, and even with the cold medicine I took, I still failed to sleep. So, I arrived in London feeling like hot garbage and I was unbelievably tired. I was not impressed by Heathrow Airport, which at that stage was still rather run down and rocking a 1970s chic that was showing its age. British Airways had arranged a "free transfer" for us, which meant that we had to wait for a bus to take us to our hotel in London. When it pulled up, it was the strangest bus I'd ever seen, more like a minivan but with room for, like, twenty people. Even the engine sounded different to anything I'd heard before.

"Where you headed, love?" the young driver asked my mom.

"The Corus Hotel on Lancaster Gate," she replied.

"Righty-o, get in!" he said grabbing our bags and putting them in the back of the van. We waited as several more tourists got on the bus and settled in.

The ride into central London was like riding a roller coaster.

You could feel every twist and turn in that bus, which the young man drove like a racecar. I suspected he was being paid by the trip from Heathrow to London and so had to fit in as many stops as possible in a day.

Everything was alien. We spent most of the journey on the motorway and then the Westway. Then we found ourselves driving through Notting Hill and, at that stage, I thought it looked rather run down. Not like the movie at all. We drove through lots of areas that appeared like this. It turns out the area we were staying, Lancaster Gate, was an odd place (at least in 2001), where there were all these beautiful old genteel Georgian buildings, but they were all rundown or poorly maintained. However, when we arrived at our hotel, it looked nice enough from the outside and the lobby seemed okay.

Our flight had made good time over the Atlantic, so we arrived early. But I learned when we arrived at our hotel that this was not a good thing. It was only about 10:00 a.m. and our room was not ready. It wouldn't be ready until around 2:00 p.m. This really confused me. Why would the hotels not be ready for people coming right off transatlantic flights? They made no effort to accommodate us in anyway. So, after we ate some breakfast, we simply camped out in the lobby and waited until our room was ready because we were too tired to do anything else.

And I still felt like garbage.

Eventually our room was ready and we followed a series of elevators and signs through this hotel. It seemed like we were mice in a maze. We opened the door and hit the bed. This is where we learned the first lesson of travel in London that all tourists must learn. Rooms, at least in the tourist hotels, are small. Our window had a view of Hyde Park. Well, sort of. It had a view of Dickensian chimneys with a leafy tree visible beyond.

We barely had room for us and our luggage.

I promptly collapsed on the bed and fell sleep for a nap.

As we explored London over the next few days, I felt like I was in an alien world. Things that were similar to the only other big city I'd been to, Chicago, were slightly off. There were elements that were the same - like plenty of homelessness, beggars, rude people, etc. – but what really shocked me was how grimy London felt. It felt dirty. That's not a word I think anyone would use to describe Downtown

Chicago. Everything was slightly shabby, covered in grime. We had cloudy weather the whole time, and that didn't help either.

People were not nice to us.

Every time I opened my mouth, I felt like I was being judged for being an American.

There were signs everywhere warning you of pickpockets.

There were even children panhandling.

Most of all, it just didn't feel like any of the places I'd seen in movies, and feeling is important. Sure, places looked just like they did on the screen, but they didn't feel like it.

It was the first time I experienced that reality disconnect between movies and real life. How could something not feel like how it made me feel on the screen? Cool Britannia this was not.

As I wandered through London that first time, still fighting off the cold and being quite surly and mean towards my mother, I realized I wasn't falling in love with a place I had staked my personal identity on.

I felt like I was failing as an Anglophile by not loving London as it was.

How should London feel?

Because how it felt to me was not how I thought it should feel.

Everything was slightly...off in London. The people spoke English, but it was a another kind of English that I didn't fully understand. The cars drove on the wrong side of the road. Until I realized they wrote on the street which direction to look, I was honked at quite a few times for looking the wrong way. I went to the movies and had to reserve my seat even though I was the only person in the theater. There were commercials before the movie (this was before this became a thing in America). Books seemed cheap to me, and I only learned much later it's because they don't charge VAT (sales tax) on books. Traveling in London that first time felt like I'd entered a parallel universe where everything was only slightly different.

It was very disconcerting to a boy who'd barely left the Midwestern United States.

Going through my box of mementos from that trip - I keep a box from every trip to Britain I've been on - I found all kinds of strange objects. Apparently, I went to the internet café almost a dozen times. I'm not sure why I did this. I was in London, why was I wasting time on the internet? Probably writing letters home to my crush - letters long since lost to the graveyard of bytes. This was the day before Wi-Fi. If you needed to get access to the internet, you had to do it at an internet café . There are still internet cafés in London, but they're sketchy places now, more a place for terrorists and people who don't want their internet movements tracked. I haven't set foot in one in a decade. There is Wi-Fi and now smartphones everywhere now.

Riding the Tube was a fun experience. Coming from rural Indiana, I found it amazing that you could hop on this train, pay just £1.50, and go anywhere in London. It's more than £1.50 now, and it costs more the further you go, but that's beside the point. I felt like I had the "freedom of the city" to explore, just by purchasing a small little paper ticket.

We did touristy things and visited tourist attractions. That's what you do. We visited Westminster Abbey and the London Eye and walked along the Thames and went to Harrods and did all the things the guidebooks say to do when you go to London for the first time. But it all felt a bit hollow. I was finally achieving my dream of visiting London and I was not getting out of it what I expected. I was not overly impressed by Westminster Abbey and the London Eye and the Thames and Harrods.

What was wrong with me?

Looking back now, I think the real problem was that I was seventeen years old.

I just didn't know any better.

My expectations for myself, for London, and for my poor mother who bore the brunt of my surliness, were simply unfair.

Expectations breed disappointment. My expectations were simply too high.

How could seventeen-year-old me expect to have a complete understanding of London's history, culture, and context? How could I have expected myself to appreciate London's beautiful architecture? How could I have expected so much of myself when I didn't even really know myself?

By the end of the trip, I was starting to finally feel better. I finally started to get a feel for London. My mother, trying desperately to get me to enjoy myself, spotted a classical music concert she knew I would want to go to. It was at the Royal Albert Hall and it was to be a performance of Tchaikovsky's *Violin Concerto*, which was my favorite piece of music. She was brave and made a phone call to the box office and reserved the last available seats for us.

We went to the show and it was lovely. I'd never seen the Royal Albert Hall before. I had no context for how important the building was. Looking back, that was the problem, really. I had no context for anything. You can only get context for London by being in London. Nothing else can give you that context. As I sat there and took in the music and listened intently as my favorite piece was played, I realized that I was in one of those perfect moments in life.

As the violinist furiously played a piece pronounced "unplayable" by the first violinist to see the score after Thchaikovsky wrote it, I realized that London was beautiful. I'd just been looking at it in the completely wrong way. After the concert, we couldn't get a cab and struggled to get back to our hotel. Frankly, we had one of our scariest experiences in London. But, I was finally in love with London.

The only problem was that the trip was now over. I had no more time. I'd squandered that first trip. As I left London, I was sad because it was over, but I was actually upset because I'd lost the London I'd longed to visit for so long. However, I'd discovered what London really was and what it really meant to me. It wasn't a perfect city. It was grimy and cold (in culture and in temperature). Some neighborhoods had seen better days. It was filled with tourists and tourist attractions. It feels like a foreign place. I learned it's the imperfections that can make you love a thing. True love is loving something despite its imperfections. As my plane took off on that fateful trip, I couldn't wait to go back. When I visited again in 2004, this time with the love of my life, I could see the city through new eyes, and firmly fall in love with London properly. I've been discovering the real London ever since. It's more brilliant than any TV or movie could paint. I hated London on my first trip, but I couldn't wait to go back.

NOTES FROM A WILTSHIRE PUB

There is a pub. It's called Moon Under Water. It's an old Victorian place. If smoking was still allowed, it would be smoky and reek of tobacco and spilt beer. The tables are hardwood, no glass surfaces, soaked in centuries of alcohol. There are roof beams, low ceilings, a fire going in the hearth. There may be a dog wandering around. There's probably a dead animal over the mantle, covered in dust. The pub is always quiet enough to talk to your companions. The food is serviceable but you don't go there for the food. There isn't a TV, radio, or a piano. This is a place for drinking and socializing.

If this pub sounds familiar, that's probably because it doesn't exist; yet, it fits the stereotypes we all imagine pubs have. These points were actually set out by George Orwell in a classic essay about the Great British Institution that is the pub. His point was the Moon Under Water cannot possibly exist anymore. But we would all like it to. Despite classic pubs having gone the way of the dodo, pubs still play a critical role in the cultural life of Britain. Moon Under Water now exists in the minds of Britons, and every pub across the land is trying to capture the feeling that Orwell lays out.

Romance is a key part of finding a pub. More often than not, the vibe a pub gives off is the vibe that you bring with you. We have found our own Moon Under Water and came across it almost by accident, which is the best way to discover your favorite pub.

We arrived promptly at our booked time for Sunday Roast on a rainy afternoon. You must always book ahead for the best Sunday Roasts. The waiter showed us to our table, rickety and old with two very high pew-like seats. The pub was dark, and it was noisy with the Sunday Roast atmosphere in full swing. A Christmas tree twinkled in the corner. Children played while the large group of parents chatted about life. A fire crackled in both fireplaces. A black lab wandered around, hoping a scrap would fall on the floor. It was paradise.

The first task of any wayward Anglophile traveler when they visit England should be to find the perfect country pub. Don't believe the headlines that all the good pubs are closing. While there are certainly pubs closing in great numbers, the attrition rate is no worse than most other businesses. There are still over 52,000 pubs in Britain according to the Campaign for Real Ale, an organization that advocates for pubs. I once saw a Google Map of all the pubs in Britain, and it was hilarious because it was essentially on giant red Google Map location point. There are plenty of pubs in Britain and plenty of beautiful country pubs to discover. It's important to find one.

Finding the right pub is like finding a friend, it takes work, and sometimes the chemistry has to be just right. After 20 years of travel in Britain, we finally found our perfect pub, deep in the Wiltshire Countryside.

We've been to lots of pubs in our travels. Some are terrible. Some are no better than a chain restaurant. Some you can't leave quick enough. Pubs can be very hit or miss. But the best pubs, in my humble opinion, are country pubs. They're fundamentally different than a pub you'd find in London or a smaller city. Often, the pub is the only piece of community for miles around. It's a gathering place for locals, but it casts a wider net. A good country pub will also attract outsiders and become a crossroads of sorts for weekend travelers.

Many country pubs find themselves along public rights of way, so they cater to walkers who plan their walks to include a good pub along the way. This is a critical task when planning a long day of walking in the English countryside. One must stop for a pint and a meal at your halfway point (or tea if you're teetotal like me). So, country pubs are often a hive of outside interlopers and locals angling for a space at the bar. Many will have places to sit outside, some with expansive views of the English Countryside.

A country pub lives or dies based on its food. While a pub can survive if it has decent beer on tap, it will not survive if the food is terrible. In the days of Yelp and TripAdvisor, a pub with bad food simply cannot last. When someone plans their weekend around stopping at a country pub for the atmosphere and the food, you can bet they're going to expect a certain standard of quality in the food.

The best pubs are ridiculously hard to find. Our new favorite in Wiltshire was impossible for our car's SatNav to locate. This was a problem since it was night and the back lanes leading to this pub were pitch dark and single track.

When you rely on the SatNav to get you anywhere in England, there's always a good chance it won't get you there. In fact, you can end up in an unexpected body of water or at the end of a dead-end lane. As our car led us through the dark to the country pub we had never visited before, we got increasingly worried as the country track got narrower and narrower and the lights of civilization got darker and darker.

And then our SatNav told us we'd reached our destination and that we needed to get out of our car and walk the rest of the way. As this was in the middle of the road with nowhere to park and no sign of any human activity, we were pretty sure our car took us on a wild pub chase. Our GPS guide, we agreed, was taking the piss.

We drove on and a half a mile later, civilization suddenly reappeared, and we found our pub, lit up in the night like a beacon in the darkness. We parked the car, laughed that the SatNav yet again almost led us astray, and marveled at the picturesque country pub in front of us.

When we read the description in the guidebook provided by the cottage we were staying in, we knew we had to pay a visit for dinner: "Wonderfully sourced and cooked local food in unpretentious flagstoned, low-beamed old pub complete with wood-burning stove. A real find!" The romance of the place oozed from the page.

Of course, I've been to many pubs in my travels, but I have a major problem. I don't drink. Ever. I'm as teetotal as a Victorian temperance innkeeper. I can't stand the taste of alcoholic drinks - wine, beer, spirits. I detest it all. And I have tried many. I wanted to like alcoholic drinks, mostly because social drinking is a big part of British culture.

Turning twenty-one in America is usually a big deal. It signifies one major life change: you can now legally drink alcohol. And gamble. But alcohol is the big one. I was never really interested in alcohol, but felt the occasion of my twenty-first birthday elicited at least one drink. By this point in my life, I'd been to Britain three times. Each of those times, I could have taken a drink if I'd wanted one. I'd been to enough pubs. I just wasn't interested.

But when it came time for my twenty-first, Jackie came up with the best idea.

"Why don't we go up to that English pub on the North side of Chicago?" she said.

So that's what we did. We lived about ninety minutes outside of Chicago, so a trek into the city was a big deal. We'd heard about this pub. It was supposedly the best English pub in the Midwest. The Red Lion was run by a tried and true Englishman. According to online reviews, it was decorated just as an English pub would be in London and served typically English fare like fish and chips and bangers and mash, as well as having English brews on tap.

It was also supposedly haunted.

We arrived in the afternoon, and it became clear that we were the only people there. Just us and the publican, who was indeed English. It was dark and smoky like you would expect to find a pub in England. It was like the proprietor had read Orwell's essay on the Moon Under Water and constructed a faux pub to match. There were typically English prints decorating the walls - Nelson at Trafalgar, pictures of the 1966 World Cup, and various other bits of English ephemera, undoubtedly found in an antique mall somewhere in the Midwest. The publican told us how the bar itself came from England and was original. The seats looked like they were taken right out of an episode of *Inspector Morse*, with high backs and hardwood.

I knew nothing about beer. I still don't. So, the publican suggested one and I said that'd be fine.

We sat down and ordered lunch. Being in "full English" mode, I ordered fish and chips to go with my beer.

I liked that place. It really did feel a bit English, though it was easy to see that it was making a good imitation at being English. It was definitely the most "authentic" British pub I've been to in the USA. Most are dreadfully un-British; a Union Jack over the bar and Newcastle Ale on tap isn't what makes a British pub.

My beer arrived, and it was the moment of truth. It was a pint, a whole pint of Newcastle Brown Ale. I took a sip.

It was vile.

I practically spit it out.

"Beer is an acquired taste," said Jackie trying to suppress her laughter.

I truly hated it but thought the more I tried it, the more I might like it.

I never liked it.

The fish and chips came, and I ordered a Sprite to wash it down. The fish and chips were very good but not authentic - fish strips and fuzzy fries are nowhere in the cricket pitch of authenticity (it should be one slab of fish and CHUNKY CHIPS).

So, we'd traveled all the way to Chicago. I hated the beer. The food wasn't great. But the pub was lovely. We never encountered the ghost, only my true distaste for alcohol. The pub is no longer there (though the name Red Lion lives on in other Chicago bars), and I sort of miss it.

That was back in 2005. I still hate beer (I've tried several times since) and never drink alcohol. I'm well aware that drinking in pubs is a social pastime I'm missing out on. That's okay. You don't need to drink alcohol to appreciate the wonderfulness of pubs even though drinking is a big part of social life in Britain. You can feel left out sometimes. There have been several occasions where Brits have looked at me like I was from another planet when I ordered a soft drink in a pub. I just say, "I'm teetotal," and people usually leave it at that.

I still like British pubs, and you can still enjoy them without drinking. In fact, I would argue they're more enjoyable because you get to be the sober guy watching British people get increasingly more drunk as time goes on. Brits don't care if you're not drinking alcohol as long as there is any kind of drink in your hand - even if it's water.

After we'd settled into our newly found country pub, we placed our order and soaked up the atmosphere while we waited for our food. The place was filled with locals, and the combination of familiarity with each other and the lubrication of alcohol meant that they were an easy bunch to eavesdrop on. In the process, we got an insight into all the local goings on, some of which were rather exciting.

The big news story that day was that a few miles away, just outside of Salisbury, police had raided a marijuana farm. This wasn't just any farm, though. This farm was located in a disused nuclear bunker. Apparently old nuclear bunkers provide the perfect conditions for growing the popular drug. I couldn't help but notice a tinge of disappointment in the air because the place had been raided. The disappointment came not just because of the hit to the local marijuana supply chain, but that someone so clever had been caught. Who would have thought that an abandoned nuclear bunker in the Wiltshire countryside would have been the scene of a drug raid?

While everyone chatted, a young black Labrador retriever paced around the pub. He'd get caught in the legs of patrons standing at the bar. Often, he'd come by our table to get a pet or two. He'd lay down for a few minutes, but because of his age, , he was much too excitable to stay sitting for long. We noticed that none of the people in the pub were not paying any particular attention to him aside from our table.

Dogs in pubs are always a shock for us. I can never imagine a scenario in the USA where I would see a dog in a bar or in a restaurant unless it was a guide dog. However, in Britain, dogs in the local pub are commonplace. It goes with the scenery. When you go for a walk in the countryside, you take your dog and Britain, being a civilized country, isn't going to make the dog stay outside. It could rain!

One night in another pub, we saw a chap with his large dog, enjoying a pint. We got to chatting with him, and it turns out he was the owner of a different pub in town and it was his night off. So, even the publican takes his dog down to the pub whenever he gets a chance.

Eventually, we overheard why everyone was ignoring the dog.

There had been an incident earlier that day.

We didn't see it.

Those in the pub didn't see it, but everyone heard about it.

The cute little Labrador in question had escaped his owner's house and got into a chicken coop and ripped apart a local prize-winning hen.

He was merely in the pub awaiting the arrival of his owner who was away at the time. What a sense of community - you could be out of town, your dog could kill a local chicken, and the local pub will keep an eye on him until you come to collect him.

Back home, they'd have called the pound, and you'd be lucky to ever see the dog again.

The dog was extremely friendly; I simply couldn't imagine him being a murderer. Then I remembered my Labrador back home, and then I realized, yes, this friendly, stupid dog could totally be a murderer.

Before our dinner was finished, someone came to collect that dog. We were sad to see him go.

You can always get the best local news eavesdropping in a pub. Forget the Labrador incident. I'd much rather hear about the debate on where to put the new community cricket pitch, or find out who bought the large Stately Home down the lane that's been empty for a few years. And did you hear that Guy Ritchie flew into Compton Abbas airport in his helicopter a few days ago? He lives nearby, Madonna used to, but we know how that story ended.

More than anything, you feel leisure in the air. The English have a much slower pace of life, at least out in the countryside. This is what is so wonderful about country pubs; their very atmosphere is sedate. You simply cannot be in a hurry in a pub. You don't care how long the food takes to get to you, because why would you want to leave such a warm and stress-free environment?

On this particular visit, it was the Sunday Roast between Christmas and New Year's. Britain shuts down from Christmas until after New Year's; it's not uncommon for most "white collar" offices to be closed for two weeks. This isn't considered part of your allocated time off either, which is usually five weeks in Britain plus public holidays. So, the pub is filled with people relaxing. You can feel the lack of stress. It's wonderful. No one is in a hurry to go anywhere. The only purpose of this rainy Sunday is to go down the pub, have a good Sunday Roast, chat with your friends, read the Sunday paper, down a pint or two, and perhaps walk back using a public footpath.

It's a glorious place to be.

When we left, we were in awe of the starlit night. This is something that always catches me by surprise when we stay in the English countryside. The stars are so incredibly bright. Since back home we live outside of Chicago, light pollution washes out most of the night sky. It's funny that we have to come all the way to the English countryside to see more stars than we can see back home in the Indiana countryside.

We climbed back into our rental car and got back onto the dark country road to return to our cottage. We didn't need the SatNav to guide us; we knew the road was dark and narrow, but we knew the way now.

Find your country pub, and don't tell anyone about it. I'm not telling you where this one is!

FINDING A HOMETOWN IN ENGLAND, SHAFTESBURY

When people ask me for Anglotopia's number one travel recommendation, I often tell them to pick a base you can return to trip after trip. For many people, this is London. For others, it can be a village in Northern England, or a city on the south coast. As one should, I follow my own advice. My hometown in England is a town in Dorset called Shaftesbury. It's not a perfect bucolic paradise, but it has become our home base in England. It's a place I can navigate my way around without needing a map. I know the local footpaths; I know the local shops; I know the local politics. It's like home. Shaftesbury became the genesis for Anglotopia's creation, which is a long, wonderful story I'm always happy to tell.

I first became aware of Shaftesbury in the late '90s as a teenager. One day while browsing the local Hobby Lobby, I came across a poster that was so beautiful I had to buy and frame it. It was a charming English street scene with a row of cottages following the gentle curve of a hill and a beautiful view of the landscape in the background. I was transfixed by it. As an Anglophile already, I was in love.

I bought the poster and put it on my wall next to my bed. That poster was there for years. It became a beacon of hope for me. The high school years are tough for most, and whenever I would struggle to get out of bed, I would look up at that poster to get motivated. I would think that things cannot possibly be so bad because this place exists in the world, and one day I'm going to visit it.

It was an odd poster, as I would learn later. The poster was of Gold Hill. The caption on the poster simply said, "Villages of Dorset," which I would learn later is a bit of a lie because Shaftesbury is not a village, it's a town, and the English are very particular about this distinction. So, the poster was selling me a fantasy- a fantasy I ate up. Little did I know, the fantasy would turn into a reality.

I began to see the street everywhere. I would see it in shows about England. I would see it in period movies. I would see it in English travel guidebooks. I learned quickly that Gold Hill was probably the most famous street in Britain. I wouldn't learn why until much later. I only saw the place in my own little universe as a place I dreamed of going.

Gold Hill is famous because of Ridley Scott. Yes, the director of *Alien* and *Blade Runner*. He made a small hill in a town in Dorset the most famous street in Britain. Before he directed movies, Scott directed commercials. In 1973, he directed a commercial for Hovis Bread, one of Britain's most famous bread brands. I can attest that their bread is delicious. It's a period commercial that features a young boy in Edwardian clothing pushing a bicycle full of bread up a steep hill. At the end, he rides down at full speed, set to music from Dvorak's New World Symphony. The commercial was a huge hit. In fact, it's been voted Britain's favorite advert ever. The commercial made its director famous, but it also put Gold Hill on the map – sort of..

Most people couldn't figure out where it was. Because of the steep hilly scenery, most assumed the village was located somewhere suitably picturesque like Yorkshire. The stone cottages looked like something that would fit in in Yorkshire. But it's not in Yorkshire, and it's not a village. Gold Hill is part of Shaftesbury, a small town at the tip top of Northern Dorset. It's only meters away from the Wiltshire border. Gold Hill is hidden, tucked away behind the Victorian town hall, down a steep alleyway. Once you round the corner, you're presented with a view that takes your breath away every time.

Shaftesbury was put on the map due to its association with the famous Hovis Commercial, so much so that there's a giant loaf of bread sitting at the top of the hill. It's a popular stop for pensioners – or retired folks - on their tours of Britain. It's also popular with international tourists, and why you'll find Gold Hill in pretty much every guidebook about England and certainly the ones about Dorset.

The street has become a stand-in for what people think of when they think of England. That's not really fair to the rest of England, because there are so many beautiful places. I admit I've played along in this narrative so much that Shaftesbury and Gold Hill specifically are my chosen home away from home in England.

We've now been to Shaftesbury at least a dozen times over the last fifteen years. Our stays have ranged from a few days to almost three weeks. Cumulatively, we've spent several months in this one place. When you spend so much time somewhere, you learn a lot about it. We've watched Shaftesbury change a lot over the years. It's a microcosm of the changes Britain has gone through in the last few decades.

When we first started visiting Shaftesbury in 2004, the high street was very much like it was for the previous hundred years. There was a greengrocer selling fruit and veg. There was a butcher. There were pubs. There was a Post Office. There was an ancient hardware store (called an ironmonger in Britain), the kind of place that had everything down to random bolts not used in a hundred years. There was the baker making delicious baked goods. There was even bookshop. I'll never forget buying my first proper pair of Hunter Wellies in the local shoe store. There were also plenty of chain stores, the kinds you would find all throughout an English high street (their word for downtown or main street).

Despite its wonders, something happened to Shaftesbury in the early 2000s - something that happened all the time in America, but happened faster in Britain. A Tesco opened on the outskirts of town. A Tesco is the British equivalent to a Wal-Mart Supercenter - though they're still much smaller than your average Wal-Mart. When the Tesco opened, it began to suck the life out of the Shaftesbury High Street. Slowly, the old school businesses started to close. They just could not compete, and the nostalgia of their services was not enough to keep the customers coming.

The irony is that if you talked to locals, they would all complain about the Tesco and how it was killing their High Street. Yet, somebody was keeping the Tesco in business. It's a bit like pretending your house is not on fire, when in fact it is. Shastonians changed their High Street, not the Tesco. When the economic crisis hit in 2008, that was curtains for Shaftesbury's High Street. Any businesses that were hanging on by a thread closed down. There were empty storefronts galore. Then the High Street became infected with a disease that has infected all the other struggling High Streets in England- the proliferation of charity shops. Think of Goodwill, but ten of them on one street.

The high street is in much better health today. The traditional businesses may be long gone, and the Tesco has won, but there's nothing you can do about it now. Still, there's been a proliferation of small specialty shops that are always nice to visit when you're in town. There have even been some new businesses trying the traditional route like the wine merchant or the new tearoom in a 500-year-old Tudor building. The town still has great pubs, which are the heart of any town or village in Britain.

When we fly over to England, we usually hop right into a rental car and drive down to Shaftesbury. I don't even need the GPS anymore; I know how to get there. The M25 to the M3 to the A303 - the highway to the sun.

As you leave Heathrow, England is as built up as it gets. As the minutes pass on the two-hour journey to Dorset, England begins to slowly change. As you travel outside the suburban sprawl of London, pockets of countryside begin to appear. Before you know it, you're driving past Stonehenge and into the most beautiful landscapes in England. Green rolling hills are all around you. Dramatic cloudscapes float by, even in the dead of winter.

I'll never forget driving into Shaftesbury after having just left the A303, and seeing snow all around us. It rarely snows in England. It didn't last long, but the big chunky flakes were beautiful. It was like driving through a Dickens' story. Shaftesbury is the highest town in England, so it exists in a microclimate of its own. That can mean rain, snow, sun, sleet all in the same day. It's magnificent.

When you spend a lot of time in a place, you begin to learn its landscape, its public rights of way, the secret places where you get a great view or spot an old mill still churning away. The wonderful thing about England is that you learn a landscape more intimately than your own. Back home you can live your entire life in a place and not learn its landscape the way you can in England. The British simply have a different conception of property and land ownership.

When I come to Shaftesbury, I get to *explore properly*, as I fantasized about when I was a kid. I always bring an OS Map with me on my journeys to England. The Ordnance Survey produces the most beautiful, detailed maps of the English countryside. Every structure, every footpath, every road, every railway, and sometimes every tree, feature on these beautiful maps. I can spend hours poring over them. Every time I visit my town, I bring my map, pick a new footpath, and explore it.

You never know what you're going to find. The most wonderful thing is that you have the freedom to be able to do this. If I started trudging around the farmland near my house in Indiana, I would likely be shot.

Mostly though, the best part of finding your hometown in England is usually, without trying, you pick up a few friends along the way. Making friends with locals completes the circle of what makes a place homey. Now when I book our yearly trip to Dorset, I don't fantasize about the landscapes; I look forward to meeting up with our friends again, going down the pub and catching up on the latest gossip or political news (and if you want an idea of how ruthless local politics are in Britain, just read *The Casual Vacancy* by J.K. Rowling).

Anywhere in England is an embarrassment of riches for things to do, and Shaftesbury is no different. Within twenty minutes of Shaftesbury, there's a castle, a Stately Home, several good pubs, forests, hills, streams, footpaths, and so much more. It's a microcosm of everything I love about traveling in England. I love that their "local Stately Home" is Stourhead House and Gardens - a beautiful National Trust Property that everyone should visit at least once in their life. The gardens are literally an Eden (or Arcadia, to borrow a phrase the English use).

Further afield, drive an hour, and you're at the Dorset Jurassic Coastline. With more Stately Homes, more castles, and even a tired old seaside resort town, Weymouth (which isn't so tired anymore). I spent my entire life growing up in the USA without having seen the Atlantic Ocean. I've now seen it dozens of times, just on the other side of it in Dorset. I can now navigate the roads of Dorset without a map. If I need something, I know where to go to get it. If I want a good meal, I know where the good restaurants are. If I need a flash card for my camera, I know I can overpay for one on the high street. If I want to go to a decent secondhand bookstore, I know there are a couple in Bridport. My wife knows where all the knitting shops are.

Need help finding a home of your own in England? Throw a dart at a map of Britain. Go to it. Don't leave for a week. If the place clicks with you, you've come home.

Now you can spend all your free time thinking about how to get back there as much as possible.

THE COUNTY WITHOUT A MOTORWAY

My home state is Indiana. I've spent most of my life here (save for a few years in Texas when I saw a young child). I know the rhythms of its life. I know the landscape (sorry mostly flat). I know the people (a mostly rural, uncomplicated folk). I know the history (a lot of Lincoln and little of anything else). I know the culture (sorry, Indiana, there isn't much). But it's my home state, it's where I own a home, and it will always be "home" to me, no matter how much my heart lives somewhere else.

It was only natural that I found my "home state" in Britain when I started to get to know the country better. Never mind that Britain doesn't have 'states' in the American sense. In fact, you could fit almost the entirety of the United Kingdom within the borders of Indiana. No, Britain has counties. They're a bit like states, but don't tell the British that. Each county in Britain is different, much like our states are different. They have their own histories and cultures and rivalries. The recent row between Devon and Cornwall over which order to put the clotted cream on your scone is a great example of that.

Dorset has become my "home state" in Britain. It's the place I try to spend the most time I can when I travel. It's the place where I pour over Ordnance Survey maps to try and learn every nook and cranny of the landscape. It's where I get lost on long walks and visit every tourist attraction imaginable. I want to know Dorset as well as I know my home state of Indiana. It must be so. If I see a book about Dorset, I buy it. I have Dorset flag bunting hanging from the ceiling my office. I have pride for a place I've never even lived. I probably know more about Dorset than many locals, and I always want to know more.

To me, Dorset is everything that Indiana isn't.

When we visited Dorset for the second time in 2005, we stayed the night at a local B&B, and chatted with the innkeeper.

"What brings you to Dorset?" he asked.

"Oh, it's just so beautiful and quiet here," I responded.

"You know, we're the one of the only counties in England without a motorway!" he exclaimed. This gentleman was always pretty excitable.

This blew my mind, and when I looked at a map just to confirm such a boast, he was right. There is no motorway in Dorset - what we would call an interstate. There are major roads, but no massive motorway cutting through the landscape. Couple this with historically poor railway connections, Dorset can feel a bit cut off from the rest of the world - and this is truly wonderful. The pace of life in Dorset is slower. It takes forever to get anywhere, and that's lovely. Where my home is in Indiana, I live in between two interstate highways. Less than a mile from Interstate 90 and about three miles from Interstate 80. No matter what direction the wind is blowing, you hear one highway or the other. The whole of traveling America passes by my house every second of every day. I'm also under a major flightpath into Chicago, so airplane noise is constant. Not only does Dorset not have motorways, they don't have flight paths into Heathrow. Merciful silence.

My first literary exposure to Dorset was through the works of Thomas Hardy, who set many of his books in and around Dorset (and the greater 'West Country'). *Far From the Madding Crowd* was a favorite book of mine as a teenager. I loved the title. All I wanted was to enter the world of the book and live in Dorset. I didn't know, at the time, that really the story was a swan song to country life in Dorset which was forever changing thanks to the advent of railways, tractors and the overall industrialization of farming.

Dorset changed during Hardy's life, but Dorset is still very much a rural area, with more landscape than people. When they made a new film adaptation a few years ago of *Far From the Madding Crowd*, they were able to film most of it in Dorset, and in many of the real locations Hardy wrote about. That's how much in Dorset hasn't actually changed.

One of my favorite short novels is *On Chesil Beach* by Ian McEwan, which chronicles the terrible wedding night of a young couple in 1960s Britain. The landscape of Dorset also plays a big role in the background of the story with their final argument taking place on the iconic Chesil Beach - a three-mile-long spit of shingle where the rocks inexplicably change in size from one end to the other in an ordered procession. It's a remarkable place, and I can see why McEwan set his book there. When the film came out recently, I was very pleased to see that they filmed it in the real place and it added great dramatic weight to the film.

There are just so many empty places in Dorset. When you drive around on any given day, you will not run into very many people. The villages feel closed to the world, and even the big towns are not as bustling as you would think. It's remote. It's cut off from the world. And it's perfect in every way.

Of course, what I'm most in love with is the landscape. There is not a flat piece of land in Dorset. It's beautiful, green - even in the winter - rolling hills provide a dramatic and varied landscape that I never tire of looking at. I can spend hours in the dining room of our favorite cottage on Gold Hill, Updown Cottage, staring out at the Blackmore Vale, watching the landscape change as the sun rises and sets. If I ever showed you the flat and dull landscape in Indiana where I live, you would understand what a novelty curves in the landscape are to me. I'm sure there are more beautiful landscapes in Britain, and I've even been to a few places I might even say are more beautiful - like the Lake District. But that's like choosing your favorite child. I love Dorset's landscape. It's my first love and will always remain so. My soul lives in the Dorset landscape.

I've gotten to know the landscape very well. I've traversed the county countless times in rental cars, walked innumerable miles and taken thousands of photographs. I'll never forget going out with a professional photographer and learning to see the landscape in a different light. It was just two days after Christmas, and I was a big fan of his pictures. I bought his calendars every year, even in the USA. He is known for his beautiful landscape pictures of Wiltshire and Dorset. We corresponded by email and much to my joy, he agreed to take me around Dorset to photograph some of his favorite spots.

This was the highlight of the trip.

We set off early, then spent the day chasing the sunlight - the low winter golden sun paints a perfect landscape to photograph. He taught me the thought process for composing good pictures of the landscape - how to frame things, how to pause, look, and wait for the right light. I'd been taking pictures for years, but he really taught me how to hone my photography and take pictures worth printing and hanging on the wall. We drove along miles of single track country lanes. We found the empty places of Dorset, where we encountered no people and only heard sheep. We even visited an old manor house at one point, where no one else was visiting. It was a surreal day. It felt like we had all of Dorset to ourselves.

Of course, Dorset has tourists and crowds, but they focus mostly on the southern coast where there are plenty of lovely old seaside towns and villages. One ended up playing a starring role in a major British TV drama. The honey-colored sand cliffs in West Bay, Dorset became the unofficial star of the ITV Show Broadchurch. When it aired in Britain, it was an event. The show itself was about a small rural town in Dorset that struggled to cope with the murder of a local boy. The story was interesting, but it was also interesting to have such a story set in such a remote place.

It put West Bay on the map. Even when we visited in the winter, there were plenty of people talking about it. It also helps that the place is beautiful, no matter what time of year it is. On the one hand, I was excited to see one of my favorite places be part of a Major British Drama. But on the other hand, I was a bit sad that the rest of the world was going to discover my special place. When the show aired on cable TV in the States and was a surprise hit, I thought that would be the end of my solo love for Dorset.

Thankfully, years after the show has finished, I'm happy to report hordes of tourists have not ruined Dorset. It's much the same as it always was. Quiet and unassuming. I'm sure the British people reading this chapter are baffled.

Dorset?

Really?

I'm sure there are plenty of other places in Britain that many of my descriptions could apply to.

Still, none of them are Dorset because it's my home.

Just like Indiana is my home state, Dorset is my home county. I love it, warts and all. It's an irrational love. No love for your home is purely rational. You love it because it's home. I've spent cumulative months over the last fifteen years in Dorset, and I hope I can spend many more years there in my life to come. One day, I hope to know every road, every lane, every grand house, every Iron Age ruin, every barrow, every field. I know this is optimistic, but I want to learn as much as I can about my home.

Dorset calls me home every day, and I can never get back there soon enough.

RIGHTS OF WAY

When my father was a child, he went for a hike in the woods with his grandfather Amile. They were walking in the woods around the Valparaiso Moraine, a beautiful ridge in Northwest Indiana that separates the land carved out by the glacier that formed Lake Michigan and the land above it where the glacier stopped. The ridge is so big, you'd be lucky to notice it, but in spots, you can see the geography sculpted by relentless glaciers not so long ago.

The problem with their hike was they were probably trespassing. All of the land in or around the Valparaiso Moraine is privately and jealously owned. They simply ignored the "No Trespassing" signs as they went on their way. Exploring this area earlier, my father had found a dead wasp nest hanging high in a tree. It was something his grandfather really wanted. My dad told him about it and they went back with a gun to shoot it down.

As they were aiming to shoot at the wasp nest, a voice shouted at them.

"Who's there?" An older man, about the same age as his grandfather, rode up on a horse.

He was armed and pointing a gun at them.

"Woah, there," said the grandfather with his hands up.

"This is private property," he cocked the gun. "What in the hell do you think you're doing here?"

"Just hunting squirrels," said Amile.

My father, who was only a child at the time was quite scared, thinking this was turning into an armed stand-off. His day of fun in the woods away from the fighting of his divorcing parents was going to end badly.

Then, the mood shifted.

"Amile, is that you?" said the man, putting the gun down.

Amile looked up at the man and squinted, finally recognizing him. "Bill, is that you?"

They were both retired steelworkers, and they had worked together on bolting the steel together on the Sears Tower in the Chicago (back when it was still the Sears Tower). The tension was gone as the old men reminisced about working together. The dangerous situation was over.

That story always stuck with me, and I think of it often when I stop to consider land ownership in England. One thing that always seems remarkable to me when I travel there is the number of places I'm perfectly welcome to wander.

If you look at any Ordnance Survey map of England, you'll find hundreds of beautiful dotted green lines leading all over the landscape. These are the public rights of way and national footpaths. Yes, Britain has National Ffootpaths. These are places that anyone is perfectly welcome to walk through. Some of these lines go directly through a property that would otherwise look like an entirely private property. This idea that the landscape belongs to everyone, that it transcends individual property rights, is baffling to an American who cannot wander at home.

There are, of course, plenty of hiking trails in Northwest Indiana. But those are different. Most of those are within the boundaries of the national or state parks. None of them go through private land or even along it. There's a complete lack of openness. When I'm in England, I spend a lot more time walking places than I do back at home and it's simply because I have places I can walk.

I live in a rural area, but if I were to walk outside my door and go for a wander, I'd have nowhere to go. I'm surrounded by endless acres of farmland and not far from several lakes. But you would be hard-pressed to find any public footpaths. Property owners around here don't want people wandering on their land, because it's theirs. Letting people wander onto your land is a liability.

I'd have to walk along my street, which even though it's a rural road, has enough traffic to be dangerous. At the end of my street, there's a massive section of farmland - and after harvest season spends most of the year a barren field of dirt. In the middle of it is a lovely secluded wood. It's an island in the middle of the field. It looks beautiful. But I can never visit it. The field is fenced off and has ample "No Trespassing" signs. If I ignored them, I would risk meeting the meaning of America's 2nd Amendment, the right to bear arms, head on.

It's a shame.

I feel alienated and disconnected from the landscape I live in.

The first time I went on a public footpath in England, I spent weeks preparing for it. The very idea of having a wander in the English countryside was exciting. I had purchased the ordnance survey map for

Northern Dorset and spent hours poring over it on my kitchen table. I followed all the dotted green lines, everywhere they went. I imagined the places I could go, marveling at the unique names of all the places.

Butt's Knap.

Guy's Marsh.

Pennymoor Pitt.

Lady's Copse.

Long Bottom.

Melbury Hill.

That's it. That would be my target. When you look at a picture of Gold Hill in Shaftesbury, Dorset, the most striking feature, beyond the famous row of cottages are the hills off in the background. This is called the Blackmore Vale, and the most prominent hill is Melbury Hill. It looks rather tall in any picture. Measuring in at 863 feet (263 meters), it's not an unusually tall hill, but when you come from a state where the standard geographic feature is flat farmland, it's tall to me.

I wanted to climb it. Not only that, I tried to follow the path I charted using the public footpaths on my trusty OS Map. I'd spent hours gazing at that hill on my Gold Hill poster; now, I wanted the opposite view. I wanted to see Gold Hill from the top of Melbury Hill. Never mind that I was incredibly out of shape and any climb up could possibly kill me. But, hey, I was young at the time and willing to do it.

This climb would require preparation more extensive than just studying the map. I would need the right gear. After many hours spent watching the BBC flagship countryside show *Countryfile*, I knew I needed to have Hunter Wellington Boots. Their signature green country boots became a talisman of sorts for me. On my journey to fit in as an Anglophile in the English countryside, I needed to have these boots. At the time, circa 2005, you could not easily buy them in the USA yet (and they had not become the fashion accessory they were to become later on). But I was not going to let that deter me.

When Jackie and I arrived at our bed and breakfast, we asked our very British innkeeper where we could find a pair of wellies.

"Well, you can get a decent pair up at the new Tesco for a tenner," he told us. "But don't bloody go there, that place is terrible and sucking the life out of our high street. No, you want to go to Parfitt's on Salisbury Street, they'll sort you out."

Later that day we wandered to the other side of Shaftesbury to visit Parfitt's. Inside, they were happy to help. When I told them what I wanted and what size, they brought out the box that said Hunter on it. When I opened it, I smiled. There they were - those giant rubber boots in their beautiful muted green color, smelling of fresh rubber. I picked one up and admired it. I know it sounds absurd to be excited about a pair of rubber boots, but these meant something to me. They still do, I should add. I still have them 15 years later.

I tried them on, and they were comfortable. And rubbery. I felt instantly transformed into the English countryman I wished to be. One of the great compliments I ever received from an Englishman was when he told me I looked like a proper English countryman.

They were £115 and the exchange rate at the time was almost $2 to the pound. They were very, very expensive boots. So, I did what any self-respecting young college student would do in 2005. I put them on a credit card to worry about later.

I left the store with my box of Hunters, and I felt complete. Now, to put them to good use.

The next day Jackie and I set out early, just after breakfast. I was so excited to be wearing my new green Hunter Wellies. I brought along my OS Map and began to follow the route I'd been planning for months. We walked down Gold Hill, turned onto Layton Lane, then followed the map down French Mill Lane. The roads got narrower and narrower as we walked. French Mill Lane turned into a single track. We weren't on public footpaths yet, but we were close. Finally, we found it.

My first English public footpath: marked with a faded wooden point with an arrow at the top that said Public Footpath.

We stepped on.

Then, we proceeded to get lost.

You see, despite being a former Boy Scout, I was incapable of reading the map properly. But that was fine; we were on an adventure. We walked down the path and watched as the landscape unfolded on each side of us. We were basically walking through a farmer's field, and he couldn't do anything about it. The views of the surrounding landscape were incredible. Sheep were grazing in the field, occasionally bleating in the distance.

We crossed a stream and marveled. We were able to stand in the water with our wellies and not get wet (oh, the things that used to thrill me). We walked through patches of mud, some several times just because we could. We were lost but we were on a public footpath, and it was everything I hoped it would be.

Eventually, we got un-lost by following the map and found our way to the foot of Melbury Hill. Situated in the very small village of Melbury Abbas, the hill towers over you. It practically shoots straight up at a 45-degree angle from ground level. I imagined it must be magical to live at the foot of such a beautiful and massive hill. There was a public footpath the led from the street, along a farmer's field, then up Melbury Hill. It was a muddy February, so the air was brisk but clean. It was glorious.

The climb was gentle at first. Then, it became steep. At a ridgeline, about halfway up the hill, the footpath began to blend into the rising hill simply because it seemed people would make it this far, enjoy the lovely view back towards Shaftesbury, then give up because the vertiginous climb ahead looked slightly terrifying.

I was going to climb that hill.

Jackie had had enough of following me as we wandered in the Dorset countryside. I was determined to climb the hill, and in that moment, I did something that, to this day, I have not lived down. I pressed on without her, abandoning her at the ridgeline and climbing on like a freight train. It's a miracle she ever married me.

I tried to follow the path. My stiff, new wellies gripped well on the side of the hill. I was careful to keep my balance - an arrogance that was only assured by the knowledge that I was following the footpath, that damned green dotted line on the map. I was incredibly out of shape (a trend that continues to this day), and the muscles in my legs began to burn. They did not appreciate me climbing this hill. I was out of breath. I was thirsty. The higher I got, the colder I got, but I was sweating profusely in my winter parka.

But I was going to get to the top of that hill.

And I did.

Eventually, the steep path stopped, and I found myself on the plateau at the top. The cold wind blew fiercely around me as I was exposed to the full force of the Dorset winter winds. It was not late in the day and the sun shined on the hills around me, and I was presented with the most beautiful landscape my eyes had ever seen. Glowing in the late afternoon, the low winter sun illuminated the hills of Blackmore Vale. Back towards the way I came, I could see Shaftesbury and Gold Hill. To my right, I could see Compton Abbas airfield and the rumble of a small plane taking off. To my left, I could see the hills of the vale, and the rush of traffic in the distance and people drove north and south.

I was out of breath; I was thirsty. I'd pissed off my fiancée.

But I made it to the top of that hill on my first walk along public footpaths. I took approximately one million pictures. Said hello to a fellow walker coming from a different direction. It turns out if you walk from, say, Compton Abbas airfield, the walk is gentler. We talked about the weather, which is always the first order of conversation when meeting an English person.

I took a deep breath, soaked in the view one more time, and began my descent down the hill. Jackie was not pleased with me, but I think she was secretly happy I'd made it to the top after all.

We did not walk back. Conveniently, there was a bus stop at the foot of Melbury Hill, and we simply waited for the next bus.

The walk blew my mind. This idea that I could follow some lines on a map, walk through fields and hills that didn't belong to me - and weren't in a national park - was simply remarkable. Walking in the English countryside has since become one of the things I love most about my visits there. You feel free. I find it ironic how much Americans crow on about their freedom, but don't have the right to roam like the British do. Of course, there are, as always, exceptions (like the Appalachian Trail). We feel disconnected from our landscape in the USA, which is probably why so many people simply don't care about it.

This idea that the commons, that the landscape exists for everyone to enjoy, is such a beautiful thing. Still, not everyone agrees with it. There are often disputes between landowners and activists who maintain public rights of way. They can often spill into the courts. Famously, television presenter Jeremy Clarkson, of *Top Gear* fame, spent years in court trying to get a public footpath diverted from passing in front of his cottage on the Isle of Man.

The right to roam wasn't always so prominent in English history. Like all things in British history that I love, it was something that evolved over time and became crystalized with a flash point. If there is one flashpoint for the right to roam, it would be the Mass Trespass of Kinder Scout, a mountain in the Peak District.

The event sounds absurd, but in the 1930s the right to roam was not like it is today. In fact, various enclosure acts starting in the Georgian era had closed off mass amounts of land in Britain from traditional commoners (and is one of the reasons why the Scottish Highlands are so empty today, and why there are so many people of Scottish descent in North America). The right to roam simply did not exist.

Kinder Scout is one of the most prominent hills in the Peak District, and a group of activists led by the Rambler's Association found it absurd that it wasn't a place that people could roam freely. Activist Benny Rothman of the Young Communist League of Manchester was one of the leaders of the Mass Trespass, and he viewed the right to access open land as the right of every Englishman.

On April 22nd, 1932, Rothman and several hundred of his followers set off to climb Kinder Scout. In a coordinated attack on the hill involving three groups coming from three different directions, the teams trespassed on private property, battling gamekeepers along the way, often violently. They persisted in their trespassing, and two of the groups succeeded in reaching the top of the hill. Several were arrested when it was over. However, it galvanized public opinion that everyone should have the right to open access in the English countryside simply because, while it may be privately owned, it belongs to everyone to look at and enjoy.

Kinder Scout is now owned by the National Trust, an organization founded in 1895 precisely to preserve Britain's open spaces and special places for the public to enjoy, forever.

Since that first walk up Melbury Hill, I've been on dozens of walks in the English countryside. I try to plan at least one every trip. I find that connecting personally with the mud and fresh air of public footpaths to be the most enjoyable part of my trips to England and I'm still amazed by the openness of the countryside. I'll talk to anyone willing to have a ramble about it.

I was once on a writer's retreat on a farm in the Lake District. This farmer considers himself to be a steward of the land he owns and farms at the base of a great fell (Lake District speak for mountain). But, he's simply one in a long line of farmers who've worked the land, and there are public rights of way on his land.

One day during the course, we all followed the public footpath up the fell to seek inspiration and do readings from various nature writers. About halfway up the fell, we all stopped and sat down to rest - it was a pretty strenuous climb, and we were all grateful for the chance to sit, look at the landscape, and ponder our favorite writers.

As the writer leading the workshop was speaking, a couple of ramblers came walking up the hill, his hill, as was their right. I'm sure they were rather startled to see a group of people sitting the side of the mountain, and probably felt uncomfortable about interrupting something. We made room so they could walk through.

There was a short exchange with everyone, and then the farmer said, "Enjoy your walk today."

It was a perfect moment, and it really summed up how wonderful public rights of way in Britain really are.

DREAMING OF THE AQUATINT SPIRES

My vision of Oxford was heavily influenced by TV and literature. *Brideshead Revisited* is my favorite work of British literature and also my favorite British TV drama. Charles Ryder describes Oxford so perfectly; I've been dreaming of his vision of Oxford since I read it:

> "Oxford, in those days, was still a city of aquatint. In her spacious and quiet streets men walked and spoke as they had done in Newman's day; her autumnal mists, her grey springtime, and the rare glory of her summer days - such as that day - when the chestnut was in flower and the bells rang out high and clear over her gables and cupolas, exhaled the soft airs of centuries of youth. It was this cloistral hush which gave our laughter its resonance, and carried it still, joyously, over the intervening clamour."

When I visited it for the first time, I did not quite experience the visions of aquatint. No, my first real memories of Oxford are of my one-year-old son both sleeping and not sleeping. It was the Schrödinger's cat of traveling with a toddler. We did not foresee how much flying into a new time zone would mess up our poor child. We didn't foresee how much it would mess us up. We certainly didn't foresee having to make multiple circles around the Oxford Ringroad in the middle of the night trying like hell to get our kid to fall asleep in the back of the car. I'd like to say we got to see plenty of the beautiful countryside surrounding Oxford, but it was dark. We saw the 24-hour Tesco and occasionally the Mini Cooper factory in Crowley when we made our loops. Little did I know that eventually, Oxford would become one of my most favorite places to visit in England and that I would get the chance to study there one day.

The city of Oxford was always a place I knew about. I knew it was the most prestigious university in the world. I knew it was a beautiful medieval city steeped in English history and arcane culture and traditions. They gave the world the standards and structures that all other universities are based on. Yes, including Cambridge, founded by Oxford exiles. I saw Oxford in TV shows, read about it books. I knew one thing; I wanted to study there. Somehow. I dreamed of its spires and its beautiful golden colored buildings. The Harry Potter books, painted a picture of endless libraries and medieval dining halls. The idea of a city entirely dedicated to knowledge has such a romantic pull for me.

But my own studies took a different path. I ended up at Purdue University, mostly because it was local and I could live at home while attending. I got a decent education. My degree is in English, despite what all the grammar errors on Anglotopia may indicate. My school was so small, though, that I never had the chance to study abroad. And let's face it – I wasn't quite smart enough to get into a bigger school that had a study abroad program, nor could I afford one as I had to pay my own way through university. Sure, there were the few months in my junior year of high school where I fantasized about being a Rhodes Scholar. As my favorite physical activity was sitting in front of a computer, I didn't meet one key requirement: being good at sports.

Oxford was never going to be the place where I went to university. I met Jackie on my second day at Purdue, so we worked to put each other through school. We were lucky to graduate on our own when we did. Studying at Oxford wasn't going to happen. We had a wedding to pay for and a future to plan. The goal was to get school finished as soon as possible and get on with our lives. But, our university years did something very critical for us; it fostered our mutual love for England. Every spring break, we irresponsibly used the leftover student loan money to go to England (don't worry, tuition and books were always paid for, and we both worked more than full time). Our year began to revolve around our visits to London and England, cementing a love affair that exists to this day.

It turns out that spending our loan money on those trips ended up being an investment in what would eventually become Anglotopia. The knowledge from those trips filled our fledgling website with information in its early days and provided information for our first guidebooks. One place we were never able to go, though, was Oxford. It continued to be a place I dreamt about. When I finished university, I had fantasies of going to graduate school there. I was, shall we say, not much of a distinguished student, so I probably wouldn't have been able to get in. Plus, there was no way I could pay for it, and our life just wouldn't accommodate it. We'd had enough of being students; it was time to get jobs and move on with our lives.

I'm never done learning, though. I have a thirst for learning new things that's never satisfied. I'm reminded of a book I read when I was a kid, *The Voyage of the Frog* by Gary Paulsen. It's about a boy who inherits a sailboat from an Uncle, and he sails the boat alone to a homeport, reminiscing about his uncle along the way. One thing his uncle said stuck with the main character, and it stuck with me until this day. He said:

> I want to know all the things I don't know...not just about the sea. All of it. I want to know all of everything there is to know that I don't know. I want to know about other planets, and I want to know about molecules. I want to know about art and science and music and love and hate and dreams and trees. I want to know everything...

Reading this back to myself as I write this chapter, I didn't realize how much this simple passage practically became my life philosophy. I want to know everything as well; everything that interests me that I can fit into my head. It's why I have a library with almost 2,000 books in it (and maybe only half are British related – I have wide interests!). It's why I run a business that requires me to research and learn new things every day. Over the years, I've watched countless documentaries, read countless books, always learning. Oxford became a place in my mind, almost like a church, a high altar of learning. It was a place I had to visit and pay homage too.

My first visit to Oxford was achingly brief. It was the day we arrived from a transatlantic flight over to cover Queen Elizabeth's Diamond Jubilee. We had a one-year-old child with us, and we'd never traveled with him before. We arrived in Oxford, jetlagged and foggy. After a pub lunch and a recharge of the batteries, we found enough energy to take the bus into Central Oxford and have a look around. And that's all we did. We looked around. There was some major event, and roads were closed off. It was late; all the shops were closed. There was nothing to do, and we were completely shattered. We argued over finding somewhere to eat and wandered into a Jamie's Italian and had a disappointing pasta dinner. We wandered around enough to take pictures proving we'd been to Oxford. I had no context for anything, nor did we know what to see and do. We hadn't prepared because we hadn't planned . I don't even remember how we got back to our hotel.

For a place I dreamed about visiting my whole life, it was an extremely disappointing first visit to the city of dreaming spires. It would just not do.

I would not have a chance to visit Oxford again until February 2016. When planning a trip entirely to London, we realized we had a spare day in our itinerary. I wanted to take the train somewhere, to experience somewhere new. So, we decided to visit Oxford properly this time. I bought a guidebook. I prepared. I made a list of things to see. I planned every minute. I endeavored to take a walking tour. The train to Oxford is only an hour from London, and we were there before we knew it. We did not have the most beautiful day on offer by the British weather. It was cold and dreary, but at least it wasn't raining.

We gave Oxford the attention we were not able to give it on our previous flying visit. The walking tour was illuminating, and it was magnificent to wander through real Oxford colleges and get a sense of the place. It was during term-time, students were rushing about or busy studying. It felt like we were voyeurs on a life we never had, an unwelcome intrusion into the cloistered world of Oxford. We dined and drank in the Eagle and Child, the pub home of the Inklings. We visited Blackwell's Bookshop, and I bought entirely too many books. We wandered the beautiful Oxford covered market in search of souvenirs.

There was still no sign of aquatint, but I finally got to experience Oxford in a way I'd always wanted.

And I fell in love.

After that trip, I felt a longing for Oxford. I was well into my thirties; my studying days were behind me. After a second visit that year on another research trip, my new love for this city was cemented. No longer would Dorset take up all the space in my heart for England. It would now have to share with Oxford.

If only I could experience what it would be like to study at Oxford.

We don't often think deeply about email. It exists in our life; most people hate it. But it's the main mode of communication for our age, especially when you run a business; emails can change your life. Opportunities can just drop into your inbox randomly. Somewhere else in the world, someone is sitting in a room, discovers your website, finds your contact information, and thinks you should get in touch. Your life can change with one simple email.

One email can allow you to study at Oxford as a student, long after your student days were over.

The email was an update from one of our advertisers on Anglotopia. The English Speaking Union is an organization that fosters an understanding of the English language all over the world. Their US branch runs a series of tours and educational programs for teachers. One of the highlights is that they run programs that allow teachers to go to Oxford and study. When they told me that they still had spaces available and wanted to offer a discount to Anglotopia readers, I immediately had the idea to propose them giving me a place, and in exchange, I would promote the tours and their programs. I had done advertising trades like this before. I dashed off the idea, practically off the cuff.

There's no way I could have just typed my way into studying at Oxford, right?

The reply came a few hours later. They wanted to do it but had to get the necessary approvals. I'll never forget when I received an email that started with, "Exciting news – we have the green light to sponsor your trip to Oxford! In less than 6 weeks, you will be immersed in a course on the evolution of the English language." I literally stood up from my chair and jumped up and down, running to Jackie to scream the news at the top of my lungs. For a brief moment in time, I would be a student at Oxford.

***

It was but a brief moment of my trip but a major event in someone else's life. Students spent three years in Oxford, away from their family, in some cases in a completely different country, studying at the world's most prestigious university. It was surely not without its challenges. It was Diploma Day. Diploma Day is when the actual pieces of paper student's spend three years at Oxford working towards are handed out. There's a ton of Oxford pomp and circumstance to this. Families come from all over the world. Each college has its own day, and I was staying at Worcester College. On Diploma Day, the place was swarmed with students dressed in their Oxford gowns and their families dressed in formal clothes. It was quite a sight to see. It got me thinking. It made me jealous. These students had accomplished something amazing, a degree from Oxford, and now was their day to celebrate. And celebrate they did. They earned it. I was just an interloper, nibbling at the fringes of being an Oxford student.

Oxford changes in the summer. The students leave, and the tourists descend upon the city. It becomes a different place. I've visited Oxford during term time, and it's a quiet, studious time with students rushing about to their tutors or living their lives amongst the dreaming spires of Oxford. In the summer, they're gone, save for the occasional return for their diploma day. What kinds of people visit Oxford in July? Tourists do. But not just tourists. It's a chance for students from all over the world to come to Oxford and get the Oxford Experience so they can see if it's the place for them. The colleges are filled with under-18s - many away from home for the first time.

When I arrived in Oxford for my week of studies at the university, the first order of business was to check-in and get my room. I took the bus from Heathrow directly to Oxford; it took about forty-five minutes. Though, how long it actually was I'm not so sure as I fell asleep on the way. I tried like hell to sleep on the overnight flight over but for the life of me, could not fall asleep. Five minutes on a bus to Oxford and I was out like a light. The bus deposited me at the Gloucester Green bus station, a newer bit of Oxford, home to the local market, a cinema, some shops, and a lot of places to eat. Thanks to hours spent poring over maps of Oxford before the trip, I knew the exact route to walk, and within minutes, I was at Worcester College.

Worcester College was established in 1714, and it's a 'newer" college compared to many of Oxford's colleges that existed for hundreds of years more. This is reflected in the architecture, which is not medieval but more Georgian, Palladian, and later styles. The college is known for having the largest gardens in Oxford, and once you're inside the walls of the college, the sounds of bustling academia fade away, and you're in a cloistered, quiet environment the feels like paradise for learning. Some notable alumni of Worcester College include press magnate Rupert Murdoch, former *Doctor Who* showrunner Russell T. Davies and US Supreme Court Justice Elena Kagan.

The University of Oxford is college based. When you apply to the university, you also apply to a college. Your college is your base while you study at Oxford. It becomes your surrogate home. It's where you study one on one with your tutor, where you stay, where you eat and where you do your schoolwork. Lectures are run at the university level, so you attend those outside your college. Meals are served in the dining hall every day for students and visiting fellows. The menu changes and there is quite a bit of variety. Your "loyalty" is to your college, not to the university itself, and college pride runs very strong. Each college is financially independent and runs its own affairs (and has their own criteria for who they let in). Some colleges are richer than other. St John's is reportedly the richest of the colleges as they own land throughout southern England, which makes them a lot of money. Exams are run at the university level and conducted at the end of term time. The year is divided into three 8-week terms: Michaelmas (October-December), Hilary (January to March) and Trinity (April to June). Most US universities have two terms (or semesters). Consequently, you can finish an Oxford degree in three years instead of four like at a US university.

When I arrived at the college, I was greeted by the porters at the porters' lodge. The porters control access to the colleges - most are only open to the public a few hours a day so as visitors don't disturb the students. The porters are also responsible for caring for the students - arranging anything they need while they're students. During my stay, I found the porters to be very knowledgeable and helpful, even to "pretend" students like me. In addition to the porters, there are the scouts. The scouts clean your rooms and keep the college tidy. Back in the day, scouts used to have a personal relationship with you. I'm not sure if that's the case anymore, my scouts were more like maids and I rarely ever saw them. They did keep my rooms clean and tidy, however.

During my stay in Oxford, every day was the same. I woke up around 7:00 or 8:00 a.m., and either did breakfast in the dining hall with the other students, or I ate breakfast in my room. After that, it was time for lectures at 9:00 a.m. There were two lectures each morning, with a short tea break in between. After the lectures, it was lunchtime. Sometimes I'd go to lunch with a classmate (shy me actually made several new friends), or I'd plan to go to lunch myself. The afternoon was usually given away to a guided tour - of Keble College, Oxford itself, the Ashmolean Museum or the Bodleian Library. After that, we were on our own to explore Oxford. Full dinner was provided in the evenings, but it was optional - I opted for it a couple of times but chose to have dinner out to get the most out of Oxford.

One night, I was bored after eating dinner and still had plenty of the day left, so I decided to go for an amble through Oxford, taking random streets to see where I ended up. This is my favorite part of travel, discovering something new that wasn't planned. I found the Oxford Castle, took my favorite picture from the trip at Nuffield College, explored the shops, and all around soaked up the atmosphere of Oxford in the summer after the tourists had left. It was glorious. As I was in Oxford by myself, there was a lot of time to think and do some self-care. I was there to work, but I certainly got a lot out of the experience personally. I'm a huge admirer of architecture and Oxford is full of beautiful architecture, from medieval buildings to new ones. It's interesting to see them living side by side. One of the oldest buildings in Oxford is now a currency exchange and a Pret a Manger. Not something the original builders of the building could have imagined. The original Norman castle is surrounded by a shop selling everything from travel gear to books. Plop a Norman down on St. Aldate's, and I'm sure he would not recognize the place despite Oxford's seemingly timelessness.

Since I had the time after my lectures, I was determined to visit as many of Oxford's museums as possible. The place is positively packed with them. They're world-class, just like the museums in London, and it's a shame that many people don't think of Oxford for its museums. But a place that has been educating people for almost a thousand years is bound to acquire a few good museums. My favorite was the Natural History Museum. This glorious Victorian structure is a temple to natural history and has some amazing fossilized animals and dinosaurs (don't miss the dodo!). But by far the biggest treat is located through a hallway at the back of the Natural History Museum: The Pitt-Rivers museum. This place is hard to quantify. It's a massive gathering of cultural artifacts from all over the world - an ethnographic survey of cultural history. There are artifacts from every corner of the globe, and all of them are given the weight they deserve.

There are some rather macabre items on display such as some real human shrunken heads. There are also some amazing items on display from samurai armor to artifacts of indigenous tribes in North America. The sheer number of items in the collection is mind-boggling - hundreds of thousands of items have been saved, but only a few are on display at any given time. What you see in the grand Victorian central hall is a sliver of a massive collection of cultural importance. If we were to save anything of humanity in the face of the apocalypse, we should save this entire museum. The best part about Oxford's museums? They're all free.

No trip to Oxford is complete without a stop at Blackwell's, the renowned bookstore on Broad Street that has become an Oxford institution. It's basically the bookstore of your dreams. Five levels of new books plus one level of select used books. They've expanded into a music shop (frequented by a certain Inspector Morse) and an art shop. Blackwell's is a huge operation - with branches all over the UK (and even within Oxford), but their main store on Broad Street is the spiritual home of the bookstore founded in 1879 by Benjamin Henry Blackwell. The Norrington Room, in the basement, dug out of the grounds beneath the store, is home to the largest amount of bookshelf space in the world with more than 100,000 titles along three miles of shelves. If the helpful staff can't help you find a book, that book does not exist. I'm not capable of exerting self-control in Blackwell's. Thankfully, they will affordably ship your books home to the USA (mine arrived shortly after I did).

What's so great about Oxford is that it's a compact city. If you're staying in the city center, you can walk pretty much everywhere. There's so much to see, you will not have a shortage of places to visit. A highlight of my time in Oxford was actually when I left the city center for the day. I took a taxi up to Wolvercote Cemetery to pay my respects to JRR Tolkien, writer of *The Lord of the Rings* and *The Hobbit*. He's buried there with his wife in a shared grave, and it's become a bit of a shrine to Hobbitheads. After that, I walked along the main road towards Godstow, a lovely old medieval settlement home to two major attractions: The Trout Inn and Godstow Abbey. The Inn is a classic English pub made famous by Philip Pullman and Inspector Morse. Godstow Abbey is a ruined monastery that's free and open to explore. This was a great way to end my trip to Oxford and oh-so relaxing to enjoy a hearty pub meal beside the Thames at The Trout Inn.

When you spend a week in a place, you begin to get the rhythm and feel. It begins to feel like home. Every day was a treasure. From the lectures, to walking in the college grounds, to exploring a new bits of Oxford I'd not seen before, Oxford was amazing. I've come to the conclusion that I want to spend a week in Oxford every summer for the rest of my life. I think my very soul will need it. I should see about getting a doctor's prescription. Living amongst the dreaming spires is a treat that I recommend to anyone who loves learning and soaking up history and architecture. Oxford is the place for you. And there's so much there that you'll spend a lifetime finding something new every time. I only saw but a sliver of life at Oxford and I will spend a lifetime trying to see the rest.

Did my time in Oxford match the original fantasy I had set up by *Brideshead Revisited*? Mostly. Spending that time in Oxford, in the golden summer, I finally saw the Oxford of aquatint that Charles Ryder describes. And he was completely right. A piece of my soul now lives in Oxford. I want to go back. Perhaps, one day, I'll still study there as a "real" student. There was a man in the news recently who went back to Oxford in his late forties to attend graduate school and compete in the Oxford versus Cambridge boat race. There was a tremendous personal cost to him to doing this, but it got me thinking: If he could do it, then, perhaps, my student days are ahead of me yet.

ENGLISH MILES

"Curb! Curb!" Jackie shouted as the car lurched at 60 miles an hour. It's no wonder that curb rash is the most common problem on rental cars (or hire cars as the British call them).

"Oops," I said trying to continue paying attention to the road. Hitting the curb was happening so much the first time I drove in Britain that I almost didn't hear it when she shouted it. Surely, she must be making it up if she says it so often.

Nope.

The problem wasn't the driving; that was the easy bit. I had spent my whole driving life since I was 15 years old driving on the left side of the car, and on the right side of the road. When it came to switch to the other side, my brain simply could not spatially process the difference. It was impossible to imagine the physics of the car from the opposite side. As a consequence, on those first miles, I met the curb quite a bit. But, I discovered happiness driving in Britain. Pure happiness. Driving in Britain is maddening for an American. It's not the reversal of the driving; it's the tiny country lanes, the high speeds, the speed cameras, and most of all the distances. You see, English miles are different than American miles.

I don't mean that in the sense that they use the metric system and we don't. No, Britain has a hybrid measurement system where they still use miles in the American sense. But when you calculate something on Google maps or your SatNav, and it says it's only forty miles away, you think, "Oh right, I'll be there in half an hour." If you were in America, you would be right. In England, you would be lucky to get there in an hour. English miles are longer than American miles.

When I prepared to drive in the UK for the first time, I put a lot of work into it. First, I had to be old enough. No one would rent a car to me until I was older than twenty-five. So, on all our trips to Britain up to that point, we took trains and taxis and buses whenever we wanted to go somewhere. The first time I was going to be able to drive in Britain, it was going to be liberation. We could finally go everywhere we wanted. Countless readings and British TV had warned me that driving would be different in Britain, so I tried my best to prepare.

The first step was to learn the rules of the road. Thinking ahead one trip to London, I purchased the AA Highway Code, the "official" booklet that teaches you the rules of the road in Britain. I picked it up at Hatchards, my favorite bookstore in London. I had to ask for help to find it. When the chap at the till could detect I was an American, I could see a bit of an eye roll when I exclaimed I was going to master English driving before I even got on the road.

I studied that book for hours. It all seemed pretty straightforward. The biggest issue, really, was learning all the different signs. The British have so many. It seemed like they had many more than America did. I studied and studied the diagrams for the roundabouts: the one terrifying element of driving on British roads. We simply don't have roundabouts in America, so I'd never driven in one. As with most things when it comes to studying a book, it really doesn't prepare you for reality. Poor Jackie had to keep the book in her hands the first few trips while we looked up rules and signs along the way.

Our first time hiring a car came before the age of ubiquitous SatNavs. You could rent one from the car rental company, but that was $25 a day. Smartphones were still relatively new at this point and didn't work outside the USA. So, we had to by a road atlas. I turned to Stanfords, the travel bookstore in London, for this. I spent quite a bit of time staring at the shelf of road atlases in the basement.. I couldn't figure out which one was best.

"Pardon, do you need help?" asked a woman who was nearby. She didn't appear to work there. It was very odd indeed to have a stranger speak to you in Britain.

"Yes, I'm trying to buy the best road atlas."

"Oh, lovely." She then went into a Byzantine explanation, asking me along the way what I needed it for and finally made a recommendation. "It even has the speed cameras," she finished.

I mumbled a thank you and picked it off the shelf.

I still have this British road atlas to this day - over ten years later.

When I first got into an English car. I had no idea what the hell I was doing. Everything was backwards. I was on the wrong side. Jackie was sitting where I should be sitting. The shifter was in the wrong spot. At least the pedals were the same. Thankfully, I saved myself a lot of grief and rented an automatic. In Britain, most cars are stick shift, and it costs extra to rent an automatic. I looked at Jackie nervously, wondering if I should have paid extra for the insurance excess policy.

And then I turned the key.

I'll never forget the first time I heard the sound of that diesel engine, that knocking sound as it got going. It's my most favorite sound in Britain. I will miss it when it's gone. Diesel cars are being phased out in Britain because they pollute too much. I once drove a hybrid British car, and it just wasn't the same.

"Right, let's do this," I said, shifting it into gear. It took a few minutes to get used to being on the wrong side. But, you know what, it was easy, just like driving back home. And then we got to our first roundabout.

"Give the right of away," was my mantra as I navigated through one for the first time.

It was great.

So easy.

Now, I love roundabouts. America is learning to love them. My hometown in Indiana even started building them.

We left Heathrow and drove onto the M25 and headed for the West Country. This was a good way to start - highway driving is always the easiest driving to do. Lanes are wider. Single track lanes are a challenge and I do not recommend doing them right off the bat. I got the hang of it. The signs were easy to decipher. Signs you won't see billboards in Britain are billboards. American freeways are cluttered with billboard after billboard, which while gaudy and terrible also provide a mild form of entertainment on long car rides. In Britain, there are no billboards - or hoardings as they're called. Even on Britain's motorways, there are no billboards. There is nothing between you and the beautiful landscape. It was refreshing to see, even on that first drive. It also made my first drive much safer, as I wasn't constantly distracted by billboards.

I took it slow, letting people overtake me, learning that you never sit in the far right lane - if someone comes up on your tail, you get out of the way immediately. In theory, it's supposed to be like this in the USA, but no one ever gets out of the way. I kept to the speed limit, mindful that there were speed cameras everywhere. We had plotted our route in the atlas and followed it precisely, and we made it to our destination without incident and without getting lost.

When I stepped out the car, I was practically shaking. I'd done it - I'd driven in England.

It became old hat. Over the years, I've driven over a dozen times in Britain and logged over 10,000 miles. Most recently, we drove from Land's End in Cornwall all the way north to John O'Groats in Scotland - a drive of over 1,000 miles. I love driving in Britain. There's nothing better than open tarmac in the English countryside, with ClassicFM playing on the radio, enjoying a grand day out with your travel partner.

It's just we're always a bit ambitious with our plans. After all, English miles are longer than American miles. We learned this on our first expedition from Shaftesbury to Weymouth on the Dorset coast. When we mapped it out, it said it was thirty-seven miles away. No problem, I thought - we'll be there in half an hour, just like driving over to the next town in America.

I laugh at myself while I type this.

Yes, it was thirty-seven miles. But it took us almost an hour and a half to get there. Why is that? There are very few straight roads in England. And the roads from Shaftesbury to Weymouth are certainly not straight. They weave their way through a varied landscape. The speed limit goes up and down constantly. You pass through small villages that require you to slow down (speed cameras are watching your every move). You get stuck at traffic lights. Then you get stuck behind a dreaded lorry, a heavy goods semi, the entire way. When we finally arrived in Weymouth for the first time, it felt like a victory. We were exhausted, and we'd only traveled thirty seven miles!

We'd lost most of the morning. It was practically lunchtime!

There was a sinking feeling when I realized that we would have to repeat the journey back. You begin to see why British people plan their grand days out. A short journey will take you all bloody day. No wonder the trains are so popular. The Victorians didn't care about the landscape and just blasted straight tunnels through everything. Much more efficient.

It was a lesson we had to learn over and over - it will always take longer to get where we need to go in Britain than we think it will. Oh, it won't take us long to drive from one end of the Cotswolds to the other.

WRONG.

It will take all day!

Are you mad for even attempting it?

When we tell British people things like this, they sort of chuckle and give you that look of "Oh, you simple American."

I don't want any of this to sound like a complaint. When we drove into Weymouth and found a seaside car park and looked at the ocean for the first time in my life, the journey had been very much worth it.

I've had my bouts of bad luck over the last few years. On one trip, we'd brought the whole family with us and rented a station wagon (which still proved too small). It was a bloody challenge to drive, especially in the rain when visibility was bad. I had mostly good luck on this trip, but I was wasn't so lucky when I hit a metal gate. Twice. That ended up costing £700.

On another trip, we had a late afternoon flight but planned our drive back to the airport to stop at a Stately Home on the way. Petworth House had a Turner exhibition to coincide with the release of the film *Mr. Turner*, which was filmed there. So, we had to stop. It was very much worth it. The exhibition not so much, but it was a treat to see all the Turners (and all the other great works in the gallery) at Petworth. When we finished, we were rushing back to the airport and backed into a fence trying to get out of the cramped car park. I got out, and I'd broken a taillight. Crap! I spent the whole drive back to the airport nervous I would get hit with a big bill.

They didn't notice.

Whew! Dodged an expensive bullet there.

One thing I did wait to do was drive in London. That's one thing people told me I should fear.

"Oh, don't drive in London; you'll get lost and stuck in traffic."

When I finally did drive there, I had no problems whatsoever. Never got stuck in traffic and I never got lost thanks to the trusty SatNav.

My most exciting journey was driving through the Hardknott Pass in Cumbria. This is Britain's steepest road, and it's well known to reduce even the most hardened drivers to tears. We had a columnist for Anglotopia attempt it many years ago, and her manual car struggled to make the climb, and when she made it over, she was in tears. So, I approached it nervously.

When I mapped my journey, it didn't appear very long, but I knew better by this point. I allocated the entire morning to drive through the Hardknott Pass, and it's a good thing I did. I took my time, enjoying the stunning views of Cumbria as I climbed up and up with higher altitudes. Then, I found the pass. I took it slow, following the flow of traffic. It was a single track lane, but cars were very polite and gave way as needed. The hybrid car I was driving didn't really care for the hills (and I didn't care for the car either). When I reached the peak, there was a spot to pull off, and I took pictures and admired the view behind me, thinking I'd conquered a major driving challenge. It was a beautiful sunny day, so I had the weather on my side.

I crested the hill and began descending into a valley. And then I started ascending again. Then, warning signs appeared.

> *30% Gradient.*
> *Narrow route, severe bends.*
> *Road Suitable for cars and light vehicles only.*
> *Unsuitable for all vehicles in winter conditions.*

Then right after that, a National Trust marker indicated that I was now entering the Hardknott Pass.

Hang on a minute, the climb and pass I'd just made wasn't the main show?

Jackie wasn't with me on this trip, so she didn't have to sit in the passenger seat with me terrified next to her. The climb I'd just been through was bad enough; now, there was another one.

I began the climb.

And it was steeper.

And there were cliff drop-offs next to the road.

And cars coming the opposite way.

When I finally made it over the real Hardknott Pass, I needed a drink.

And I don't drink.

Thankfully, there was a steam train on the other side. That sufficed!

It took me all morning to climb the Hardknott Pass, passing through the most beautiful scenery I'd ever seen at that point. There was a stop at the Hardknott Roman Fort and stunning views of the Irish Sea. I'd taken my time and was richly rewarded. I spent all day driving through there, and then visited a castle at the other side (along with a steam train ride on a narrow gauge railway). Even after a decade of experience driving in Britain, I was caught out by English miles.

When my day was over, I still needed to get back to my hotel. Which was back over the Hardknott Pass, and I certainly wasn't going *that* way again. I had to take the long way, which, of course, didn't seem that long on the map.

That's the thing about English miles. They always catch you out, but you don't mind. English miles are longer than American miles, and you want them to be longer so the journey never ends.

THE CHURCHILLIAN

It's always weird when you're watching a social media firestorm in real time on the internet. It started off rather innocuous enough. I've followed Commander Scott Kelly since he spent his record breaking year on the International Space Station. I've even read his autobiography. He and his brother are the closest we have to superhero astronauts. His time in space and his subsequent public profile has gained him quite a following on social media. And it never really bit him until one day, he dared to quote Sir Winston Churchill on Twitter: "One of the greatest leaders of modern times, Sir Winston Churchill said, 'in victory, magnanimity.' I guess those days are over."

Never mind that he had a point. What followed was a social media firestorm that ended up with days of debate and think pieces about Churchill's legacy in the modern world. How dare he quote Churchill, he was a terrible person. An imperialist. He killed three million people in the Bengal famine. He was a mass murderer, just as bad as Hitler. Most of this is, of course, wrong. Most of it is complicated. But the sheer ignorance of the social media mob about Churchill, his life and what he did to save Western civilization, really gave me pause to think that we may actually be doomed as a society. Why? Because I'm a Churchillian.

On the surface, I should not be a Churchillian. If you've read Anglotopia for any length of time, you should have no idea what my political stances are because we don't talk about current politics on the site. If we do talk about politics, it's only in a historical context. While history can be very political, we focus on the indisputable history. We focus on the facts. You can bring your beliefs into it in the comments section, but we try to be impartial. So, you don't know that I'm pretty liberal. Liberal in the classical sense. I often joke that I'm "left of Marx." I'm not a communist or communist sympathizer. I grew up watching Star Trek, which imagines a communist utopia without want. But we'll never abolish want unless we can abolish scarcity. Until we can abolish scarcity, capitalism is the best system we have to work with.

If you put up a Venn diagram of my political beliefs and Sir Winston Churchill's known beliefs, there would not be much overlap. I've spent the last fifteen years of my life learning as much about him as I can. To me, he is the greatest Briton, and he did more to ensure we live in a more peaceful, freer world than when he left it. I disagree with him on many points, but that doesn't matter. Churchill saved the world. He wasn't just a politician; he was a writer. A painter. An orator. A family man. A hero. And he did all of these things well. There's so much more to Churchill than any mistakes he made in his life. People are complicated. There's so much we can learn from Churchill, so it was crushing to watch the social media mob just completely dismiss him. When Scott Kelly issued his mealy-mouthed apology, I lost a lot of respect for him.

Churchill would never have done such a thing.

I wasn't always a Churchillian, but I became one. I'd always had an interest in World War II history growing up. I grew up with the generation that had the History Channel in its 90s heyday. The joke was that it was the Hitler channel. I soaked up anything about the war. Churchill was just one of many faces in the tapestry of war. I never really focused in on him. I knew nothing about the man or his life. That all changed when I started traveling to Britain. The entire country lives in his shadow. I saw it, even on my first trip to London in 2001.

Since I was so interested in World War II, my mum and I made time to visit the Cabinet War Rooms. They were hard for us to find, as we didn't know London very well. I remember walking amongst the grey government buildings of Whitehall, stately in their post-imperial glory and wondering where this place was. Eventually, we found the unassuming entrance between two buildings. We bought our tickets and stepped into an elevator, descending down into a world I'd never seen before.

When you step off the elevator with your audio guide, you're immediately taken into an experience where you're given the background of the blitz. There are sirens playing and airplanes flying overhead. A voice narration paints a picture of wartime London. Then, you hear his voice. It was the first time I'd really heard his wartime words in a context that made me stop and listen. They were beautiful.

"Never in the course of human events has so much been owed to so few."

As the audio-visual presentation went on, I began to realize something I'd never understood back home. World War II was a big deal to the British, a much bigger deal than it was to America. World War II is a big deal in America, but on the home front, it didn't really affect daily life because the war was happening elsewhere. All Americans knew were occasional shortages of imported goods, the occasional letter about a dead loved one, but the wartime economy was pumping. The war was *over there*. In Britain, the war was present every day. It was a daily existential battle for survival. I had no idea until I visited the War Rooms.

I listened more intently to that audio guide than anything in my life. I soaked in every word. The War Rooms are very much so focused on Churchill. He spent the war here. It was his space. It was designed to make fighting the war as frictionless as possible for him. He even had a bed there. There was a microphone for his speeches. It was an incredible place, and as my head filled with stuff about him, I knew I had to learn more.

So, as we exited through the gift shop, the first thing I did was pick up a short biography of him. That was an excellent springboard for me. It ended up turning me into a Churchillian. Several books about him, several films about him, several documentaries about him later, I like to think I know quite a bit about the man. When I learned there was a word for enthusiasts about Churchill, I knew the title immediately belonged to me.

Ever since then, I've tried to connect with Churchill on a deeper level. The more you learn about him, the more you learn that he was a complicated individual. He made mistakes. He was occasionally not nice. He was both a skilled politician and a failed politician. He felt like he was never good enough to live up to the hype he had built up for his father. He would sometimes back the wrong side, such as his support for Edward VIII during the abdication crisis. He was not a perfect man. There are no perfect humans. Only humans. But when Britain needed a hero during World War II, he was there. When he was called up to serve, he led the entire country to victory.

When the film *The Gathering Storm* came out in 2002 on HBO, it instantly became one of my favorite films. It painted a beautiful portrait of a complicated man. It inspired me to be better. I loved the interplay of the relationship with his wife Clementine. When I watched the film for the first time with Jackie, who was only my girlfriend then and probably felt like she was forced to watch the film, she said to me, "You realize, you're Churchill reincarnated, right?"

"Why do you say that?" I asked, rather shocked.

"You're an asshole.. You love England in the same way he did. You have red hair. You like to write instead of paint. And you want to live in a Stately Home like him. You're Churchill, reincarnated."

Even nearly fifteen years later, she still says this about me, even if she was being cheeky about the asshole part.

Now, I don't believe in things like reincarnation or astrology, but I like to think she had a point.

I made it my mission to visit all the places in Britain connected to him so I could be closer to him and understand him more.

I had to visit Chartwell. Chartwell was his beloved home. Located in the Weald of Kent, positioned with great views of the English countryside, Chartwell was where Churchill's soul lived. After he bought the house, against the wishes of his wife, he set about turning it into the perfect English idyll. It would be his daily inspiration, even during the dark days of World War II. I had to visit.

In 2011, I was in London for a wedding. A local couple by the name of William and Kate, just a small affair. The kind where one million people line the Mall to watch it unfold. That sort of thing. After the wedding festivities were over with, I had one day left in England. It was a bit of a stolen day. I was in England to cover the royal wedding for Anglotopia. This normally would have been fine, but Will and Kate have the temerity to schedule their wedding for three weeks after Jackie had given birth to our first son. Every moment I was away, I was away from them.

But I had one more day, and I was determined to make the most of it because I didn't know when I would get a chance to get back to England. We weren't brave enough to travel with a baby yet, but were by May 2012. I decided I was going to go to Chartwell. I made an early start. Chartwell is not particularly easy to get to if you don't have a car, so I had to get there by train. Thankfully, I got good advice on how to get there. I got on a train at Charing Cross, then took it to Sevenoaks in Kent. Then, I took a taxi to Chartwell and arranged with the driver to pick me up in a few hours. It was actually really easy.

The house works on a timed entry system, and, thankfully, it wasn't too crowded that day. You walk through the house in a self-guided fashion. It's not a grand house by any means compared to Britain's other grand Stately Homes (like Blenheim where he was born). It's a very intimate place. It doesn't take too many people to feel like it's crowded. There is a docent in every room happy to chat about interesting things . The rooms are filled with artifacts from his life; his beautiful paintings grace the walls. The house is a living shrine to him.

However, the house was a financial drain for him. Churchill spent his entire life in financial difficulties. He always lived better than his actual income allowed. While he was a member of a "great" aristocratic family, he didn't get much money from them because his father was the younger son. Members of Parliament in those days were not paid, so he had to rely on income he made himself from writing. He would spend his whole life catching up, promising future books for income (as a full-time writer, I sympathize). Even after the war, he was not in a great financial position, and when word got around that he was considering selling Chartwell, his rich friends could not countenance such a thing. Surely, the man who led Britain to victory deserved to keep his home. They pooled their funds together and bought the house from him, giving him financial stability and allowing the family to live there until they died, at which point the house would be given to the National Trust (the heritage organization that runs many of Britain's Stately Homes).

I felt enormously privileged to be able to walk through his home. It wasn't a mausoleum. It was a monument to his life and greatness. My favorite room was his study and library where he wrote many of his great speeches and books. I noticed a small door at the far end of the room and enquired what it was.

"Oh, that's his bedroom. It's closed off to the public. Mrs. Churchill asked that one room be kept private since it was his personal space."

I nodded. Makes sense. How nice that there is still a bit of the house that his to this day. After seeing the house, I spent hours wandering the grounds and enjoying the beautiful place. The grounds of Chartwell are laid out exactly as Churchill intended - he even dug the ponds himself. You see his idealized view of England by walking through his gardens. If you do visit, be sure to go through the garden, observe the brick wall he built with his own two hands and then visit his studio. There, you can see dozens of his paintings, where the easel is set up as if he just popped out for a cigar and will be right back.

The next year, I was able to visit his birthplace at Blenheim Palace. Before we arrived, we pulled off in the small village of Bladon to visit his grave. Churchill wanted to be buried with his illustrious ancestors. We parked in the pub across the way and walked up the hill to the churchyard where he's buried. It's a piece of old England, the kind of place you would expect him to be born. The churchyard is right next to an elementary school, and during our visit, the children were screaming with joy and playing. There was a lone woman, tending graves in the churchyard.

When I found his grave, I was really surprised at how unassuming it was. Compared to the Duke of Wellington or Horatio Nelson at St. Paul's Cathedral, Churchill's rather simple stone slab in the Bladon churchyard was understated. It was definitely showing the wear of many years (it would later be restored into better condition). I remember being moved by the fresh wreaths of poppies from European countries, grateful for his service in saving their homes. I paid my respects, which is rather odd. I'd never known the man personally, but he was such an important influence in my life. He felt like a relative.

We popped into the church, which was a typical small village church. It smelled of damp and rotting wood. They were Churchill mementos on sale - including a DVD of his funeral. You paid for things in the honesty box in the wall. Despite going out of my way to buy that DVD, I've never been able to bring myself to watch it. I'm afraid it would be too upsetting. At least my pounds went to the upkeep of the grave.

After visiting the grave, we drove down the street to Blenheim Palace, which is a proper Stately Home - one of the finest in Britain. It was a gift from Queen Anne to the first Duke of Marlborough and his wife Sarah Churchill, for leading the British to victory at the Battle of Blenheim. The Spencer-Churchill family became a dynasty in British politics and history. So important was the family, it helped Churchill think that he too was destined for greatness. His father, Randolph Churchill, was the second son of the current Duke in the late 1800s. While he and his very pregnant American wife Jennie Jerome were visiting the house, she went into labor.

The birthing room is now open to the public. In fact, it's one of the first rooms you see when you begin your house tour. It's a rather strange room, unassuming and probably one of the smallest in the house. Yet in that place, with the peeling wallpaper and the simple steel bed, one of the most important people in history was born. You don't really have time to linger since the room is so small; the crowd has to move through it quite quickly. Still, Blenheim is more of a proper monument to Churchill's greatness.

While Chartwell was where Churchill's soul lived, his spiritual home was Blenheim. It was the fount of his aristocratic bearing, the source of his ability to trace his family's role in British history. He spent a lot of time there in his childhood and as an adult. Blenheim was the "old England" Churchill was fighting to defend. The England of primogeniture, aristocratic dominance, great houses, servants, grand gardens, and empire. It was an England that only exists in a much smaller form today (and that's not a bad thing). Churchill was defending an ideal during his life, and that ideal is very antithetical to the world we live in now. Churchill was defending his empire. The empire did not last after the war (and again, that's not a bad thing).

If Chartwell was where he wrote, and Blenheim was where he played, then the House of Commons was where he worked. He went into politics at a very young age, hoping to become a big important man like his father. He also hoped he did not descend into a joke as his father did. Parliament is the final monument to Churchill that any Churchillian should visit. And I don't mean the statue of him they put in Parliament Square. Churchill spent more of his adult life in the House of Commons than he did anywhere else.

Many don't realize that when he made his famous speeches in World War II, he made them to the House of Commons first, which did not have radio or recordings in those days. When we hear many of his speeches now, they were either recordings made later that day at the BBC or made years later when he was trying to make some extra money by recording and selling his speeches. His fellow MPs got to hear his stirring words before anyone else. What a privilege.

Visiting the House of Commons is a surreal experience. You can feel the presence of him. He's so respected by Parliament that they put a statue of him right outside the door. The House of Commons we see now is not the one Churchill spent most of his life in. That one was destroyed in a bombing raid in World War II; the current House is a post-WWII creation - made to look as close to the old version as possible, though more austere to reflect the post-war economy of Britain. The picture of Churchill inspecting the damage is quite moving when you realize how much of his life he spent in the room. It made the war all the more personal for him. Right outside the door, next to his statue, you can still see the bomb damage in the stonework that was never repaired as a silent monument to the war damage.

The House of Commons represented everything he stood for and everything he defended during the war. It's easy to sit and complain about our politicians, call them liars and the room a den of snakes. Regardless, I still have a lot of respect for anyone who can become an MP and serve in the house, even if I disagree with everything they believe in. Parliament is an almost 1,000-year institution, and many parliaments around the world are based on it. It's an amazing place to visit.

I'm always amazed to hear that at the age of forty, Churchill took to painting and mastered it. Well, mastered it as much as an amateur could. Churchill wrote a great essay on painting – "Painting as a Pastime" - that stipulated any well-rounded person should also have a hobby. Not just any hobby, but a hobby that forces them to create and to practice and to become skilled. It helps work the mind, and bleeds into your "real" life. Painting, for Churchill, was a pastime that helped him focus and helped him emotionally. After seeing his paintings at Chartwell and a few elsewhere, I'd always hoped to see more. That led me one day to go to Atlanta, Georgia.

I'd been to Atlanta before many times to DragonCon, a multimedia, multi-genre convention held every Labor Day weekend. So, I was familiar with the place. I got word that the Millennium Gate Museum was putting on an exhibition of his paintings, the first time they had been shown in America for quite some time. I had to go. The problem was that Anglotopia was keeping me very busy (this was the heyday of Anglotees, a business that has since almost died) and I had two young kids. Leaving to go to Atlanta for any amount of time by myself was a non-starter.

That year, though, Jackie gave me as one of my Christmas presents a free pass to go to Atlanta for the day to go see the paintings.

She knew how much it meant for me to be able to go see these paintings. We wanted to go together, but finding a sitter in those days was difficult, so I'd have to go alone. I also had to do it on a budget. Thankfully, I'd accrued enough air miles in my account to book my ticket to Atlanta. It only cost me $5 to fly. I booked a flight out early in the morning and then booked a flight back later that same day. It seems absurd to fly to a place for one day and then return home, but Chicago to Atlanta by plane is not far and I used to work at a company where people would do it every week to visit clients. I tried to treat it as no big deal.

On the day I was due to fly, I was so excited. I was recovering from a 24-hour stomach flu. Despite this, I was still determined to still go. Churchill would not accept anything less! I drove to the airport and got on my plane to Atlanta. I was there in just over an hour. I rented a car and drove right to the museum as it was opening. I saw the exhibition, and it was a real treat to see Churchill's paintings in person again. They had some of his best, and these paintings were special - many hadn't been on public display before because they were still owned by the Churchill family (some of whom now lived in Atlanta, thus why the exhibition was there). The real treat was Churchill's painting of Marrakech, which was the only painting he did during World War II - and he did it in the presence of Franklin Roosevelt during one of their summits. It was a true artifact of historical importance and inspiring to see in person.

I took my time, taking in the paintings. After all, I'd flown a long way to see them. When I was done, I got back in my car, drove around Atlanta bit, then returned to the airport to come home. I never wrote about the experience for Anglotopia simply because I didn't think anyone would be interested. That was an error on my part. It was pure laziness in those days. But I'd wanted the experience to be for me, not everyone else.

In all the years that I've run Anglotopia, Churchill has been an invisible force behind the website. He's my daily inspiration. I have his painting of Chartwell on my wall and a bust of him on my desk next to me. Running a business has its up and downs; the last few years there have been more downs than anything. "Never give up" is one of my personal mantras and there have been many situations where I almost threw in the towel. But I didn't. I stayed the course. That's what Churchill would have done. Wars are not won by retreats. You don't achieve greatness by hiding. If you want something, you work bloody hard for it.

Last year, I visited Chartwell again, which was strange after not having been there since 2011. I was in a much different place. I was no longer in my 20's. I was not a young father. I'm in my mid-thirties now, and I have an 8-year-old and a 6-year-old. One thing that was important to Churchill was family, and I'm proud to say that it's very important to me too.

This time I was led around on a private tour by the staff - the perks of being recognized as a publication. I was researching an article on Winston Churchill at home, and they agreed to show me around. I came in a couple hours before closing and got a "behind the ropes" tour with the very knowledgeable staff. It was a real privilege (shameless plug, search the website to read the article). Anyway, towards the end of the tour, the house was beginning to close for the day.

After my guide finished, she turned to me as said, "All right, you have two choices. We can pop down to the studio to look at his paintings, or we can go back up, and you can see his private bedroom."

This was one of the most exciting moments in my entire Churchillian life.

"The bedroom please," I said trying to keep my cool. "I've been to the studio."

She led me back through the house, up to the studio where he did most of his writing. She led me over the barrier designed to stop wayward tourists.

An alarm went off.

"You can ignore that."

She took out a key and unlocked that small, unassuming door I'd seen back in 2011. The door opened into a rather small room.

It smelled like an old room; the dull sunlight from the rainy day was shining through the window. She didn't turn the lights on. You could see the view over the Weald of Kent out the window. To one side, was Churchill's rather small bed. Some of his paintings were laying on it.

"The room is a bit askew right now as we're in the middle of conservation work," she said.

I wasn't allowed to take pictures, but she kindly let me have a moment. I'd entered Churchill's private inner sanctum. The room where he slept. Where he lied his head and composed his speeches in his head (or shouted at his long-suffering secretaries outside the door). I so wanted to sit in one of the chairs and just inhabit that place for hours. But as the chair was original to the room, no one gets to sit in it. Churchill was probably the last person to sit there.

I only had five minutes in the room, but it was one of the biggest treats in my life.

I'm a Churchillian. I'm proud of it. I will defend him to my dying breath. But I understand the nuance that he was not a perfect man. He had terrible opinions that horrify modern sensibilities. He stood for Empire and Victorian values. He was the discredited British aristocracy in living form. Still, he was a hero. He was human. He has been there for me in dark times, as he was there for Britain. Anglotopia would not be where it was if it wasn't for him. The world would not be where it was if it wasn't for him. So, Scott Kelly, in the rare chance you might be reading this, you were absolutely right, and you should retract your apology.

CHRISTMAS ON GOLD HILL

On a cold December night, as we digested the consumption of a rather unsuccessful Christmas, Jackie and I began to look ahead at the coming year. Christmas hadn't been a big success for us that year – financial, familial, and weather-related problems proved challenging. While we were always grateful for whatever Christmas we could provide for our family, we felt the urge to get away from the Christmas rat race. We had enough of ticking the boxes of a perfect American Christmas. We had heard from our friends that their cottage in Dorset, Updown Cottage on Gold Hill in Shaftesbury, which was usually booked for Christmas every year, was available.

Looking at each other, I said, "Why don't we just spend next Christmas at Updown Cottage?"

"Yes," Jackie responded.

It was all she needed to say. I immediately messaged our friends and reserved the cottage for Christmas and New Year's.

Now, we had a year to figure out how to make it happen, let alone pay for it. The next year proved to be a busy one – the most notable event occurring in June when our second child was born. But we never lost sight of the goal to spend the Christmas holidays in England, and try to have the most English Christmas vacation we could have. It was an amazing and stressful journey but so rewarding that we're planning on doing it again.

Our week in London before we went to Dorset went by in the blink of an eye, and before we knew it, it was time to pick up the rental car and head to Dorset for the grand event. We were quite ready to leave the pre-Christmas chaos in London. We left in the early afternoon, and we had no trouble with traffic. Shaftesbury is about a two-hour drive from London, and it's always a pleasant one. I really enjoy driving in England at any time of the year. When we pulled up to Updown Cottage for our dream Christmas, we found it already lit up and decorated for the holidays.

It was quite a welcome. The cottage owners had come down and decorated the cottage just for us – that included a tree with all the fixings (lights and ornaments). As soon as we opened the door, we stepped into an English Christmas. They'd thought of everything to make sure we had the perfect English Christmas, including leaving us some lovely gifts. More on those later; they were hidden from the kids!. Our son was very excited to see all the decorations, and we all felt like it was finally Christmastime.

One thing that's hard to get used to when you're in England in the winter is the early nights. Because Britain is further north than most of the US, it gets dark very early in the winter. The sun starts going down at 3:30 p.m. and it's gone by 4:00. These short days with a low winter sun cruising across the horizon make you want to make the most of each day: early starts and early ends. Thankfully, places still stay open to their normal times; it's just dark out. It takes some getting used to. The flip side is that in the summer, sometimes the sun doesn't go down until past 10:00 p.m., leading to very long days and trouble falling asleep if you go to bed early. So, it was a real treat as we pulled up to the cottage and found it lit up for Christmas. It was right out of a postcard.

We began thinking about our Christmas dinner months before our trip. Our goal was to have as traditional a British Christmas dinner as possible (with a few American embellishments to make sure the kids ate it). We discovered the main dish for Christmas dinner in Britain is usually turkey or goose, but most people do turkey these days. We found this intriguing as turkey is the dish of choice in America for Thanksgiving. We decided on turkey since neither of us liked goose. It was a bit odd that we would be having turkey twice in one year – it also turns out that many of the side dishes in a British Christmas dinner are also the same as an American Thanksgiving dinner.

For months, we had fantasies of our British Christmas dinner in our perfect little English cottage in Dorset. After speaking with our British friends, we discovered that while you can find turkeys in stores, it's not as common. They recommended ordering a turkey from a local butcher. We could order the exact size we would need and have it delivered right to the cottage. This seemed like the best option for us, so we didn't have to search for one. It also kept the money in the local economy and ensured that our turkey was locally sourced and raised. When the bell rang on our cottage door, and the butcher made the delivery (we also bought some other meats we thought we'd eat), we were shocked at how small the turkey was, it was maybe half the size of what we would have at Thanksgiving. But that didn't matter, it was only the four of us, and our daughter wasn't even on solid foods yet. It would be plenty. The turkey was fresh, butchered the day before, just for us. We had it delivered two days before Christmas and stored it in the cottage's fridge until the big day. We joked that we drove by our turkey grazing on the way down from London.

In Britain, they don't have Santa Claus. They have Father Christmas. Father Christmas has roots in anti-Puritan sentiment, and he became a symbol of merrymaking. As time progressed the idea of Father Christmas and Santa Claus merged. It's also less common for children to visit him and tell him what they want for Christmas. There are some places that do it, but often you have to book months in advance (like at Harrods, sometimes you need to book as far ahead as August). We hedged our bets and took the kids to see Santa back at home before we left. We had to explain to our oldest that Santa would find him no matter where we spent Christmas. Once we did arrive in London, however, we did manage to run into Father Christmas on a visit to Selfridges, so the kids were thrilled about that.

As we settled in for our stay at Updown Cottage, Christmas went from "that event we'll worry about once we get to Dorset" to "Uh-oh, Christmas is in two days." We still needed to do some Christmas shopping, knowing full well that we had to keep it simple so that we didn't overfill our luggage. We had a lovely time visiting the High Street in Shaftesbury and buying gifts for the kids that they couldn't get anywhere else. One of them, a small bell toy for our daughter, became one of her favorites. We also ventured out and visited a mall in Southampton for the first time. We were able to pick up lovely Christmas pajamas for all of us, a tradition that Jackie insists upon, so we were properly attired on Christmas morning. Jackie and I also separated and did a bit of secret shopping so we could buy gifts for each other without spoiling the surprise.

Before we knew it, the night before the big day arrived. We had a lovely dinner and watched *The Snowman* – a charming cartoon that encapsulates British Christmas perfectly. I'd never seen it, but knew it had become a TV tradition in many British households, so I was looking forward to seeing it for the first time with my kids. *The Snowman* was a cartoon just thirty minutes in length that was produced in the 1980s. Based off the children's book by Raymond Briggs, *The Snowman* is about a young boy who magics his Christmas snowman to life and goes on a grand Christmas adventure. There is no dialogue in the entire short film. It's told entirely with visuals and music. The song in the middle, "Walking in the Air," sung by a young boy, is the most beautiful evocative song that captures the magic and joy of Christmas, but also the melancholy that comes with the holiday. You will hear the song everywhere in Britain during the festive season. When I saw it for the first time, in that cottage in Dorset, I cried. It really encapsulated British Christmas for me. It was a moment of pure bliss.

I dare you to watch *The Snowman* (and the recent sequel - *The Snowdog*) without tissues.

The kids were bubbling with anticipation, and for once, we didn't have to fight them on going to bed at the proper time. After they went to bed, Jackie and I spent the rest of the evening wrapping their presents and watching British telly (and sneaking away to wrap our secret presents for each other). By the end of the night, despite our apparent restraint, there was quite a number of presents under the tree, and we were quite chuffed. We could not wait for the kids to get up and see their presents, their first British Christmas.

Of course, they woke ridiculously early, and who could blame them?

The next few hours were a dizzying array of wrapping paper flying everywhere and copious amounts of tea to make sure we could wake up for the day. We eagerly opened our presents from Jane and Simon, the cottage owners, and they were truly lovely and thoughtful. Mine was a specially made Ordnance Survey map of Shaftesbury and its surroundings – perfect for walks!

And then, at 8:00 a.m., the bells started. This was probably my most favorite memory from the trip. Our cottage on Gold Hill is right down the hill from the local church (which was built in the Victorian Era). On Christmas Day, it was truly lovely to hear the bells ring out for what seemed like forever. It was raining, but it was worth it standing outside the front door to listen to the bells toll. And when they had finished, another church in Shaftesbury followed suit. The cascade of bells on Christmas Day was beautiful. It was something we simply didn't have back home and could only hear in England. It was magnificent. The kids loved it too. I will never forget the bells and will spend my life trying to get back to England for Christmas to hear them again.

After that, it was time for a Christmas breakfast, and then

Jackie got right to work on our Christmas Dinner. My job for the day was to keep the kids out of her hair as she struggled to cook on foreign cookware with foreign directions. Sourcing all the ingredients had been a challenge – between getting the bird and finding all the ingredients at the local grocery stores (which kept odd hours at that time of year and sometimes weren't even open when the door said they should be). The kitchen is on the bottom level of Updown, so it was easy to keep the kids occupied with all their new presents while she cooked. By mid-morning, the house was already filled with the beautiful smells of what was cooking. One British Christmas tradition we could not abide by was Brussel sprouts; we all hate the taste (and the smell is even worse), so we did not include those in our dinner plans.

When our daughter went down for her nap late in the morning, my son and I suited up and went for a walk to Melbury Hill, the tallest hill in the area. It's quite a climb, but the views are amazing. The temperature dipped to a proper winter cold. And what really struck me was the silence. Back home, we live near major roads and industry, so even if you live a bit out in the countryside, there's never much silence. But in Shaftesbury that Christmas it was completely silent. There were no cars on the roads, there was no industry clanging away, there were no airplanes in the sky, there were no trains rumbling along. It's just you and nature and a quiet community getting on with Christmas Day. Occasionally, the silence would be lovingly interrupted by the sound of bells tolling from some distant church.

It's safe to say that it was probably the loveliest Christmas Day I ever experienced, and it wasn't even over yet!

By the time we returned from our walk and recovered with warm cups of tea, it was time for the main event: Christmas dinner. The turkey turned out amazing, and Jackie had no problems roasting it properly in the English oven. All the fixings turned out perfectly. For someone who had never prepared a British Christmas dinner, Jackie hit the ball out of the park, and everything was perfect. The food was great, as was the table setting (and, of course, we popped Christmas crackers). Jackie made homemade Yorkshire puddings for the first time in her life, and they were memorably delicious. Though some things didn't quite turn out so perfectly, like the *hors-d'oeuvres* that ended up burnt. Sadly, we didn't have the family dog with us to scarf them up instead. As we ate our bountiful Christmas dinner, we watched as the sun began to go down on our English Christmas across the Blackmore

Vale below us. Smoke billowed out of the smokestacks of the cottages and farms in the distance.

Soon bedtime came around again, and the kids went to sleep like champs. How could they not? They were exhausted! British Christmas had run them ragged (and us too). After they were sound asleep, we started a fire in Updown's sitting room, opened a bottle of wine, and enjoyed the various Christmas specials on TV. I believe the line-up that year was *Doctor Who* and *Downton Abbey*. It was a treat to watch our favorite shows as they aired in Britain in an old cottage by the fire. I'm not afraid to admit that we did not last long into the evening ourselves; we nodded off in post-Christmas happiness, having had the perfect British Christmas.

In America, most people go back to work on December 26th; the retail stores open back up, then return season begins. There are usually big sales. Many employers will get the day off, but if they're not, shall we say, enlightened, most people are back at their desks on the 26th. In Britain, December 26th is Boxing Day, and it's a Bank Holiday, meaning most things are meant to stay closed. Things have softened in recent years (which is a shame), and most bigger retailers are now open on Boxing Day for limited hours (usually 10:00 a.m. to 4:00 p.m.). The Boxing Day sale is a huge event in the British retail calendar; people go out to buy the things they didn't get or return the presents they didn't want. But as most non-retail employees have the day off, it's still a holiday in those households. We knew this and planned ahead.

We have good friends in Shaftesbury who were kind enough to invite us to their Boxing Day lunch, which was a very special treat. It gave us an opportunity to visit our friends and try some foods we hadn't yet tried. We tried meat pies for the first time, and Jackie fell in love with British pickle spread. It was a lovely and relaxing way to spend an afternoon, and it reminded us that after fifteen years of travel in Britain, the best things we've gotten out of our travels are our friends, not the souvenirs we've brought home. We did miss our families a bit during the holiday period, as they missed us, but we all had celebrations before and after we left. And even though we were far from home, all our friends made us feel right at home, and the spirit of Christmas was plentiful.

Most employers in Britain shut down for the two weeks over Christmas and New Year's, at least in the white-collar area of jobs. The kids are also off school as well. This means the space between Christmas and New Year's is a great time to visit Britain's tourist attractions. We took advantage of this, and visited ruined Corfe Castle, finally rode the Swanage Railway, visited Portsmouth Historic Dockyard and HMS Victory, Longleat House and Safari, and Jane Austen's Home at Chawton (we've written about all of these things on Anglotopia.net). It was a whirlwind. Many of them were not crowded at all, and it was a great time to see so many places (and the weather did improve).

Before we knew it, it was New Year's Eve, and we rang in the new year watching Big Ben bong on the telly rather than watch the ball drop in New York. The next day it was time to begin wrapping up our English Christmas vacation. With much sadness, we packed our bags and headed on to our next destination, the Cotswolds. We packed up our hire car, and strapped the kids into their car seats. Jackie and I looked at the cottage, still decorated for our Christmas. It was a very emotional moment – tears were shed – as we drove away from our perfect British Christmas. We can't wait to do it again.

RIDING IN BLACK TAXI'S

In most major cities, taxis don't really get much love or affection – that's why Uber is so popular now. Then again, most cities aren't like London—a city that loves its iconic black taxis and appreciates the work it takes to learn The Knowledge (the name of the training all London Cabbies go through). I've been riding in London taxis for more than twenty years, and every time I'm in London, I immediately feel at home. Drivers of black taxis are generally nice, know their routes, and keep their cabs clean. Over the years, I've had many lovely adventures in taxis. Despite the love and affection many people have for black taxis, the future of the black taxi industry is uncertain as the London cabbies face unexpected changes .

I don't remember my first black taxi ride, but it happened sometime in the summer of 2001 when I traveled to London for the first time with my mother. There is one experience from that trip that really stuck out and endeared me to drivers of black taxis. As it was our first trip to London, we wanted to be sure to see and experience a lot of culture. We discovered that while we were there, there was a concert at the Royal Albert Hall and we wanted to see it. I can't recall the theme, but I know it featured Tchaikovsky's *Violin Concerto*. The concert was fantastic, but it ended very late. Being new to London, we still didn't know our way around, and from our limited knowledge, we didn't think we could get the Tube back as we didn't know where a station was. Oh, the days before smartphones.

We saw crowds of people head for night buses, but we didn't know what the routes were, leaving us with no idea about which what bus to even take. Our hotel was directly across Hyde Park, so we thought we could walk it. It turned out the park was closed for the evening; although, even if it was open, it would not have been a good idea for just the two of us to walk through it in the dark. We stood around and waited for a taxi. We stood for quite a while and started to get annoyed that no taxis were arriving. Surely, I thought, they knew there was a concert this evening people would have to get home from? We didn't know the neighborhood at all, and all we wanted to do was get back to our hotel. We started walking, hoping we would have better luck finding a taxi on another road. I was only seventeen at the time and still had a lot to learn about how the world works, so both my mother and I got increasingly worried when we could not find a taxi.

Eventually, we were able to find a taxi whose driver was on duty, and he took us back to our hotel. He was incredibly kind during our ride back to the hotel. As some of you will note, a taxi ride from one side of Hyde Park to the other is not cheap nor short. When we arrived at our hotel, we were so happy and relieved to be back, we gave him a very generous tip that worked out to be more than our taxi fare.

"Are you sure?" he yelled as we walked away.

Now, we know tipping is rarely something you have to do in London, but back then we thought it was a suitable thank you for picking us up in an unfamiliar neighborhood and getting us safely back to our hotel. He couldn't believe we would tip him so much. If you do tip a cabby, the general rule is to merely round up to the next pound. From then on, we always felt safe getting into black taxis. Having only ever ridden taxis in Chicago (which are terrible), it was a relief to have such a well-educated taxi industry.

Many people don't know it takes drivers nearly three years to learn how to navigate London's confusing spaghetti noodle layout. They call it the Knowledge, and it's been scientifically proven that as potential black cab drivers learn their trade, the part of their brains responsible for mapping increases in size. Drivers of London's black taxis must memorize every road, attraction, hotel, and monument while being able to navigate between them at any given time. It's a massive commitment on the part of the drivers, but as far as I know, most cities do not make their taxi drivers go through such a grueling course. Black taxis are heavily regulated (and many drivers agree that they're a bit too regulated) to protect the safety and pocketbooks of their passengers. Fares in all black taxis are the same in London. There is another class of London taxi drivers who aren't regulated and don't have to go through as much rigorous training: mini-cab drivers.

Many years after our first positive adventure with a taxi driver, I traveled to London for the first time Jackie. I'd planned the trip for quite some time, and I had a huge surprise in store for her. I was going to whisk her to Paris for the day. She had studied in France and missed it. I decided this was where I would propose to her. This was before High Speed 2 made the Chunnel journey about two hours. Back in 2004, it took almost three hours to ride the train from London through the Chunnel to Paris. This meant that we had a very early morning to make sure we made our train on time. We had to wake up at 4:00 a.m., which is quite early, especially when you're on vacation and nervous about asking a woman to marry you.

We walked from our hotel towards the Tube station, and when we got to the door, we discovered that the station was closed. This was the moment we learned that London's Tube network does not run 24 hours and, in fact, closed at night. As of 2016, there is now a limited Night Tube service. It didn't reopen until 5:00 a.m. The problem was we needed to be at Waterloo to catch our train to Paris and we could not walk it (this was before the Eurostar moved to St. Pancras). We needed a taxi.

There were not a lot of taxis around at 4:30 in the morning. So, with the clock ticking until our train left without us, we started walking, hoping we could find a taxi. When we got a few hundred feet from the Tube station, a man sitting in a silver car with a cigarette hanging out of his mouth tried to get our attention.

"Need a taxi?" he asked.

We turned to him and thought we were saved.

"Yes," I said. "We need to go to Waterloo."

"Well, I'm a taxi, get in," he said.

Something wasn't right. It was rather odd that he was just sitting on the side of the street. He wasn't driving a typical black taxicab. It was a silver passenger car. I did not see a taximeter. And in the dark of 4:30 a.m., the man looked rather scary.

We declined his offer and continued walking until we finally came across a black taxi who whisked us to Waterloo, offering us something of a tour of London's landmarks along the way. This was the first time I heard Buckingham Palace referred to as "Buck House." We learned later that the man we ran into was probably a mini-cab driver. Mini-cab drivers are not allowed to pick up passengers on the street; they can only pick people up if it has been scheduled in advance. Mini-cab drivers don't go through the same training at Black Taxi drivers do (if they go through any at all). They rely on SatNavs to get where they're going (which is not a perfect solution in a country like Britain where the roads never make any sense). They also charge higher rates. More than likely the man who picked us up would have somehow fleeced us in some way. Thankfully, I felt something wasn't right, and we went on our way. However, it was still scary.

When we returned from Paris late that night, we learned about a new taxi phenomenon we hadn't learned of before: the taxi rank. When three hundred people from an international train are deposited into a train station at 10:00 p.m., they all make a run for the taxi rank where, hopefully, there are just as many taxis waiting to take them where they need to go. The British have had a long time to figure these things out, so there are guidelines throughout the station that lead you to the rank. What the guidelines don't tell you is how long the line is when you get there. We couldn't believe how long we had to wait for a taxi, and admittedly, after spending all day in Paris and being exhausted from events of the day (the aforementioned successful proposal), we were in no mood to wait. But we ended our day as we began it, ferried to our hotel by a black taxi driver.

You can always get the pulse of London by talking to cabbies. Some love the city they live and work in, some hate it (and won't hesitate to tell you). Many will happily talk about politics or at least ask you what brings you to London. Most of the time, they're curious to know what Americans find so fascinating about London. Most cabbies are usually polite and happy to talk. Occasionally, you'll get one who doesn't want to chat, and that's fine. We've even come across a very rare sight in the male-dominated London taxi trade – a female black taxi driver.

There was one time when my appreciation for black taxis failed me. Back in 2010, Jackie and I were in London for a quick visit because I had an interview about a possible job with a company based in London. It was an opportunity that would require us to relocate our entire lives to London–something we both had wanted to do for a long time. We traveled over and settled in, and on our first full day there, I put on my nicest suit and headed to the interview. To keep my suit nice and pressed, I wanted to avoid the Underground. It was July, and the Tube is usually very hot. I didn't want to arrive drenched in sweat, so I hailed a taxi.

He pulled up next to me and rolled down his window.

"Can you take me to Tooley Street?" I asked.

"Sorry, what?" he asked.

"I need to get to Tooley Street," I said expecting him to nod and signal me to get in.

He looked at me with a quizzical look (I'll never forget it), and he drove off as fast as he could without a word.

I stood there in my nice suit watching the taxi that should be taking me to my dream job interview drive away. I could not believe it. I don't know what I said wrong. Perhaps the driver didn't know where it was and didn't feel like figuring it out. Perhaps he didn't want to drive that far. Perhaps he didn't want to cross the river (the interview was in Southwark). I don't know, but it's bothered me since then that he just drove off. That was the first time I got slighted by a taxi driver and thankfully it was the last. I eventually found another taxi; the driver was very friendly and knew exactly where I needed to go. I arrived at my interview sweat-free. I was eventually offered the job, but ended up having to turn it down (see the chapter about that).

Many drivers of black taxis have hobbies outside of work; sometimes these elite cabbies even have a second job. Because drivers must have an encyclopedic knowledge of the London streets to pass the "Knowledge" exams, many cabbies end up becoming amateur historians. I've been in quite a few cabs where the driver was more than happy to wax historical about something or other. Sometimes, this is very welcome. Sometimes, like when you're wrestling with two kids under age three, you don't appreciate it quite as much.

Back in 2013, the Anglotopia family spent a week in London before the Christmas season. It was a magical time (something we can't wait to do again); there's nothing quite like Christmas in London. On one of our last days, we decided to spend the day out to visit the Imperial War Museum, which was something we'd been meaning to do for years. We took the Tube, then walked to the museum. Having never been to Lambeth before, we were astonished at how far the museum was from the nearest Tube station. Short walks become much longer when you're pushing two strollers and all the attendant baby gear. Destinations south of the River Thames have always been rather underserved by public transport, and that lesson was reinforced to us that day in London.

We greatly enjoyed our visit to the Imperial War Museum, yet enjoy isn't quite the right word. The kids loved it. There were many wonderful displays about Britain's war history—some fascinating, some downright terrifying (the Blitz Street recreation requires a sedative after experiencing it). We enjoyed a nice lunch with the kids, exited through the usual gift shop, and found ourselves standing on a street corner in Lambeth pondering the long walk back to the Tube station. We simply didn't have it in us that day.

Luckily, a black taxi drove right by, and we hailed him. I will always remember this as one of our best experiences in a taxi. The driver was very friendly, there was ample room inside for our strollers and baby gear, and the whole family sat comfortably. We knew we were in for an expensive cab ride back to our rental flat so we sat back to enjoy the London scenery as it went by. Then the cabby started talking. Turns out, he was a bit of an amateur historian. He proceeded to give us a guided tour all the way back to our flat. Georgian building this, Victorian event that. It was lovely. Being a writer, who makes his living writing about London and Britain, I was familiar with much of what he had to say, but I still learned quite a bit. It was nice to sit back and relax to a guided tour of London while the kids nodded off,. I should add, his history lesson did not alter the correct route in anyway—another hallmark of the London cabby. They will always pick the quickest route. The usual custom is to tip a London cabby up to the next pound, but we were more generous that day as it was such a lovely ride.

London can sometimes be a city of moaners (the British call it whingeing). They moan about everything: the skyscrapers, the property prices, the government, motorists complain about cyclists, and cyclists complain about motorists. And, yes, Londoners even moan about their taxi drivers. They moan about how expensive cabs are, how slow cabs are when they get stuck in traffic, then moan about how expensive cabs are as the taximeter goes up slowly sitting in traffic, they moan about taxi drivers who are too friendly and won't shut up, they moan about taxi drivers who are unfriendly and don't talk at all, they moan about any who dares to share their political opinions (and, oh my, do cabbies love to moan as well if they have the opportunity).

Many would say that this is why apps like Uber and Lyft have become so popular in London. It allows people to get picked up by something that's like a taxi but can cost a lot less. But, you know what? London's legion of black taxi drivers are always there. They know their routes, and they have to deal with an ungodly amount of ill-will towards them (not to mention drunk passengers, bloody passengers, and the occasional birth on the side of the road). Uber drivers and mini-cab drivers don't have the knowledge of London that black taxi cabbies have. They never will. Remember: You get what you pay for. Now, Londoners moan about Uber drivers that don't speak English, urinate in people's front gardens while they wait for jobs, don't know the routes and rely on GPS (which can quite often be wrong). So, it's not surprising that London's black taxi industry isn't going anywhere.

The iconic black taxi isn't just a ride; it's also the office of 30,000 small business owners in London—the drivers themselves. The Hackney Carriage—as they were called at first—is a very British invention. In fact, any are still made in Britain, despite being owned by the Chinese. It's a symbol that's recognized the world over—a sign of Britishness. Most modern London taxis are made by the London Taxi Company, founded in 1899. Ironically, they're not built in London, but, in fact, are manufactured in Coventry. The taxi has had to adapt itself to the modern age as the years have gone on.

There are many rules that dictate the design of the taxi as well. It must have a 25-foot turning radius; legend has it, it's so cabs can make a U-turn at the Savoy Hotel entrance. More than 130,000 London black taxis have been produced at the London Taxi Company's Coventry site over the past sixty years. Annual production averages between 2,000 and 2,500 units per year. Around two-thirds of production goes into London via a dealership in Islington while the rest usually enter service in British cities that have adopted codes similar to London's. As part of the conditions of carriages, taxis must not be older than fifteen years, so there's always a strong market for new taxis. The London Taxi Company's new Chinese owners, Geely, have big plans, including a new plant. They also plan to begin marketing the taxi abroad as a British icon, so we may begin to see black taxis all over the world. Mercedes-Benz also manufactures a cab, the Vito London Taxi, released in 2008, which is a people-carrier vehicle based on a van. It should also be noted that they're not always black. Most are, but colors can vary. Some have also become mobile advertising billboards and find themselves covered in ads.

There are always a number of people learning the Knowledge. While there are courses in classrooms, they're also easy to spot on the streets of London. Part of their training requires them to travel on London streets on a motorbike with a map in front of them, going sector by sector, learning every single street in London. You can see them at all hours of the day. They must learn every single street. Not only that, they have to learn all possible routes to and from that street. You can see why it takes three years to complete the process.

After many trips to London, it's pretty easy to see all London's cabbies as the same. They're usually cut from the same working-class cloth, and more often than not, they have a bit of an East-End/Cockney accent. Admittedly, they become a bit faceless, but I mean that in a good way. The faceless cabby driver of London will always get you where you need to go (unless he decides to drive off on you). Cabbies are trustworthy, and you can't buy that kind of trust. Even in the days of Uber and Lyft, people will still remain loyal to the black taxi. I know I will. Black taxi drivers are changing with the times, albeit slower than most people would like. Many now use the apps which allow you to hail a taxi anywhere in London. And, crucially, these apps allow passengers to pay by credit card—a major innovation in itself. London Taxi drivers are required to take credit cards, but they all generally hate them because of the fees credit card companies charge. So, more often than not, you'll find the card reader "broken" or "not working." Apps somewhat solve this problem and make sure you always have a way to pay for your ride.

I have a lot of happy memories in London's black taxis. The good memories begin when I rode home from a symphony concert with my mother, and I fell in love with the city. There was riding back to the hotel after spending the day in Paris and proposing to the love of my life. The memory of my children screaming with glee over the excitement of riding in the back of a taxi for the first time still makes me smile. There was being deposited back at my hotel quickly and efficiently while I suffered through a bout of sickness after seeing a play in the West End. Most of all, I remember the sound of the diesel engine in a black taxi as it stops to pick you up and take you on your way, ready to explore London. It's a lovely rumble. It's the rumble of home.

AN ENGLISH COTTAGE

It's the smell I love most of all. When the old wooden door opens and you enter, then open the internal door, the smell hits you. It's not a bad smell by any means. It's the most wonderful smell. It's the smell of a 400-year-old building. A mixture of cleaners, old wood, furniture, carpets, and clean English air. It's glorious. We're all used to the smells of our homes because when you inhabit a space, your nose gets used to it. But when you leave for a while, then come back, you smell it again. It smells like home. The smell of my dream English cottage is the key code to my Anglophile soul.

I love the doorbell next. The owners of the cottage don't even know where it came from or where to find a replacement in case it breaks. It's a lovely brass bell. Connected by a pulley system through the entryway to the front door. Outside you pull a lever, and it makes the most wonderful noise. When you're inside the cottage and the bell rings, it fills the entire cottage with its song. Yes, every cottage needs a proper bell. An electronic substitute will just not do.

At home in my relatively modern house, I don't have any views. I live in Indiana. We have vistas, but they're mostly flat and contain corn or soybeans. Every window from this cottage has a view of something. From the front sitting room, your view is Gold Hill, the most famous street in Britain, and a ruined abbey wall from the 10th century. When you walk back to the piano room and towards the kitchen, your view is the Blackmore Vale, a sweeping green valley surrounded by gently rolling hills. No matter the time of the year, you can watch the sun rise and set along the entire length of the vale. Off in the distance is an old Victorian church. Right below you are the back gardens of the cottage under Gold Hill. It's a slice of England. When you go upstairs, the views don't stop.

One of the smaller bedrooms, where we usually put our children when we stay, also has a view of the Blackmore Vale, but in a more easterly direction. When you lay there, late at night with your children, you can watch the cars go up and down the curving roads, miles away. They're like snakes in the night. In the turquoise room, where we always sleep even though there is a larger bed upstairs, it's perfectly compact and also has a view of Gold Hill and the abbey wall.

Even in the cold of winter, we open the window and let the cool breeze in at night. It's the best way to hear the sounds of the town.

And, surprisingly, there isn't much sound. That's one of the most surprising things about the English countryside - how quiet it is except for the occasional bit of wildlife. At night, Gold Hill is completely silent save for the occasional punter stumbling back from the pub down in St. James. If you're really lucky, you'll hear the church bells at the top of Gold Hill on Sunday morning. Then, shortly thereafter, you'll hear the bells of the other church in town echoing its calls.

Climb another flight of stairs and you're in the final bedroom. This room has expansive views of the Blackmore Vale and is the coziest room in the cottage because it's in a converted loft with low ceilings. The bed is practically lying on the floor. When you're lying in it and hear the winds of the Blackmore Vale push the cottage and force it to bend and creak, the cottage begins to talk to you. You hear the stories of hundreds of years of people who have lived there.

The views are perfect, from every room. I want to die with this view within my sight.

The cottage is old, as I said, but it's still a modern home. It's not a museum. Compromises must be made to function in the modern world. I've had to fight with the toilets on more than one occasion when they didn't work correctly. At one point, I had to disassemble it with the cottage owner on the phone telling me what do to. Then there are the extractor fans, required by modern planning regulations. They're automatic. They open silently when you turn on the light, then proceed to make the loudest whine you can imagine. It doesn't stop when you turn the light off either. It continues until it's satisfied no dangerous fumes of any kind remain in the bathrooms.

TVs are hidden away so they don't detract from the history of the rooms. It's always fun trying to cook in the kitchen. Everything is different. Not just different, English different. I've burned quite a few meals by assuming that everything would be the same as it was back home. Thankfully, there are smoke detectors and I've never had to call upon the services of the local fire service. It's an odd mesh of modern home conveniences in an ancient building. It's wonderful. The British are the master of the bodge. There is no other way to live in a 400-year-old cottage than to bodge things and make the best of it.

Cottages like this were built for the lower classes. They were built cheaply and, in some cases, shoddily. That's why, when I leave the bedroom, my six-foot-tall frame has to duck so I don't hit my head on the 400-year-old beam outside the door (rumored to be from the bow of a ship). Why not just fix it? It's load-bearing. The whole cottage would collapse without it. So, mustn't grumble and just remember to duck.

I have forgotten to duck on several occasions.

It's built of stone, and all different kinds of stone at that. Usually cottages like this are constructed with locally sourced materials. In some cases, builders simply looted the abbey ruins across the street for building materials. The echoes of the long destroyed abbey (looted during the Dissolution of the Monasteries - thanks Henry VIII) are literally in the walls of Gold Hill. Recycling out of necessity creates sublime beauty. Stone buildings are funny creatures; they're hard to set up with modern HVAC units. This building doesn't have an air conditioner - most houses in England don't. It doesn't get hot enough to need one usually, but occasionally it does get sweltering - 90 degrees is hot to the British. There's no way to retrofit the house with a forced air HVAC system. So, it has radiators. Good luck getting the temperature just right, though. It's either chilly or boiling hot. One day, we'll get it right. It doesn't help that the thermostat is in Celsius and that might as well be Greek. I just don't know what "20 C" means in any real sense.

England's low winter sun is perfection in the winter, and this cottage is perfectly situated to get the most of it. I've wiled away many winter days, sitting on the sofa in the piano room, reading a book and bathing in that warm winter glow. ClassicFM is always playing in the background. Cups of tea are required. Cake too.

There are millions of cottages like this, all over Britain. Their look and feel varies. They are often built of stone. Some have thatched roofs. Some are run down. Some have been abandoned to time because no one can be bothered to give them the care they require. But these cottages define a picture of England that is enduring around the world. No one thinks about Swiss Chalets like we think of English cottages. Most are unassuming. They are simple homes, nothing special. But the people that live in them, treat them as something special.

Cottages need special care. They need a lush garden. Cottages are not for everyone, but if you ask most city-dwellers in England, what they dream of, they will tell you they dream of living in a small cottage in the country. The English soul, and now my soul, lives in a cottage in the English countryside. During World War I, Britons were encouraged to send postcards to their loved ones on the frontline featuring scenes of cottages in the English countryside. Propaganda posters featured lush English landscapes filled with cottages. People literally fought and died for England and its conception of its cozy cottages.

It's weird to be in a loving relationship with a place, especially a place you do not own and probably never will. Our favorite cottage is self-catering, rented out by the owners for anyone to enjoy. They bought it for sentimental reasons, but run it seriously as a business. It's an investment to them, albeit one with special meaning. We have no claim to ownership over it. I happen to know what the place roughly sold for when they bought it. As random chance would have it, we both saw it in the Sunday Times when it went up for sale in 2006. I will likely never be able to afford to live there permanently.

So, we visit whenever we can, which is not often enough. The owners, as fate would have it, have become very good friends of ours, almost a surrogate English family of sorts. They know how much the place means to us and they have bent over backwards to accommodate us in the past. A few years ago, they realized that they were no longer getting the reward they wanted out of the cottage from the constant work, stress of dealing with guests, and the all-around tribulations it takes to run a small business. They decided to sell the cottage.

This was the most devastating news to us.

The idea that it could be sold and turned back into a private home and that we might never be able to stay there again was so upsetting to us; I cried when I heard the news. We immediately booked a trip so that we could be amongst the last regular guests to stay in the cottage. It was a very different trip. Most of our previous trips had been to do something specific or research something interesting. This trip was literally to stay in a place one last time and make the most of every moment.

And that's what we did. We still did things in Shaftesbury, but we spent as much time as we possibly could in the cottage. We watched telly, cooked meals, read books, slept in the comfortable beds. We took long leisurely baths in the enormous bathtub with views over the Blackmore Vale. We were there the week of New Year's, the Christmas tree was still up, but Christmas was over. It was another English winter, the cottage groaned and swayed in the winter winds.

In my journey to Gold Hill, I finally found a cottage located directly on it. I had achieved many dreams, but all that was behind me. Now it was a place that was mine. It was a place I had lived, if only for a few days or weeks at a time over the years. It had gone from a place I put on my wall, to a place where I had real memories. Spending those final days in the cottage was like saying goodbye to a friend you knew you would never see again.

When we packed up and said our goodbyes, I cried harder than I ever cried in my life. Pathetic, I know. It's just a building. But it's so much more than a building to me. It's an English cottage, my English cottage. My special place in the world.

English cottages are a place to be at peace with the world and yourself. Leave your smartphone outside, the computer at work. Bring yourself and a book or a Sunday newspaper. I love spending time in this cottage so much because it allows me to spend my time in the way I like to spend it - being one with a place and focusing on the things I love the most. One day, I'll be able to have this experience all the time. Until then, I'll stay in short bursts and make the most of every single moment.

I never really leave the cottage. A piece of me always stays there, waiting for me to come back. Yet, the piece of me that wants to go back is always bigger. A year after our final stay, we got word that they just weren't able to sell the place, no matter how hard they tried. So, they decided to keep it for now and continue to rent it out. I will have a chance to stay there again. Goodbye was not necessary. I can't wait to go back. And, hopefully, they'll hold onto it just long enough until we're able to buy it. It's a dream. Certainly a dream that requires purchasing lottery tickets.

But dreams have a way of coming true.

THE 4,000 MILE COMMUTE TO WORK

The commute. Talk long enough to any person who works, and they will inevitably end up talking about their terrible commute to work. To Americans, complaining about your commute is akin to the way the British talk about the weather. It's not uncommon for most Americans to spend an hour or more trying to get to work. It causes lost productivity. It causes depression. It causes anger. It's killing our planet.

I love my commute, but that's because mine is a bit different. Instead of getting up early and driving into Chicago, I leave in the late afternoon and go to the airport for an overnight flight to London.

My commute to work is 4,000 miles and about eight hours depending on the tailwinds.

I love my commute.

Running my website and magazine means that I need to travel to the UK as often as I can for research purposes, to keep the content fresh. We average at least one trip a year. But, I also travel because I love it. I love going to the UK. I'm extremely blessed because my work and career are based around British culture and history. When I take my 4,000-mile commute to work, I get to spend every moment in England doing what I love - spending time in the country and learning as much as I can while I'm there.

The only way I can realistically get to the UK is by flying. Instead of getting in my car in the morning, I get on an airplane with 300 other people. Instead of getting stuck in traffic, my "car" travels at 600 miles an hour.

Flying is a glorious thing. We take it very much for granted these days. On the hierarchy of things people complain about, having to fly somewhere will usually be the next topic they'll want to complain about after the commute. To understand how amazing flying is, you need to look at history.

In the past, travel was difficult, so much so people didn't really do it. Most people didn't leave their own towns. A horse could only get you so far. Then, trains came and travel as we understand it became a thing. Trains revolutionized the way people got around in America but also in Britain. Almost overnight, Britain's economy changed thanks to trains - and they even invented the modern tourist industry as a consequence.

Even as America and Britain developed their rail networks, you couldn't take a train to Britain from the USA. You had to take a boat. Granted it was a sight more comfortable by the 19th and 20th centuries than our original pilgrim forefathers. Traveling across the ocean took *time*. It was so rare to travel between the two countries that most people who did the journey only did it once and never went back the other way. It was expensive. It was disruptive.

The journey took so long it was an adventure in itself. It was a trip so disruptive to your life that it was rarely done. If you were wealthy, you may have done it once. If you weren't, you might have done it once if you were emigrating somewhere. When you would arrive home, you would be a completely different person than when you'd left. The journey would change you. You could get sick on the ship and die. You could meet the love of your life, or have a torrid affair.

If we traveled as we do now in the early 1900s, our children would be strangers to us. A journey to England would take months. We could leave with a baby in someone's care and return to a baby who could walk. This is why a key point in many important historical figures' lives is the absence of their important parents. Thanks to the modern conveniences of air travel, our children barely notice we're gone (much of this is thanks to the excellent care we leave them in).

On ship, a microcosm of unique culture would form. The classes would stay very much separate. They'd have dinners, parties, lectures. Most people didn't really have anything to do, so personal dramas often unfolded. A key part of the classic British novel *Brideshead Revisited* takes place on a ship crossing the Atlantic Ocean. A love affair rekindled, and lives changed from the journey. These days, your life isn't likely to change from the moment you board the plane to when you arrive at the destination.

Modern day flying almost speeds up time. Instead of taking two weeks through rough water to get to London, I get there in eight hours. Remarkable. I love every aspect of travel. I love my local airport, O'Hare International.

I think what I love about it the most is the smell and the feeling. Every airport has a unique smell — a mixture of cleaners, recycled air, and jet fuel. But, the feeling is also unique. It's the feeling of infinite possibility. At the international terminal at O'Hare, you can fly to dozens of places around the world, then connect to infinitely more places if you so choose. A new route was recently launched direct from Chicago to Addis Ababa by Ethiopian Airlines. How amazing is that? You're one plane ride away from the heart of Africa.

I've had the commute from hell. I used to work in Chicago while living over an hour away in Indiana. Every day, I'd get into my Honda, drive to work, find a parking space in Chicago, and then drive home. Roundtrip including work, this would take up to twelve hours. What was the point of even going home? I did this for several years, and it was terrible. It was a hamster treadmill that I desperately wanted off.

When I was fired from my job in 2011 and began to work for Anglotopia full time, my "real" commute was down the hall into my home office. But, there's only so much work you can do in your home office. So, whenever I can, I have to get on an airplane.

England is my real workplace.

When I'm in Britain, I basically don't stop until I leave. Between new exhibitions I need to visit, new attractions to review, meetings to take, friends to see, and visiting places I've never been before to build up our photo and video archive, I don't stop. Every minute I have in England is expensive. I must make the most of it.

There have been many trials and tribulations along the way. Travel, no matter how well planned, never goes smoothly 100% of the time. There was the time the toilet broke next to our cheap coach seats. Smelling raw sewage for eight hours is not an experience I wish to repeat. Travel with your children can be a joy, but eight hours in a metal tube is trying to everyone's excitement, and now we don't travel with our two young children. It costs too much to bring them and creates so much stress; it's just not worth it. Hiccups happen.

One time we were hanging out in the BA lounge at O'Hare (we got upgraded for free - bonus) and the Captain himself came into the lounge to tell us that we would be delayed. They couldn't get the flight computer to boot up.

"And it's something we absolutely can't fly without," he said. My wife and I immediately wondered what problems they *would* fly with.

A hazard of planning a trip in January or February is that you'll get delayed by snowy weather. Recently, we sat on the plane for a good two hours while we waited for it to get de-iced. The feeling of sitting there, trapped on the plane, is made worse by a lack of movement. The excitement of going to England fills me with adrenaline, and it has to be sated by take-off. I can't think straight or even read.

Many people ask me why I always pay a bit of a premium to fly British Airways. It's about the experience. Look, there are plenty of cheap options now with the rise of the budget transatlantic carriers. But you get what you pay for when you fly. If you pay for a cruddy flying experience, that's exactly what you're going to get.

When you step onto a British Airways plane, you've already arrived in Britain. The planes don't live in Chicago. They live in London. The crew is British. The plane is stocked with British newspapers, British drinks, British everything. They pipe classical music over the speakers. The flight safety video is British to the core. Even in coach, you feel like you're getting a particularly British experience.

Working in Britain is always interesting and a challenge. Finding good Wi-Fi is always a problem. It's usually fine in London but the further into the countryside you get, the worse the internet gets. I once launched an entire new business on a dodgy internet connection in a cottage in the Cotswolds. The only way I could get a signal was to sit in the unheated conservatory in January and aim my laptop at the perfect angle. It was a miracle it worked.

One time, we agreed to do a series of Instagram posts for an organization. We'd do them while we were there, so the content was fresh and in the moment. The problem is that the cell phone internet signals at most National Trust properties in the countryside is terrible, if it exists at all. Luckily, things get better with every trip.

Sometimes the best parts of the trip are to disconnect completely and just enjoy being there. When we stay in our favorite cottage in Dorset, I spend more time just soaking up the atmosphere than working. I can work back at home. You can't quantify how a place will change you until you write about it later. It fosters inspirations. Sometimes I start writing in that cottage in Dorset, and I cannot stop.

As an outsider, you learn to observe everything. Britain is very different than America, and it's mostly different in the smallest of ways that you would never think of. That's the glory of traveling there - discovering all these little things that are different — and then writing about them. As a consequence, I'm always "on" when I'm in England. Everything I see, or do, or hear is fuel for the business. Sometimes it's exhausting, but I never lose sight of how lucky I am to be able to make a living from this strange passion.

Like all commutes, the worst part is the way home. The joy of flying is slightly made worse by the simple act of leaving a place I love so much. It doesn't help that due to the headwinds, the flight home takes a third longer. You're sitting in a chair, in the sky, being forcibly taken away from your own idea of paradise at 600 miles per hour. Still, it's not a bad gig, and I wouldn't trade it for anything in the world.

ORDNANCE SURVEY MAPS: A LOVE AFFAIR

I still remember seeing them for the first time, like it was yesterday. Their beautiful orange spines, taking up an entire bookcase in a side room of the Travel Bookshop in Notting Hill. Being the Anglophile movie fan I was, when I first went to London with Jackie, we were determined to visit the Travel Bookshop. It was the one that supposedly inspired the film *Notting Hill*, one of my favorites as an Anglophile. Of course, I had to go. The Travel Bookshop was one of those great little London shops that sadly have faded away over the years as real estate prices and taxes in London have gotten out of hand. There's still a bookstore in the spot, but the Travel Bookshop is long gone, and that's a shame.

When I visited for the first time in 2004, it was travel nerd heaven. If there was a place you dreamed of going in the world, you could find books about it. And maps. Oh, my, the maps! If you wanted to climb a mountain in Asia, they had a map that could guide you on your journey, and if they didn't have it in the store, you could order it. I should add that my love of this travel bookstore predates my discovery of Stanfords, a much older and more famous travel bookshop in London. Anyway, being completely ignorant of travel in Britain, my favorite part of the shop was the side room off the main store that was dedicated completely to British travel.

It was wall to wall guidebooks, history books, London books, and, of course, maps. Any map of Britain you could desire was in this room. I was a poor college student in those days, and I remember the pain of having to decide which one or two things I could afford to buy. Then, I saw the maps on the wall, taking up an entire bookcase. One section was orange and the other purple. Not knowing what they were, I pulled out an orange map and discovered a whole new world of British geography. I'd discovered Ordnance Survey maps.

Knowing I could only afford to buy one map, I quickly thumbed through the little catalog of all of them and found the one for the area I wanted to know the most about: Shaftesbury, Dorset. I learned it's number. Map 118. Shaftesbury and the Cranborne Chase. There was a lovely picture of Gold Hill on the cover, which was a scene very familiar to me. I needed the map because I was going there and would need it to learn my way around. It was only £6.99, which seemed like an incredible deal to me when you consider the amount of information contained on an OS map. They cost £8.99 today, which still seems too cheap to me.

When I got back to our hotel and opened up the map fully, I was in love. I quickly found Shaftesbury and looked at all the names of all the places surrounding the town. I gazed at all the geographic features, helpfully identified. The nice thing about OS maps is that they're very intuitive to read; it's easy to tell a green blob is a forest, a blue line is a river, or a bunch of clustered contour lines is a hill. The green dotted lines were my favorite things to find. They indicated public footpaths, an alien concept to this American. They were paths along and through private lands that people were free to walk through whenever they liked. OS maps reveal a magical world that you don't get from Google Maps (which was still in its infancy way back then).

The British have been taking inventory of their islands all throughout their history. The first thing William the Conqueror did when he won Britain as his prize after the Battle of Hastings was to order a survey of everything he inherited, which became the Domesday Book, an invaluable resource for what a medieval economy was like. So, it was only natural that the British government would do this over and over through history. During the Napoleonic wars, fears of invasion spurred the government to create a commission to take a survey of England's southern coast. This was a military-led operation, and it created the first surveyed and accurate maps of Britain.

Eventually, this was done to the whole country - it took sevnty years for the first Ordnance Survey of Britain, and the maps still survive today. When you look at these old maps, they contain an incredible amount of detail and accuracy. It's a heritage that the Ordnance Survey maintains to this day. It's a strange organization. It's owned by the British government, but has long been separated from its military roots and is now run by civilians. Their core role is still to keep accurate maps of Britain. Selling tourist maps is a sideline that turned into a profitable business for them. America has the US Geological Survey, but their maps are not for consumers. The OS's main product after their data gathering expertise are the maps they sell to consumers. I often wish I could buy an OS-like map of the area where I live in Northwest Indiana. I bet the information it would contain would be fascinating, but such maps do not exist. There are commercial maps of my state, but none compare to an OS map.

The Ordnance Survey has mapped every square inch of Britain, and it's become a staple of British life and culture. They've taken Britain's beautiful and varied landscape and translated it to a flat, 2-dimensional map and a thing of beauty. They are Britain's "official maps," and anyone can go down to a bookshop and buy them. During the Cold War, Soviet spies even did such a thing to get accurate maps of Britain! Men work in the field every day taking measurements. OS maps are a peon to British perfectionism, a pedant's best friend. If it's not on the OS map, it doesn't exist.

I took that map home with me, and in the next year, whenever I had free time, I would take it out and try and memorize all the things around Shaftesbury. I was determined to go there in person and take a walk, following the footpaths on the map. I had to make sure I knew my way around. I would take the map with me to school in my backpack, and when I had free time studying in the library, I'd take the map out and pour over it until my eyes practically crossed. I memorized all the interesting place names: Butt's Knapp, Melbury Hill, French Mill Lane, Compton Abbas, Guy's Marsh, Donhead St. Mary, Holyrood Farm, Higher Coombe, Lady's Copse (teehee), Bittles Green Farm. The map made everything around Shaftesbury sound exotic and interesting. It gave names to such a beautiful landscape. I so wanted to learn the language of the landscape and the best way to do that was to study the OS map.

I became hooked on OS maps, though. I just needed to learn how to use them better, and the only way to do that would be to go on as many walks as possible. I now buy an OS map = of anywhere new we travel in advance. My shelf of OS maps is a graveyard of walks I've never gone on. It's a bit of a problem. I love OS maps, looking at them, and studying them intently, but my OS map shelf is really a lazy man's shelf of broken dreams. I've gone on far fewer walks than maps I own. I intend to go on the walks; I really do — one day. And I better have the right map just in case!

At one point, I was planning to walk Hadrian's Wall (well, to be fair, I'm still planning to, but it's been like six years since the planning started). So, I did the dutiful thing and purchased all the OS maps of the entire route. I remember spreading them all out in my basement, scaled from one end of England to the other. I studied those maps for hours, from England's east coast to the west. It was magical looking at all those places, then Googling the interesting ones to see what they looked like. One day, I'll actually do the walk, and when I do, I'll be prepared!

The Ordnance Survey has innovated and moved on with the times. They were one of the first mapping organizations to go digital. Now, all their maps are made on computers and printed in factories. There's no longer a draughtsman sitting at a large table with a pen. In a server room at the Ordnance Survey headquarters in Southampton is a "master map" that has hundreds of millions points of interest in Britain. It's the biggest mapping database in the world, and it's only of one country. That tells you how seriously the British take knowing what their small islands contain.

Paper maps are an anachronism in the modern day, but OS maps are different. They're a tangible thing, made by people that map the British landscape. Google Maps will usually get you where you want to go by road, but it won't guide you through the public footpaths of Britain. Besides, it's free — you have to pay for the best maps. The best maps are the ones you have to spread out and pore over, the way it's meant to be. Screens don't have scale. You can't see a landscape in context on a phone screen. But you can on an OS map. I should add, though, that the Ordnance Survey apps are fantastic, and, helpfully, give free access when you buy a paper map.

My British friends are well aware of my love for OS maps, and when they bought me a special Christmas present one year, they got me the one thing they knew I would appreciate. They got me a custom printed OS map of Shaftesbury, Dorset in all its glorious detail. They called it Jonathan's Map to Gold Hill. It's one of my most prized possessions. So is my tattered map of Dorset that I bought back in 2004; it's served me well on many trips to Dorset and will continue to do so. Ordnance Survey maps are remarkable things, and I can get lost in them for hours. Then, lost in the countryside for real, because I'm hopeless at navigation. I'm getting better at it. The only way to get better at it is to take my tattered map into the countryside and get lost. The Ordnance Survey will always lead me home. Eventually.

RAILWAYS TO NOWHERE

I'll never forget my first steam train. I've had an affinity for trains my whole life. I grew up in Ogden Dunes, Indiana, which is right by a set of several railroad tracks. The sounds of train horns was background noise for my whole childhood. Most of those trains were freight trains, never really something interesting to look at. They always hauled coal, or steel, or cars. And they moved slow. I spent large chunks of my childhood and adulthood waiting at those railroad crossings, waiting for a stopped train. Though, it was great to be late to school and it not be your fault. I never had much exposure to passenger trains except for the South Shore Line, an interurban commuter rail line that runs from South Bend, Indiana to Chicago, Illinois. Living where we did, it was an easy way to go into Chicago without having to drive. Hop on the train, and you're there in an hour. I loved it. But, passenger trains were never a big part of my American life.

I learned in my travels to Britain this was not the case for British people. They take the train everywhere. There are people who go their entire lives without ever driving a car - which was always a foreign concept to me. The British invented trains, so it makes sense that they still use them. Their entire transport infrastructure is set up to accommodate trains. Some would argue that Britain's trains are terrible, and sometimes they are. However, what they fail to see is that they *have* trains. If I want to go anywhere in the US, I have to fly or drive. Other than commuter lines, people just don't take trains between cities in America. It's slow, expensive, and prone to massive delays. It's a wonder Amtrak, America's nationalized railway company, is able to survive at all.

Not only does Britain have a well-developed railway system, they have an entirely separate railways system of heritage railways, cut off from the mainline railways. When I first learned of the existence of these railways, I didn't quite understand them. How can you have a self-contained railway separate from a railway network? The whole point of a railway is to go places. A heritage railway is a railway to nowhere in particular.

Heritage railways are all pretty much the same. They operate on a former branch line, usually in the middle of nowhere. They usually host a steam train or two but are also known to have diesel engines. They have stretches of tracks that vary in length from a mile or two, to 22.75 miles. Train carriages are antiques. Stations are conserved to look like they're from the "Golden Age of Steam" - meaning the early 20th century. They are not generally profit-making endeavors (though some are a proper business) and most are entirely run by volunteers, who spend their holiday weekend playing with steam trains and running a railway.

What a peculiarly British institution heritage railways are.

In typical British fashion, I experienced my first heritage railway in the rain. It was during a trip in 2013 when we had spent the Christmas holiday season in Dorset. I had planned our stream train jaunt with two children in tow - a two-year-old and a six-month-old - months in advance. Dorset has a heritage steam railway, and I was determined to visit it. The Swanage railway runs on a stretch of line from Wareham to the Dorset seaside town of Swanage (though I should add in 2012, it didn't yet reach Wareham). It now has 9.5 miles of track in standard gauge. The line snakes through the Isle of Purbeck - a green and hilly bit of land that, despite being completely connected to Dorset, is called an isle because of its remoteness, and a ridge separating it from the rest of Dorset. The ruins of Corfe Castle are situated right in the only opening of the ridge, and when the steam trains go by, it's basically the erotic dream of railway enthusiasts.

So, being aware of it and wanting to get my first taste of steam, I booked tickets months in advance for the Santa Train, a Christmas-themed special train that would involve the kids getting a visit (and a small gift) from Father Christmas) while we steamed our way through the Dorset countryside. It was going to be the perfect fantasy of my railway dreams.

It was not to be.

I don't want to use the word hurricane, but that's basically what hit the southern British coast while we were visiting. Britain was lashed by strong storms - so strong that it was not safe for the trains to run, or safe to do much else other than stay holed up in our cottage as it creaked and groaned around us in the wind - we even lost a gutter at one point. The Santa Train was cancelled. I was devastated. The kids didn't care because two-year-olds don't care about anything other than eating and six-month-olds are barely aware of their own existence. I suspect Jackie was relieved she didn't have to spend the day on an old train.

After the storms abated and Christmas had passed, the lines opened back up. The Santa trains were already done (and I didn't get my money back, unfortunately), but I was determined to ride this darned stream train, one way or another. So, we piled into our hire car and drove an hour down to the Dorset coast to Norden, where the train started. When we left the house, it wasn't raining. When we arrived in Norden, it was pouring down. We considered turning around and driving back, but we'd come all that way.

I looked around. The car park was filling with other passengers, and they were suitably attired for the weather - waterproof coats, wellies, and umbrellas. The British people weren't turning around - they expected this weather.

"Sod it", I said, to borrow a British phrase. "We're doing this."

We bundled up, bought our tickets, and dutifully waited on the platform for our train in the rain. Norden is not one of the original stations; it was built later to accommodate a car park big enough to handle the passenger numbers. The train arrived on time, and I got a thrill as, for the first time, I watched a steam train chuff into view and take its position at the front of the train.

I can still hear the whistle of the conductor.

The train cars were vintage, as everything is on a heritage railway like this. The plan for the day was to spend it on the rails. We would take the train to the end of the line in Swanage, have a nose around, eat some lunch then take the train back to Corfe Castle to explore the ruined castle and surrounding village (which is completely owned by the National Trust). I'm glad we persisted with this plan as the rain did eventually end, though the sun never came out. The train cars were still decorated for Christmas. They were basic and smelled old. They were lovely. The kids loved it. The entire experience was designed around stoking the railway wonder in children. The train ticket for our oldest even said "My First Train Ride" on it.

One thing you learn right away about Railways to nowhere is that they are not in a hurry. It takes about forty-five minutes for the train to travel 9.5 miles. It's purposefully slow travel. It's designed to give you a maximum steam experience while enjoying the countryside around you. It's all about the day out, and the first thing you learn is that you have all day. There's no rush. The train isn't in a rush. Much steam is expended. Horns are sounded. There's a couple stops where people get on and off. Your train ticket allows you to ride the line as much as you want that day.

Eventually, we arrived in Swanage. It's an interesting place. It's one of those old seaside towns whose heyday was long ago, but still holds onto to the mantle of a seaside resort. It's not a place foreigners would visit; it's very much a place for Britons to holiday by the sea. We walked around the town. I found a nice bookstore. We had lunch in a restaurant overlooking the sea. Our oldest played in the sand. Soon enough, it was time to catch our train back to Corfe Castle. We explored the village around Corfe Castle, then climbed to the top of the castle - a wonderful castle ruin with incredible views of the surrounding countryside. It was beautiful, even in the sunless gloom. Watching from the top of the castle, we got the treat of watching the steam train go by along the line. Keeping an eye on the schedule, we headed back to the train station and caught our train back. The station was lovely, restored to look like a station from the early 20th century.

Why do these heritage railways even exist?

Most have their roots in the era led by a man named Richard Beeching. To mention this man's name to any rail enthusiast is to invoke Lord Voldemort from Harry Potter. Some people are of several minds about him. For most train enthusiasts, he destroyed Britain's railways. For others, he saved them. If a town used to have a train connection and no longer does, or if you're on a heritage railway, it's simply because of "Beeching Cuts."

Post-war, Britain's railways were in a sorry state. Technology was behind; passenger numbers were declining. The car was supplanting the rail network. After the war, all of Britain's railways had been nationalized into one publicly owned company called British Rail. It became a byword for the failure of socialism. The biggest sin of British Rail was it chronically lost money. Cue the 1960s Conservative Government of Harold MacMillan. Richard Beeching was a successful businessman, and he was brought in by MacMillan to modernize British Rail. Cars and motorways were the future, not trains. They were old-fashioned. Reports were commissioned, and Beeching recommended closing 2,363 stations and over 5,000 miles of railway lines. This was over 55% of stations and 30% of the mainline railway network. It was akin to cutting off your legs and arms, and still being able to live like you still have them.

The report was accepted, and the changes implemented. This led to the wholesale abandonment of railway stations and lines all across Britain. Many small villages, which had previously been linked up to the national rail network, saw their connections disappear overnight — connections built during the Victorian era and relied upon. Men who like railways (also colloquially known as railfans, trainspotters, or anoraks - after the waterproof coats they are known to wear) have lamented these changes ever since they were implemented.

But the British being British, many people were not going to accept this lying down. All across the country, groups of people banded together to buy the defunct railway lines, rights of way, and stations before they were demolished. Slowly, over many years of free work, dozens of privately run heritage lines began to appear throughout Britain. Most followed former British Rail routes scrapped by Beeching. Today, the heritage rail industry is worth billions of dollars and many heritage railways are some of the most popular tourist attractions in Britain. I should add they're very popular with the British; most Americans are unaware they even exist, and they're hard to get to, so are generally left off American itineraries.

For my next heritage railway, I wasn't even supposed to be there that day. I had planned something grander. In addition to the numerous heritage railways around Britain, there are also companies that are allowed to run special steam train excursions on the mainline railways, so it's pretty common to see a steam train along the main railway routes in Britain. Whenever a famous steam train appears at one of the major London terminus stations, it always makes the news (like the Flying Scotsman). The excursion I booked was to start in Bristol Temple Meads, then steam through the West Country through Somerset, Devon, and ending in seaside Cornwall before turning around for the return journey. It was a trip that would scratch a lot of Anglophile itches; I would get to ride a real steam train on the non-heritage rail network, and visit areas of England I hadn't yet been. It was expensive as I could only book a first class ticket. It cost £220 for this privilege, and I don't think it even included food.

While I was in Oxford for something else the few days before the journey, I got word that my steam excursion had been cancelled.

I was devastated,

but also pleased I would be getting £220 back.

This forced me to reconfigure my itinerary a bit. Looking around online resources, I found a heritage railway line nearby and thought, well, that's better than nothing. I was by myself this time, so only I would have the joy of spending the day on a steam train. Looking back, I probably looked a bit weird with my fancy camera in tow and backpack, gawking at a steam train by myself. Then again, I probably fit right in with all the other "men who like trains."

The Gloucestershire Warwickshire Steam Railway is a former branch line (closed in the aforementioned Beeching cuts) that runs for fourteen miles through the beautiful Cotswold countryside. While the trains are the attraction here, the real star is the countryside the train goes through. It's breathtakingly beautiful. It's a bit more developed than the Swanage Railway - they have more track, more stations, and more steam trains. The terminus was Toddington (though they have since expanded to Broadway), and I dutifully arrived early to check things out before my departure. I felt like I had the place to myself. It was a weekday, so there weren't many families about.

Toddington Station was beautiful. Like Swanage, it's conserved to look like a railway station from the 1950s. Staff is attired in older uniforms. Most of the people who work there are of a certain age (a British euphemism for elderly). Many are retired and work as volunteers simply because they love railways. Stations like this are always the same. They have an old waiting room, often with a fire burning if it's cold. There's a ticket office, replete with old bars just like in the old days (though you can pay with a credit card nowadays). There's often a secondhand bookshop with old railway books. I've heard that old railways books are always the bestselling books in Britain's secondhand bookstores. These little shops, usually unattended and working on an honesty basis, apparently do brisk business.

Paging through the books, they will only really interest serious railway enthusiasts. They're usually very specific books about very specific railway things. They're dry to read and are usually a monument to railway pedantry. I'm sure I'll get letters for all the inaccuracies in this chapter - I once called railways 'railroads' on Anglotopia and got quite a telling off. In addition to the secondhand bookshop, there will also be a gift shop. In fact, every station will probably have a variation of a gift shop. Souvenirs help keep the railway running, and it's important to sell the railway experience with something you can take home. If you have kids, I'm sure a Thomas the Tank Engine will find its way home with you.

My favorite things to browse are the DVDs. You won't find them anywhere else. When you drive by railway tracks anywhere, often you'll see cameras by the side of the rails. They'll stand there for hours. What do they do with this footage? They put it on DVDs and sell them in heritage railway shops. These DVDs will have hours and hours of "traction action." It's amusing to read the descriptions on these DVDs as they sometimes sound vaguely sexual.

Here's a description from a DVD I recently saw:

"The Keighley & Worth Valley Railway, one of the very few complete branch lines in the UK, is renowned for holding their annual Spring Steam Gala. An important event on many enthusiasts' calendars, for featuring a varied range of trains running along the picturesque five-mile branch line. Running over the cold, damp mornings of March 2019 a collection of engines tackled the steep gradients from Keighley to Oxenhope. The 2019 Spring Steam Gala saw the return of LMS "Jubilee" Class 4-6-0 No. 45596 "Bahamas", having recently returned to steam, "Bahamas" hauled its first heritage railway services."

How positively exciting.

I'm tempted to buy this DVD myself. . . .

All these heritage railways will also have one bit of key infrastructure that's absolutely necessary for the operation of the railway: a café (pronounced 'kaf'). If you're planning a day out on the railway, you're going to have to eat lunch at some point. I've had some of my best meals at these small cafés . They're always busy, but you can reliably get an acceptable burger and chunky chips (that's thick fries in American). You can also get your requisite cup of tea and cake because no day on the railway is complete without a cuppa, even when it's July and 80 degrees out. Many of the heritage railways still have a tea trolly making its way through the train carriages.

One thing that strikes you about these heritage railways is that they are not run by people playing railways. They're professionals, even the volunteers. They take fare dodgers as seriously as they do on the "real" railways. To be able to run these machines, they have to be fully trained in doing so, as if they were an actual mainline railway company. Britain is a land of government bureaucracy (they practically invented it), and they ensure that these lines are safe. As a consequence, heritage railways keep to their timetables and bloody well run on time. My train departed at 10:00 a.m. on the dot.

I practically had the train car to myself, which was a bit surreal. There were a couple of families and excited children. I tried to contain myself and keep my excitement quiet, but I was in my Anglophile zen place. I was on a heritage steam train, chuffing through the Cotswolds, one of the most beautiful geographies in England - especially in July. I did the nerdy thing and filmed the whole journey. Like the Swanage railway, it took almost an hour to go fourteen miles. There was no rush. There were a few stops and people would get on and off. A popular thing for people to do is schedule their walks into the countryside around the train timetable, start the walk at one station, and end it at another.

At the end of the line, at Cheltenham Racecourse, we got the treat of being able to watch the steam engine decouple, then shunt its way to the front of the train for the return journey. There is always much ceremony, chuffing, and tooting of the horn when this happens. Everyone with a camera was in the front recording it, including me. There wasn't a race that day, and I didn't have time to venture into Cheltenham, so I simply waited for the journey back. It was wonderful. A journey on the Gloucestershire Warwickshire Steam Railway is worth the journey alone for the views of the varied landscape along the way. You even get the joy of going through one of the longest heritage railway tunnels in Britain.

Heritage Railways are a microcosm for many things I love about Britain - a respect for the past in experience form, conservation, countryside views, fellow travelers, steam trains, the simple joy of getting on board something old, and going on a short adventure. If you're out and about exploring Britain and you see a Heritage railway, do yourself a favor and check the timetable. Go on a journey. You will not regret it.

GREAT BRITISH WEATHER

Most of all, I remembered the rain. I spent a large chunk of my childhood on the Texas prairies outside of Waco. We lived in a log house in the middle of a town that barely existed because it has been mostly destroyed by a tornado a few years before. Even the library was temporary.

This log house sounds basic, but it was a standard modern house, just built out of logs. It's most striking feature, besides the faux rustic-ness of the logs, was its bright red tin roof. In Texas, they don't really have weather. They have sun most of the time, then an occasional roaring thunderstorm. It was those storms I remember most of all.

In my spartan frontier style child's bedroom - complete with a barn door closet that made a great hiding place - I would lie awake at night, dreaming of the stars, but mostly listening to the rain. The sound of rain on a tin roof is one of the most sublime and wonderful man-made sounds. I came to love the rain. It was rare in our part of Texas, so, when it came, you were grateful.

I still love the rain.

Britain gets lots of it. Though, I should say it doesn't get an unusual amount of rain. Britain just believes it does. Residents of Seattle, Washington would probably agree they get more rain.

Britain's climate is one of the foundational characteristics of its culture. If you want to break the ice with any English person - no matter the situation - talk about the weather. They're continually talking about it, and they're continually apologizing for it.

I've experienced all kinds of weather in my travels around Britain. I've been there in every season of the year. Without fail, whenever I meet an English person, we talk about the weather. And when they realize I've traveled 4,000 miles, their first instinct is to apologize to me.

"No, you don't get it," I want to say. "I love your weather, even when it's terrible."

I used to say, "I don't travel to Britain for the weather."

But that's not true.

I'm in my happiest place when I'm in an English cottage and rain begins to fall, even if it has dashed my plans for the day.

A common joke about British weather is that it's ridiculously easy for you to experience all four seasons in one day. The British are prone to hyperbole, so it's easy to dismiss it. Do so at your own peril.

On my second visit to Britain, we visited Shaftesbury, Dorset for the first time. When we got off the train in nearby Gillingham, the sun was shining, and it was rather warm, even for March. As our taxi weaved through the country roads to Shaftesbury, clouds gathered.

By the time we arrived in Shaftesbury, it was raining – we were not prepared.

We didn't even have an umbrella. This lesson only had to be learned once - always have an umbrella.

Shaftesbury is one of the highest towns in Britain and has its own microclimate. The weather can change suddenly, then just as quickly it returns to normal. As we walked down the cloistered alley to Gold Hill for the first time, it was pouring, or bucketing down, or pissing down, to borrow some favorite phrases the British use.

It did not spoil my view of Gold Hill for the first time. In fact, the dramatic clouds only enhanced the beauty of the landscape. Off in the distance, the sun was still shining on the Blackmore Vale. Just not on Shaftesbury.

Then the rain stopped — enough for us to have a cuppa in the café at the top of the hill. We still had plenty of time on our hands before our taxi would return and take us back to the Gillingham train station. So, we decided to go for a walk around the town. The rain had stopped, after all.

As we walked down the high street and gazed at all the foreign shops watching people get on with their lives in a busy market town, the hail started pelting us. The wind shifted, and suddenly our light spring jackets were too thin.

It hailed. Then rained some more. The temperature dropped a good 20 degrees (on the Fahrenheit scale). We shivered through our short walk down Shooter's Lane then back up Gold Hill.

Then, as if by divine providence, the clouds parted and Britain's golden, low winter sun reappeared, bathing Shaftesbury, Gold Hill, and the Blackmore Vale in the most beautiful golden sunlight. The humidity rose as all the water began its journey delicately back into the sky. Suddenly, it was warm again, and we began sweating in our light jackets.

Jackie and I just looked at each other, bemused at our misfortune for weather that day. Only later did I learn that this had all been perfectly normal for a nice spring English day. There was no use complaining to anyone. It was just the way it was.

And it was amazing. Refreshing. Exhilarating.

A sodden Jackie might disagree.

The British don't really realize how wonderful their weather actually is. I come from a land of oppressive heat in the summer that regularly tops 100 degrees Fahrenheit. In the winter it's not uncommon for us to be buried in two feet of snow with temperatures below -40 degrees Fahrenheit. If Britain had weather like this, it would be a national emergency. For us, it's just a Tuesday in February.

The British Isles may be further north than the continental USA, but their weather is comparatively mild. The warm waters of the Gulf Stream keep Britain warm year round. On the south coast in Cornwall, there are even tropical plants. I joke with Jackie that Britain is actually a Caribbean island of sorts. It is warmed by the same waters, after all.

Winter has turned into our favorite time to travel to Britain. It's certainly not a warm paradise in the winter - and bad storms from the Atlantic can create misery. But compared to our winters here in Indiana, going to Britain in the winter can be a welcome change of weather. It's usually much warmer. Even if it's in the '40s, it's pleasant. The low winter sun fuels my soul. Nowhere else I've been can match it. It's a unique golden sunlight that I have not experienced anywhere else. It's glorious. It feels like even England is in the sun. The highlight of our blizzard-induced Indiana winters is always when we leave and go to Britain for the better weather.

I'm sure any British person reading this has just spit out their tea.

"He truly is mad, this American Anglophile," they would say, tutting endlessly.

When there isn't snow, our winter landscape in Indiana is dead and brown. If you suffer from Seasonal Affected Disorder, it just makes it worse. Go to England. The grass there is green year round. Even in the deepest, coldest winter in Britain, the grass on all the hills stays a verdant green. A sunny winter day, gazing at a green landscape, with a picnic or warm cup of tea is the cure for any ailment, physical or mental. I could not survive without it.

We'd spent the day on the road, and this wasn't even on our itinerary. We happened to be nearby, and it was serendipity that we got to visit. It turned into one of the nicest experiences we had on the entire trip. I'm talking about Lulworth Cove, a half-moon-shaped sheltered bay on the Dorset coast. We'd tried several times to visit over the years but never made it. It was February. Yes, we'd gone to the seaside in February, and we weren't the only ones.

There's a lovely little café right on Lulworth Cove. We stopped for a bit, had a cream tea, and enjoyed the sea view out the window. It was wonderful. Off in the distance, you could see the angry winter ocean breaking on the rocks. Inside the cove, it was calm and sedate as the water lapped up against the store. There were a few people about. It wasn't that cold, but it certainly wasn't warm enough to swim. Children played in their wellies in the water and on the rocks. It was the perfect way to spend a cold English February day.

I've learned over the years that the English complain about the weather not because the weather can be terrible and they don't want you to have a bad time. No, they tell you this because they really have the country to themselves and they don't want anyone to know how truly wonderful it is. English winters are truly spectacular, and it's a great time to explore the country.

Stately Homes are at their best in the winter - at least when they're open. Most either close for the winter or are only open on the weekends. Still, a winter's day out to a place like Kingston Lacey is the best way to spend a winter's day out. You practically have the house to yourself. There isn't a long line in the café , and you can usually eat your meal in the warmth of the stables (and there's no problem finding a table). We've been there in the summer too, and it's still excellent, but that loveliness quotient lessens with more people. There's no room to sit, and there's barely enough room to get around the house without bumping into anyone.

No, it's much better on a day when it's empty, and you can wander from room to room as if you have the place to yourself. It almost feels untoward, having a poke around someone's house by yourself. You feel like an intruder. When we visited Chatsworth for the first time, we were the first ones through the gate when the house opened. We had all the great rooms to ourselves. It was amazing.

Then there's a Stately Home like Longleat, which is so much more than a Stately Home. It has a zoo. A zoo that you drive through. In fact, they were the first safari park in Britain and pioneered the whole cars mingling with animals thing. A bleak winter's day, when you've all got a little bit of cabin fever, is the perfect time to drive through a safari park located in the Wiltshire countryside. Your kids will laugh with glee when you go through the monkey enclosure and they start climbing all over the car. Though, you might freak out slightly when you realize you didn't get the insurance excess policy as you watch the monkeys disassemble the cars in front of you. You rather feel a bit sorry for the animals who have to live outside in the English winter. The stately lions certainly don't belong there, but they'll still scare the crap out of you when they rub against your car.

The weather in Britain is just another feature that makes it perfect. You just have to be prepared for it. Always have an umbrella with you. Why? It might rain. It sounds obvious, but it's not a lesson I learned until I was caught out enough to realize it was needed. An umbrella saved me at an outdoor concert at Blenheim Palace once. It was July; it was cold, more like March, and it was raining. But, that certainly wasn't going to cancel the concert. I sat there under my umbrella and enjoyed the music as long as I could stand it.

Hardy British people managed to make it through the whole concert because they were prepared. They were dressed in waterproof clothes, had umbrellas, and canopies, and blankets. All I had was an umbrella, and it kept me relatively dry until it didn't. The weather defeated me, and I had to retreat back to my hotel. You should even prepare for winter conditions in July. I also learned that lesson from my wet, wonderful evening.

I have now discovered a sound better than rain on a tin roof. When I was staying at Worcester College in Oxford for my course, the room I was staying in was a new building, not the old timber and stone types you'd see in *Brideshead Revisited*. I was on the top floor in a loft style room. The bedroom part of the loft was right below the ceiling with only the roof above.

As I lied down to go to sleep one night, it started to rain, and the large open room was filled with the most wonderful sound. Rain on a slate roof. It took me back to my childhood in Texas. I'd come full circle. I fell asleep in a zen-like state, the rain a soft lullaby on that stone roof.

100-PICS in souvenir pullout

THE Sun
ON SUNDAY

41 PAGES OF COVERAGE
Greatest royal wedding ever

By EMILY ANDREWS

PRINCE Harry and Meghan Markle kiss tenderly yesterday — after a modern fairytale wedding that changed the Royal Family for ever.

The billion worldwide who watched on TV were treated to a ground-breaking ceremony that was a far cry from the stuffy protocol of past

Continued on Page Three

THE SUNDAY T

BRITISH NEWSPAPERS: A LOVE STORY

Due to a mix-up with taxis, I was almost late to my BBC interview but I managed to arrive just in time, thankfully. One does not want to have a reputation at the BBC of being late. It was the day after the royal wedding of Prince William and Kate Middleton (now titled the Duke and Duchess of Cambridge), and I was in Britain covering the event for Anglotopia. This was my final appearance on the BBC, and one of the reasons I had risked everything to cover the wedding. The previous day had been amazing and I was a bit melancholic that it was now all over.

I checked in at the front desk of the BBC, feeling like things were surreal. I waited for someone to come get me. I was dressed in my tan suit that I'm now too large to fit. I was ready for the BBC. Bby this point, this was my fourth appearance during the trip, so I liked to think I had it down by this point. I was also there with another American who traveled over for the wedding - we were to be interviewed together. I was greeted by a kind producer and taken through a maze of elevators and corridors to a small unassuming door that looked like it led to a cupboard.

She opened the door, and it was indeed basically a cupboard.

But sitting in that cupboard was Simon Schama, noted television British historian.

What reality had I just entered?

I was there to be interviewed on the BBC Breakfast program.

Apparently, so was Simon Schama.

Arriving in that green room, I was quite literally star struck. The producer showed me to my seat. Sitting across from me in the green room was Simon Schama, noted British historian who'd taught me British history on his TV show *A History of Britain*. Next to him was Arthur Edwards, the official royal photographer at *The Sun* newspaper, someone who had captured the most important moments in recent royal history, a man whose photos were in the very Sunday papers sitting on a table in front of us.

They were both very nice chaps, and we all sat there reading the Sunday papers, which were helpfully left by the BBC, while we waited for our allotted interviews. I chatted about Anglotopia, and about the day before. We discussed the contents of the newspapers. It was truly bizarre to listen to Simon Schama talk to me about something in the Sunday papers. I doubt either of them remember meeting this strange American who loves Britain, but I'll never forget that moment in the green room at the BBC. The one thing I remember most was the newspapers. Even in the green room at the BBC, there were Britain's Sunday newspapers, ready to be discussed.

When I was growing up in the '90s, newspapers were still a thing - as in printed objects you could go down to the store and buy or have delivered to your house. The internet had not yet supplanted them as the primary way to consume news. I liked newspapers very much. In my quest to know things about the world and what was going on it, newspapers played a critical role. I'd always thought American newspapers were really good, especially my local newspaper. I'd always thought the *Chicago Tribune* was the gold standard for being a "proper" newspaper - until I'd experienced British newspapers for the first time.

My start with British newspapers was inauspicious. I was traveling with my mum in England for the first time. I remember getting up early one morning before she was ready and venturing out to find a donut and a newspaper. I found a local newsagent that served giant donuts and had every newspaper imaginable. I bought the giant donut and a stack of newspapers - seemingly every single one. I had to try each one out, right? Get the feel for what would be my paper?

That's when I discovered *The Sun*. I didn't know anything about the paper or its seedy history. It just had shouty headlines that sounded slightly "yellow" (a term I'd picked up in journalism class in high school). But, none of that mattered, because when I opened it up to page three, there was a naked woman.

Hold on.

I was seventeen years old.

Crikey!

I'd just been sold a newspaper with a naked woman in it.

And my mother was in the same room as me.

Let's just say the newspaper went into the garbage rather quickly. I found the British tabloid newspapers shocking. They were filled with sex and naked women. That's not something you would ever see back home except in the back of the bookstore behind a black curtain, or you had to ask the cashier for it, and they would check your

ID to make sure you were eighteen.

Britain was some kind of progressive utopia where you could buy a newspaper with nudity in it, and no one cared. It turns out, a lot of people actually cared. Only Rupert Murdoch, the paper's proprietor, cared less).

One thing was sure: I liked British newspapers and not just because they had naked women inside them!

It's often said that you can tell a lot about a British person by what newspaper they read. The chosen newspaper is a social cue that helps British people understand who they are and who they're communicating with. The classic comedy show *Yes, Minister* summarized it best:

> Jim Hacker: Don't tell me about the press. I know exactly who reads the papers. *The Daily Mirror* is read by people who think they run the country. *The Guardian* is read by people who think they ought to run the country. *The Times* is read by the people who actually do run the country. *The Daily Mail* is read by the wives of the people who run the country. *The Financial Times* is read by people who own the country. *The Morning Star* is read by people who think the country ought to be run by another country. And the *Daily Telegraph* is read by people who think it is.
>
> Sir Humphrey: Prime Minister, what about the people who read *The Sun*?
>
> Bernard: *Sun* readers don't care who runs the country as long as she's got big tits.

For the most part, a lot of that still holds true when you're talking about British newspapers. A few aren't on that list. One of my favorites is the *Evening Standard*. The *Standard* is a London focused newspaper. When I first started traveling to London, you had to pay for it, but now it's a free newspaper, handed out at Tube stations to anyone who wants a copy. It perfectly encapsulates London. Whenever I visited, I had to pick up a copy and learn what Londoners cared about that day. It helped me fantasize about being a Londoner and worrying about the issues of the day.

Tube fares are going up again? Oh dear.

There was a stabbing in Croydon? How awful. At least you don't have guns.

Oh, there's a new play starring Ian McKellan in a limited run? Must try to dash to that.

How nice, a guide to the best suburbs with affordable rents. I better file that for when I'm living here one day.

That's what you can expect to read in the *Standard*. It's gone through ownership and format changes, but it's still essentially the same newspaper. It's printed every day in the afternoon with the latest headlines of the day, and it's one of the last papers to publish an evening edition in time for commuters to read on their way home from work.

Then there's the Sunday papers. They live in a whole different world from the daily newspapers. In fact, most of the Sunday papers have completely different editorial staffs and production teams. It's not uncommon to read an interview in the Friday entertainment brief, then read another deep dive interview with the same person in the Sunday edition. But, the Sunday one will be better in *every* way.

Sunday papers are these massive beasts of printing. The best ones are still broadsheets. You struggle to carry them in one hand. Often they come wrapped in plastic because they have so much packed inside them. There's often a free gift given away as well as a book, a CD, or a toy. When you open up one of the big Sunday broadsheets, they're massive. You have to properly spread your arms out to read them like old newspapers. Even the Sunday paper back home gets smaller and smaller every year. The Sunday papers in Britain have resisted this. The dailies have not; most are tabloid shaped now.

The Sunday papers are a tradition with Britain's literate classes. Most will buy several on a Sunday, then go sit in a café or sit in their flat, brew a pot of tea and spend several hours reading the papers. And let's be clear here, several hours is not enough. I've found myself taking bits home to read later simply because they are so packed full of content it's impossible to read it all in one sitting. They're the best way to get the pulse of the nation, to find out the big news stories affecting Britain, to read the movies and TV shows coming out soon. The culture section is my favorite. There's so much to read, and it's so marvelous.

So, which British newspaper do I prefer? Surprisingly, not the one with naked women.

No, I'm a serious man.

I read *The Times*.

Yes, I read the paper read by the people who run Britain. It makes me feel important. And it's just called *The Times*. Outside of Britain, we have to call it the *Times of London* because half the newspapers in America are called *The Times* and you don't want to confuse it with *The New York Times* (the closest equivalent we have in the USA). *The Times* is the British national newspaper of record. It's where the nation goes to read its news other than the BBC. If *The Times* and the BBC say something didn't happen, it didn't happen. It should be noted that ironically *The Times* is also owned by Rupert Murdoch, but it's serious and boob-free (and has an independent editorial board that he can't control). *The Times* is where it's at. But in Britain, it's not *The London Times*. It's just called *The Times* because it was essentially the first newspaper with that name.(*The Times* since 1788, the *Sunday Times* since 1821).

If I happen to be in Britain on the weekends, I plan my Sunday around two things: reading the paper and having a Sunday Roast in the pub. Those are the only two elements you need for the perfect Sunday in Britain. Reading *The Times* regularly is the one way to get an idea of what's going on in Britain and making sense of it. It's written for people who know how to read; it's not like *USA Today*, which is written at a sixth grade reading level. It's a serious newspaper for serious people, and, yes, I do realize I sound like a snob. Perhaps I am a bit (Jackie reading this is probably thinking "A bit?").

Newspapers are so important to the national conversation in Britain that the BBC has an entire TV show dedicated to discussing what's in the next day's newspapers. This is not a joke. Late at night, commentators will sit with tomorrow's newspapers, fresh off the presses and talk about what's in them. On Sunday morning talk shows, they'll sit with the Sunday papers and talk about what's in them. It's remarkable. I can't remember ever seeing a newspaper on the *Today Show*.

I love reading *The Times* so much, I've gone to great lengths to read it here in the USA. In the early 2000s, it was still pretty common to be able to find foreign newspapers. There was a store in Chicago called Europa Books that carried foreign newspapers and foreign language books. They carried *The Times*. It was always a few weeks out of date, but it was the best I could do. When I was a poor college student, I would count my change to be able to drive up to Chicago and buy a single newspaper.

During the dark times between trips to Britain when I missed it so much, I felt physical pain. I could easily feel better by simply finding a *Sunday Times* and cracking it open. With a cup of tea in one hand and the paper in the other, I could pretend I was there. I was gutted when the store stopped carrying the paper altogether and moved to a "Print On Demand" service, which totally ruined the experience of reading British newspapers. It was essentially a Xerox of the newspaper. Still, at least you could get that day's paper.

I was so obsessed with getting the paper one time, we were actually on our way to the airport to go to Britain and I insisted we stop on our way to buy $50 worth of newspapers so I could catch up before we got there. I remember paging through the papers at the airport, too excited to really read them, then throwing them away. It was absurd. I really didn't need to put that on a credit card. But I did. It was worth it to me. It's all building towards something, right? I try not to think about the free newspaper I was handed on the plane. That $50 I wasted on papers could have served us better on the trip.

When Europa Books stopped selling the papers, I moved my custom to another store in Chicago. It was at this point in my life that I lived in Chicago, so it wasn't far. This massive bookstore had every magazine and newspaper you could imagine, which means they carried British newspapers. So, when I had the money, I'd drag Jackie down to buy British newspapers. I did this until they stopped carrying them. *The Times'* international strategy shifted, and they didn't distribute *The Times* in America anymore because they wanted to sell a new "international edition" which wasn't available in Chicago and wasn't the same anyway. I wanted the British one. I even switched to *The Telegraph* for a while, but that paper just didn't fit me. Jim Hacker was right.

In fact, my search for getting proper British newspapers was one the nuggets that lead to the founding of Anglotopia. I desperately searched the internet for information on where to buy real British newspapers. It was my Moby Dick, and I Ishmael in search of that Great White Broadsheet. I once found a company that would sell me a subscription that would be sent every week from the UK. It cost almost $500 for one year.

I seriously considered paying this money.

I was broke, post-college, and couldn't even dream of affording such a luxury.

The information was hard to find, but once I'd found it, I reasoned that there must be other mad people out there who would want to know this information. Anglotopia was for them.

As Anglotopia grew, we made friends and gained advertisers. It was still early days, so I was not above doing a trade in exchange for advertising. So, I sold a prime advertising space in exchange for British newspapers. Every month, the advertiser (who ended up becoming a good friend) would send me a selection of British newspapers, direct from the London newsstand. I was so deliriously happy when my *Sunday Times* arrived in the post. All I had to do was put a banner on a website! Anglotopia was magic.

I've evolved, and now I settle for the *Sunday Times* on my iPad. The shipping rates are really expensive now and *The Times* makes it deliberately hard to get it over here. So, I've reconciled with being a digital subscriber. I pay £5 a month for my subscription, and it gets me access to the *Sunday Times* and the daily newspaper. If I ever want to know what's going on in Britain, I merely have to take my phone out of my pocket. Sunday's are still daddy's newspaper day in our house, and I still read the *Sunday Times* from cover to cover, it's just now on an iPad. It's not the same, but it's good enough.

When we go to Britain, though, I leave the iPad at home. I still go out on a Sunday morning and find the local newsagent to buy my *Sunday Times*. We always set aside time to read through all of the Sunday paper. It's bliss.

And now, here I go, looking to see if I can find someone to send me this weekend's edition.

TEA TIME

After waiting a long time at the National Trust Café , I sat down with my pot of tea and brownie. I grabbed the fork and took a reasonably sized chunk out of the brownie and put it in my mouth.

It was brownie heaven.

I washed it down with a swig of hot tea.

I was instantly warm and refreshed. It didn't matter if I was sitting outside in January in the cold and drizzle.

I was having tea and cake at the National Trust Café , and there was really no place better on the entire planet Earth I could be at that moment.

There are plenty of jokes in popular culture that the British drink a lot of tea, but it's not funny because it's true. Not only do they drink a lot of tea, but their entire travel infrastructure is built around having a tea break. There are even sketchy looking roadside tea cafés along stretches of roads deep in the English countryside.

Tea is a serious matter.

One day, it struck me how seriously the British take their tea. I was browsing through an old school British department store on the high street in a Dorset town. These are the kinds of places you're shocked to still see open - most have been put out of business because of larger chains or the local Tesco. But some persist. Anyway, in this store, I found the most British invention I've ever encountered.

It was a tea kettle.

Not just any tea kettle, either. It was a portable tea kettle.

You could plug into the cigarette lighter in your car in case you absolutely had to have a cuppa at seventy miles an hour going down the M4.

I immediately had a hilarious picture in my mind of a dutiful wife in the passenger seat, not navigating as you would expect, but carefully fixing a mug of tea just the way her husband likes it — just a little bit of cream and two sugars – at seventy miles an hour in a ceramic mug.

The journey can continue.

Back home in the USA, we have a different definition of what tea is. Most people only like the iced variety, which is an affront to

British people. As a consequence, getting a decent cup of tea is practically impossible anywhere. Even Starbucks makes terrible tea, in my opinion (it's often too hot to even drink). Lipton is a dirty word in the Anglotopia household.

But in England, you can get a cup of tea anywhere, and not just any cup of tea. A *good* cup of tea. And there's usually cake. You must have the cake. Don't pass up the cake.

The British may not have invented tea, but they've perfected it to be the perfect refreshment after a day exploring castles and Stately Homes. My favorite place to get a cuppa is always a National Trust Café. They do tea properly. My wife will always get the cream tea - this is a standard tea service that includes the tea, a scone, clotted cream, and jam. I usually opt for the cake. Both are delicious. It's really the clotted cream that makes the perfect tea service. It's just not something you can reliably get in the USA, and even when you can, it's not the same.

My desire for National Trust tea and cake is so strong that I'll now go out of my way to visit a National Trust property just to visit the cafe. I'm perfectly willing to visit one we've been to before. I'll tell you a little secret; if we've already been there, we won't even visit the house or garden. We'll just have tea and cake, and go on our way. I've visited the Stourhead National Trust Café more than I've visited their beautiful gardens, which are a true wonder of the world.

Stopping for tea is a great British tradition, and it literally means stopping. The thing about a fresh cup of tea is that you have to stop and wait for it to cool down to drink. This forces you to be in the moment, to slow, to chat with whomever accompanies you. A good cup of tea is about quality time with someone special. As with the weather in Britain, a cup of tea is so much more than a simple drink. It's a way of life. Stopping for tea is an important lens to experience Britain through. I guarantee you, British people will do it, and the best way to enjoy Britain is to enjoy it as they do.

What makes the perfect travel café cuppa? Never a Styrofoam cup. If you come across a place that serves their tea in these, and you won't find many, don't you dare get tea. Styrofoam ruins tea. No, it must be in a ceramic or china mug. If that's not available, a good recyclable paper cup is acceptable. But never Styrofoam. Also, opt for the brown cane sugar in the brown packet. This is proper sugar. White bleached sugar just doesn't do it, and don't you dare put an artificial sweetener in your cuppa. True intimacy with a British person is knowing how they take their tea - how much cream and how many sugars.

The real purists reading this are probably horrified that I put sugar in my tea at all.

Yes, I do. Sorry.

Sure there are ways to serve tea "properly," but the best way to serve a cup of tea is the way you enjoy it the most. I don't want to get into a religious argument about methods here.

Something along those lines recently happened in Devon when a local National Trust property created an incident that was eventually dubbed "Sconegate." You see, the property had the temerity to publish a picture of a cream tea service with the clotted cream spread *before* the jam. Cornish patrons (Devon and Cornwall are neighbors) were appalled.

"Jam goes first," they howled in the ensuing social media firestorm. It almost devolved into a second English Civil War. Even the Queen weighed in when her royal chef announced in a statement that the Queen is firmly on the side of jam first. Who said the Queen stays out of politics?

Thankfully, the proud Cornish didn't cross the Tamar River and invade Devon to settle the matter.

Besides, couldn't they all argue about the bigger issues? Milk before or after you pour the tea?

Brits choose their tea like they choose a football team: for life. When British expats visit "home" they often bring back an entire suitcase filled with their preferred tea, which is often hard to find in the USA (though it's getting easier). There is "builders' tea," which is popular with the working classes. There's Yorkshire tea. There's P&G Tips. Typhoo, an Irish import. There's Cornish Smuggler's Tea. There's Twinings. There are so many varieties in tea. They even have an entire aisle in the grocery store just for the various teas. It's not just mixed in with the coffee like it is here in the USA. When Brits pack to travel to the European continent, they'll often bring their own supply of tea with them because they do not trust the tea on the continent. And let's face it, the French and the Germans do not have the same appreciation for tea like the British do. I know British expats here in the USA who carry tea bags with them wherever they go because they don't trust there will be good tea when they order one. There is even a company that makes tea wallets!

The entire infrastructure of Britain is set up to facilitate a cuppa and you can't fake a good cup of tea. If a British person is served a terrible cup of tea, they will tell you about it. Styrofoam cups are not an acceptable receptacle from which to drink tea. It must be in a porcelain or china mug, or a teacup. At worst, a paper cup is acceptable in dire circumstances.

Having a nice cup of tea and a sit down is a great way to cope with any emergency.

Did the Germans just bomb London? Let's have a cuppa.

Were there football riots just now? Let's have a cuppa.

Was your husband just murdered? Let's have a cuppa.

Did you just agree to host a sleepover for twenty children? Let's have a cuppa.

Did you just move into a new house? Time for a new electric kettle and you better make cuppa for all the people helping you move (even if you're paying them).

Did someone just ring to say they're on their way over? Put the kettle on immediately.

I've attended many lectures and talks in Britain, and tea is always provided. It's almost a requirement (this is something America could learn). Where there is tea, there are biscuits. Inevitably, it'll be the British person who will exclaim, "Oh, biscuits!" upon seeing a tray of every kind of British biscuit imaginable. Even when they come across an unexpected tea stand somewhere, you will hear someone exclaim, "Oh, tea!" Tea is always appreciated, even when it's not served correctly.

And tea is not a gendered thing, either. British men care just as much about a good cuppa as the women do. I made a friend in my favorite town of Shaftesbury. Bernard was an older English gentleman, and he embodied what we all imagine an Englishman to be. He owned a small B&B and was the friendliest chap I ever met. He was tall with a mustache like Basil Fawlty, but he was as far from Basil Fawlty as you could get. In addition to running his B&B, Bernard also had an interest in flying.

I'd stayed in their B&B quite a few times, but it had been a long time between visits. Once we had kids, we preferred to rent a self-catering cottage rather than subject innkeepers to the horrors of our young children. I also had an interest in flying, and during one trip had a lovely experience when he took me up in his airplane. We flew about the green hills of Dorset all the way down to the sea and back. After the trip, I made a small book of all the pictures I took and sent it to him.

I made a friend for life by doing this. He was chuffed to bits.

So, next time I was in town, I invited him over to our cottage for tea to catch up. Jackie was out with the kids, so I would be doing the tea service all by myself. Bernard arrived bang on time, as I expected he would. I boiled a kettle and put out mugs and biscuits. I was quite proud of my little tea setup.

I put the bags in the mugs and poured the tea.

As I was pouring, he exclaimed, "Jonathan! You're overfilling the teacup!"

I looked down; it didn't look like I was overfilling it.

"You've got to stop here, so it doesn't overfill when you add the milk!" he said, schooling me on making a cuppa.

I looked down again at my tea and thought he might be right. I stopped pouring and let it steep for a few minutes while we chatted.

I took the teabag out and poured in my milk. Sure enough, as I went to mix, the tea spilled over and it got everywhere.

"See," he said kindly. "Mustn't overfill the teacup!"

Of course, he was right. One of the many lessons I've learned over the years from traveling in Britain.

Now, even years later, when I'm pouring boiling water into my beloved Emma Bridgewater mug (Union Jack motif, obviously), I hear Bernard in the back of my head telling me not to overfill it.

And when I do, I hear him again setting me right: "See, you've overfilled it, Jonathan."

ENGLISH TIME

When doing business with Britain, one has to learn how to tell time differently. The English operate on a different clock and calendar. I don't mean the time difference, that's easy to work around. My solution is to have second clock on my computer that keeps UK time all day, I only need to glance to know what time it is across the pond. No, the British have a completely different concept of time and how they spend it.

In America, you work to live, and your entire life is dedicated to working in some capacity. It's our Protestant work ethic, drilled into us from a young age. The British don't have this baggage. They work, but they don't work nearly as hard. They work smarter. And they value the importance of time off. Britain had its own labor movement that was born in the Victorian slums, and they fought hard for their rights as workers, so they make sure to jealously guard the things in which they're entitled. And that's great.

You have to understand most salaried British people get twenty-eight paid days off a year - some get more. Twenty-eight days! And this is set in the law! Most Americans are lucky to get two weeks of paid vacation, which works out to just ten paid days off, and there is no law to enforce this. Often, that also includes sick time. Your twenty-eight days off in Britain does not include your sick time. If you're sick, you're not penalized. You're entitled to not have to work when you're ill. The time off doesn't end there; you have to add in the statutory holidays. Things like Christmas and New Year's and bank holidays. Usually, this adds another seven to ten paid days off per year. If Christmas falls on a weekend, you can basically expect Britain to shut down for two weeks around Christmas and New Year's.

One of the most frustrating things to deal with when working with companies in the UK is understanding when people aren't at work. Your inbox will quickly fill with autoresponders of people who are on annual holiday or annual leave. And they will certainly not be checking their email while they're away. This means oftentimes, major decisions are delayed, sometimes by weeks. I've had to learn that anyone I work with could go on holiday at any point while I'm dealing with them. So, never count the money egg before the person returns from holiday.

This patience is very necessary, because you realize that the British spend more time not at work than they do at work. What a remarkable way to live - this idea that you shouldn't have to spend all your time at work to live. As an American small business owner, who must work more than the average person, I find the situation frustrating straddling the two worlds. On one hand, I admire their time off directives. On the other, I can never have that kind of time off, even though I run my own business and set my own policies. I recently went on a proper vacation for the first time in my professional life; it didn't involve a trip to Britain, and I still found myself working!

As a traveler in Britain, it's important to understand British time because it can affect how well you enjoy your trip. I'll never forget coming to Britain in February and counting on visiting several exhibitions at London's major museums. When we went to the Natural History Museum on an unassuming weekday, we found the line wrapped around the building, merging with a line for the Science Museum next door. What was going on?

When we spoke about this to a Londoner friend later, she laughed.

"It's February half-term!" she exclaimed.

She had to explain to us what that was. It's the one week break during the school term. The school year is divided into three terms, and there's a break in the middle and in between terms. It's a busy time for Britain's free tourist attractions because it gives families something to do that doesn't cost anything. So, as a consequence, museums are packed, and you'll have to wait in line - not just at the museum but also at the restaurants around the museum, and expect the Tube and rail lines to be crowded. Now we make sure to check when half-term is before we book our trips. Just Google "England half-term dates" because it changes every year.

Then there are bank holidays, which are guaranteed days off spread throughout the year. When you add up all the vacation time, all the bank holidays, all the half-term times, etc., it's very clear that there are very few weeks where the British are actually at work for five full days of the work week. It's maddening. But brilliant.

Being in Britain at Christmastime is to see an entire country at rest, enjoying its best life. Most white-collar employers will simply shut the office right before Christmas and resume operations after New Year's. No one is getting any work done. As someone who has gone back to work in an office the day after Christmas, only to not really do anything but still having to be there, this seemed so enlightened. And most places won't make you use that time towards your statutory holiday time! So, add fourteen days to twenty-eight. It's really starting to add up.

We had a rude awakening when we traveled in Britain at Christmastime. Bits of our trip were arranged with various tourist authorities around Britain, but good luck trying to contact anyone between Christmas and New Year's! They'd all turned their email off. Most independent shops have limited hours and they, along with the big chain stores, shut down completely on Christmas and Boxing Day (or have limited hours). Coming from the land of 24-hour grocery stores, it was a bit of a challenge to source food while Britain was shut down. You have to plan ahead. There's no popping out for any ingredients you forgot. Everything, and I mean everything, is closed. We had a startling realization on Christmas Eve in our rented cottage when we realized that we basically wouldn't be able to leave for a couple days other than to go for a walk.

Once the public holidays are done, things start to slowly reopen. Pubs and restaurants open to cater to all the people who are off work. At most good restaurants, you will require a reservation just to get a table. Spontaneity is very difficult at this time of year. Planning is key. Many of Britain's Stately Homes, which usually close up for the winter, will open up for limited hours during this period, so it's a good time to see some heritage while you're traveling. But be warned, come January 2nd, most will shut back up again.

One of the most popular things to do during the Christmas season is to plan your holiday time around what's going to be on telly. Unlike America, which shows mostly reruns during the holiday period, Britain saves some of its best dramas, movies, and documentaries for the time when people are most likely to be home and bored out of their minds. It's not uncommon for grown adults to still buy a copy of the *Radio Times* - Britain's equivalent to *TV Guide* - and circle all the things they plan to watch over the festive period. The latest shows are talked about on telly or in the papers. You will get some of the best British TV during the holiday period.

This is all alien to us Americans, but this is a rhythm of life in Britain, and the British are perfectly used to it. They're never in a hurry to do anything, and when a holiday comes around, they don't care that the stores might be closed for a few days. They plan ahead to work around it. Mustn't grumble. Make do. Let's have a lovely holiday! A British person never thinks that they shouldn't go on holiday, they just go on holiday, and their job is waiting for them when they get back. They're never made to feel like bad people for staying home when they're ill.

These are a people that will pack up the car, drive to a Stately Home on the weekend, and literally spend all day having a grand day out. There will be a picnic. There will be ogling of the Stately Home. There will be cups of tea, and that will be the entire point of the day. Simply existing in their wonderfully built and historic landscape. They're in no rush. They're having a grand day out. It makes me jealous every day. It makes me want to be there every day.

There's a reason one of their most popular TV shows revolves around a man (now a woman) traveling around the universe in her own time machine which also contains its own pocket of time. The entire island of Britain is its own TARDIS. It follows its own rules of time and space. And, as the good Doctor would say, *allons-y*!

TURNER, CONSTABLE, AND LEARNING TO LOVE ART

In 2005, I learned about art. Well, British art, at least. This was the time period when BitTorrent was a new thing, a way to share large files over the internet. Pirates loved it. I discovered dark corners of the internet where people uploaded every British TV show and shared them over BitTorrent. This became my renaissance in British TV; I discovered so many great shows and began to see them as they aired in the UK, long before they aired in the USA. I felt like I was joining an exclusive club.

One of the first shows I discovered was called *A Picture of Britain*, and it explored the history of Britain through art and consequently how art influenced Britain's own perception of its landscape. It was one of the most educational shows about Britain I'd seen in my life at that point, and I loved every episode. The presenter David Dimbleby, who is part of the Dimbleby TV dynasty and a hugely respected political commentator - who still stays up all night to cover elections in Britain - was the perfect guide to this aspect of British history that I'd never known before.

I'd always had an appreciation for Art with a capital "A," but I'd never really known much about it. Art History was not exactly topic for discussion at my rural Indiana schools - even when we had art class, we didn't really talk about the history of art or even admire works and their contexts. We just made things or tried to draw. It was a real disservice. By watching *A Picture of Britain*, I discovered a whole new world in art I'd never experienced before.

It was the education in art I'd never gotten.

It's where I first discovered the names Turner and Constable.

When we imagine Britain in our minds, and the British do the same thing, we imagine this idyllic pastoral utopia of green rolling hills, charming villages, and hardy working people. This is not an accident. Our perceptions of the English landscape have been shaped by the art that was inspired by it. But what's interesting most of all is the actual works of art have now created this perception themselves.

Mr. Dimbleby focused a lot on a work of art I'd never seen before called *The Hay Wain* by John Constable. It's a pastoral scene of an ox cart fording a river near a mill. It's considered the preeminent masterpiece of the British landscape. Don't get me wrong, it's a beautiful painting. This painting alone is responsible for how the British think of their own landscape - a green and pleasant pastoral idyll that may not have ever even existed because the painting itself is a fiction. Though, the location in the painting - Flatford Mill - is a real place you can visit, and, bar a few modern additions, still looks much the same.

In addition to Constable, Dimbleby also spent a lot of time discussing J.M.W. Turner, another painter I'd never heard of, but who played a huge role in Britain's art history. I had no idea that his iconic paintings were even his and that they played a big role in other art museums. For example, his painting of Carthage, on display at Tate Britain, inspired the final scene in the Lord of the Rings, one of my favorite films. It was a revelation to learn about *The Fighting Termiere* and *Rain, Steam and Speed.*

I was so intrigued by these paintings and how important they were; I knew I had to go see them. It turns out, they're the most important pictures in the collection of the National Gallery in London. So, the next year when Jackie and I visited, we finally went to the National Gallery to see these paintings. By that point in my life, I'd been to art museums - I was a regular visitor to the Art Institute in Chicago. While the collection in Chicago is fantastic, the National Gallery in Britain is on a whole other level. Chicago has gathered the greatest works of the world and brought them to a place where they wouldn't normally belong. The National Gallery is filled with paintings created in Britain. They belong there.

We spent hours wandering that museum for the first time. After following the very confusing map, we finally found the room with the Constables and Turners. It felt like I was in the presence of a religious figure. The first thing that struck me when my own eyes gazed upon *The Hay Wain* for the first time was how enormous the painting was. It took up a massive amount of space. It was so big you could imagine yourself walking right into the picture. How Constable managed to paint such a massive picture, mostly from memory, is proof enough of how much of a master he was.

Gazing at that picture for the first time, I understood it perfectly. Now that I'd been properly educated on its importance by David Dimbleby, I connected with it on my first viewing. While the painting was responsible for creating Britain's conception of its own countryside, it was now a critical part of my own understanding . I fell in love with the painting. When I exited through the gift shop later, the first thing I did was buy a print for home. There are big gorgeous leather benches right in front of the painting, and I sat down and stared at it, trying to make out every detail, trying to have an emotional experience, and I did.

My love for Britain cemented that day. A place that could produce art this beautiful and sublime deserved my lifelong love.

When I walked to the other end of the room and found the Turners, I was again struck by their massiveness. Things always look so small when you look at them in art books or see them on a TV screen. The amount of detail you can make out in person is just incredible - and you can get so close. It feels like such a privilege to be in the presence of these priceless paintings. Next time you're there yourself, take a look at *Rain, Steam and Speed* and see if you can find the hare hidden in plain sight.

While I love Constable, Turner became my favorite British painter. I must confess this happened to coincide with the greater interest in Turner's life that came about when the film *Mr. Turner*, starring Timothy Spall, was released. I was so excited to see the film that we actually went to a special exhibition at Petworth House, where scenes from the film were shot. Turner had a personal connection to Petworth as the lord of the day was one of his patrons, so there's a massive art gallery onsite that has several Turners. It's bizarre walking into the room and there being almost more Turners than you can count, like they were just vacation snaps someone took a picture of and put on the wall.

The real treat, though, was being allowed into a part of Petworth that was normally closed to the public because it was unrestored and unconserved. It was like venturing into an abandoned Stately Home. It was cold. It had the most wonderful musty smell. It was dark, filled with paintings covered in centuries of grime. The stairs creaked like an old dog waking from a nap. The reason for allowing visitors into this part of the house was because we were going to see the old library, which was actually used as a studio by Turner because he frequently visited the house. They used the same space for the film.

It felt like walking into a history book and the film. We did eventually see the film, and I loved it. Jackie didn't like it so much. It had a little too much time focused on Timothy Spall spitting into the paintings. His immersion into the role of Turner was perhaps a little too intense, but the film is beautiful, and it's a great insight into the life of a complicated man who had a singular talent. It says something when, two hundred years later, we're still shuffling through art galleries to look at his paintings.

As I said, here in America, Turner and Constable weren't really a part of my art education or heritage. However, that doesn't mean that they don't exist here. After I discovered these artists, I did some digging and discovered that the local Art Institute of Chicago actually has two Turners on display along with a Constable. Whenever I visit the Art Institute, I'm sure to see the paintings. It's like visiting old friends. I know most people are there to see the Monets or the Suerats, not the Turners and Constables, so I like to think I'm giving them a little extra love they wouldn't normally get.

They have a very similar painting to *The Hay Wain* called *Stoke-by-Nayland*, and it's another romantic English idyll. It even features an ox cart. Constable knew that if he was good at something, he should keep doing it. It's a marvelous painting - just as massive in person as *The Hay Wain*. When I stand in front of it and admire it - along with the Turners in a different gallery down the hall - all I can think is that they don't belong there. Those paintings should have never left Britain. They should be with the others in the National Gallery or Tate Britain.

But, I'm glad they're not, because I get to visit them and get a little bit of Britain in Chicago.

In the years since that first visit to the National Gallery, I've visited so many times I've lost count. That's the glorious thing about the National Gallery; it's completely free to visit. So, when you're near Trafalgar Square, you can just pop in to look at your favorite paintings and pop out. The Art Institute is very expensive to visit- almost a $100 for a family of four - so you're better off making a day out of it. What a luxury it must be to live in London and be able to visit such great works of art completely for free, whenever you feel like visiting them. It's an enormous privilege I take advantage of whenever I'm in London.

Sitting in the main gallery, gazing at *The Hay Wain*, I'm at peak Anglophile happiness. I love the painting, and through that love of the great art that Britain has produced, I come closer to understanding Britain and its rich history. I have David Dimbleby to thank for that.

That, and an appreciation of the Land Rover Defender, the car he drove around Britain when he visited its great art. That car is another icon of British art and design. I would like to have in my garage.

MR. BEAN AND DOCTOR WHO, OR BRITISH TELLY, A LOVE STORY

I cannot write a book about the influence of Britain on my life without writing about British TV. Other than traveling there, the number one way I can connect with Britain is to watch its television. For most of my life, America has only gotten the scraps of British TV networks think will be hits in the USA. I was desperate for more and I had no idea what I was missing out on until I began traveling to Britain. British TV is the number one way Britain exports its "soft-power" to the world. British comedy is synonymous with good humor. Many famous American TV shows were actually remakes of British originals. British TV is wonderful, and until fairly recently, I had one problem in my life: I could never get enough of it. My desire for British TV, and to read as much about it as possible, were two of the things that led to the creation of Anglotopia.

The first episode of British TV comedy I can remember seeing was *Mr. Bean*. I caught it late at night on PBS; it was probably the summer, when I could usually stay up late with no consequences. *Mr. Bean* is the bumbling adventures of a man who never speaks as he ventures through life in early '90s Britain. I'd never seen this silent man before, and he intrigued me greatly. But most of all, the country he lived in intrigued me. What an interesting looking place, where cars with three wheels were common. The episode in question was the one concerning the school open day. I thought it was hilarious, and I almost shed a tear at the end when Bean's iconic lime green mini was run over by a tank.

Despite the fact that he used no words, Mr. Bean spoke to me. Portrayed by Rowan Atkinson, here was an unattractive man, unable to speak to let the world know about his frustrations. Sometimes, being a shy young American in middle school who could not get girls to talk to him to save his life, I felt like Mr. Bean. Though on rewatching *Bean* as an adult, I realized he was kind of a jerk, but, then again, so are most twelve-year-olds.

The Britain of *Mr. Bean* was an alien looking place. It always seemed to be cloudy. Everything looked "old" and outdated, and I don't mean Victorian or Georgian. I mean the 1970s or 1980s. This was Britain before "Cool Britannia," when it still seemed like it was stuck in the past. I quite liked it and wanted to go there. The show gave me an insight into British culture I'd never gotten before from films and TV shows. It's a show that did this not without trying at all - but simply by existing. The British people who made the show didn't think, "We need to educate the viewers about what Britain is while they're watching this show." No. They just showed the country they lived in and let you fill in the blanks. So, you get to see Britain completely lacking in pretension, unlike what you would get from shows about Stately Homes and detectives.

I was in love. These were the days before DVRs, so I had to work hard to make sure I watched *Mr. Bean* whenever it was on. Thankfully, my local PBS station in the '90s loved cheap or free British TV, so they showed it over and over. I was disappointed to eventually learn that there were only fifteen episodes of *Mr. Bean*. Why weren't there more? This show was fantastic. This was the heyday of *Friends* on TV - twenty-six episodes per season, all of consistent quality. Why couldn't the British make more *Mr. Bean*? The less said about the two *Mr. Bean* movies, the better.

I had a similar introduction to *Doctor Who*, the British sci-fi show that's now been on the air for over fifty years. Again, I found it late at night on PBS. I found it completely incomprehensible. I had no idea what was going on. There was a man with a long scarf running around like a mad man (I would later learn that this was a feature, not a bug of the show). What really caught the attention of this middle school boy was the pretty young assistant running around in a tiny skirt. I watched that show despite having no idea what was going on.

I was determined to become a *Doctor Who* fan, but my local PBS station made it very difficult. It simply wasn't on very much. I was too young to be able to afford the VHS tapes, and this was long before you could just queue up the episode of *Doctor Who* you wanted on the streaming service of your choice. Anglophiles coming of age now are really spoiled. But then in 1996, it was announced there was a *Doctor Who* movie coming out, and on Fox TV no less. I knew nothing about it, but I thought this must be a big deal for a British sci-fi show to be premiering on a major TV network. I counted down the days.

The day finally arrived.

And it was terrible.

Apparently, this was the general reaction at the time, which meant that *Doctor Who* spent almost another decade off the air until it was successfully revived in 2005. I was all in for the 2005 return. I was still in college in those years, much more of an Anglophile, and someone who gained a far bigger appreciation of British sci-fi since I'd been young.

"Run!"

I was in love with the "new" *Doctor Who* from episode one and have watched almost every episode since, some several times Top five: "Blink," "Girl in the Fireplace," "The Empty Child," "The Day of the Doctor," and "Gridlock." While I loved Christopher Ecclestone, David Tennant was my Doctor and always will be. I like to say I was a *Doctor Who* fan before it was cool, but then that makes me sound like a classic *Doctor Who* fan, who would say the same thing. Before my time, *Doctor Who* was practically a secret society, with fans trading bootlegged VHS tapes in small local groups around the US because their local PBS stations didn't air it. Those original fans deserve to be on their pedestal.

Doctor Who is now one of the most popular shows on the planet; it's become a force in the entertainment world. Whenever a new Doctor is cast, it makes headlines around the world. It's aired on major cable networks and they even have viewing parties at local cinemas all around the world. If you would have told me back in 2005 when *Doctor Who* returned after it's long slumber, I would have laughed at you. Now, it's cool to hate on *Doctor Who* again. The show is like marmite, you either love it or you hate it. Still, you also go through phases where all you want is marmite, and sometimes you go through phases where you can't stand it anymore. That's where *Doctor Who* is for me right now as someone who still hasn't finished watching the last series.

As I went through my college years, I was educated not only in school but in my personal time as well. My subject? British TV. I was determined to find and watch the best British TV I could find. I was sick of the scraps that aired on PBS, so I began to find other ways to find shows. My local library was a great resource. They had hours and hours of DVDs you could rent for free. There were other cable networks that aired British TV at odd hours. Then, there was the advent of BBC America, which has been a disappointment for most of the last twenty years. And that, my friends, is when I learned how to be a pirate.

I discovered many brilliant British classics in these years.

During college, Jackie and I were very busy people. We both went to school full-time (at the same school but on different days). We both worked full-time jobs. She worked in a party store in a nearby town. I worked for my father's cleaning business. We were young and had limitless energy. When we weren't in classes or doing our coursework, Jackie was at work, or I was at work. Then in the evenings, we would go to work together cleaning a series of car dealerships spread across Northwest Indiana (and not cleaning them very well, to be honest). We had very little free time.

But when we did have free time, we discovered and watched some of our most favorite British TV. One of the first TV shows we ever binged (and this was before "binging TV" had entered our cultural lexicon) was *Jeeves & Wooster*. This delightful '90s British comedy was based on the books by P.G. Wodehouse and starred Stephen Fry and Hugh Laurie in their heyday as comedy partners. I don't remember where or how I got the DVD boxed set, but when we did and watched the first episode, we were hooked. It encompassed everything that I was interested in as an Anglophile. Comedy. Stately Homes. Britain in the interwar period. Bumbling aristocracy. Biting social criticism. We loved it. Typing this, I realize I haven't watched the show in over fifteen years, and now I really want to.

We became addicted to the show. In the precious hours we had between work and school, we'd watch an episode, then find ourselves watching another one. Before we knew it, we were neglecting the state of our house and not doing our coursework (and I wasn't writing the great American novel I was supposed to be writing). We had a codeword in our house because we knew that sitting and watching hours of *Jeeves & Wooster* was something we simply didn't have time for.

All Jackie or I needed to say was, "Weeves and Jooster?" and we would nod at each other and pop the next DVD in the DVD player. Those are some of my happiest memories of our early days together as a couple, sitting in our old Victorian apartment in Valparaiso, Indiana, binging a classic British TV show.

Another show that was critical to my Anglophile development in these days was *Yes, Minister* (and its following series *Yes, Prime Minister*). I'm a politics junkie in general, but I'm fascinated by British politics. After I read a textbook on British politics (in my free time, mind you, this had nothing to do with my university courses), I was hungry for more and discovered this classic comedy. Honestly, I don't remember how I discovered it. This was long before YouTube so there was nowhere to stumble across a show like this. I think these were the days when we had a Netflix DVD subscription, and I got the show there. Come to think of it, I think that's how we watched *Jeeves & Wooster* as well. I was hooked from the first episode.

Yes, Minister starts right after a British general election when a new party is swept into power in a zeal to reform the government. The show follows erstwhile Jim Hacker, a party politician who becomes the Minister for Administrative Affairs, basically the bureaucrat of bureaucrats. He comes into the ministry full of energy to reform the place, cut red tape, and make government *work*. For the people, you see. This is all well and good, but the government functions perfectly well without ministers. That's where Sir Humphrey Appleby comes in. While the minister is appointed to run the department, Sir Humphrey is the official who actually runs the department.

Most episodes consist of Hacker or the government trying to do something and the British civil service trying to stop them. This sounds incredibly boring on the surface, but it's absolutely hilarious. It's a cynical but funny look at how humans create institutions, then perpetuate their stability and existence. Sir Humphrey is the perfect caricature of a government bureaucrat seeking to maintain the status quo and prevent radical change. After all, according to him, it's worked so well for hundreds of years.

The three main characters, Jim Hacker, Sir Humphrey, and Hacker's secretary Bernard Wooley, create the most perfect comedy trio to ever grace British TV screens. Their banter back and forth is amazing, and while some of the jokes are very dry and droll, the show has important things to say about the nature of government and political service. The show was a huge hit in the 1980s during Margaret Thatcher's reign. It went on to have three seasons along with two further seasons when Jim Hacker miraculously becomes the Prime Minister (the less said about the 2013 revival, the better).

Most Americans know the actor Nigel Hawthorne for his role as George III in *The Madness of King George*, but to me, he'll always be Sir Humphrey Appleby. When you consider he was a trained Shakespearean actor, the fact he can do comedy so well is simply astonishing. Paul Eddington, who played Hacker, knows how to balance an air of authority and knowledge with the bumbling absurdity required to be a Minister of the Crown. Derek Fowlds rounds out the triumvirate as Bernard Wooley, who always, always had the perfect pithy retort to whatever Humphrey and Hacker are arguing about. You can easily find the show on various streaming services, watch it if you can. It's wonderful.

By far, though, the one show that had the biggest impact on me was *Brideshead Revisited*. I'd read the book in college, and it was one of my favorites. I'd also read another book called *The Decline and Fall of British Aristocracy* by David Cannadine. You could say that I had a particular interest in the decline of the British aristocracy. When I watched the first episode of *Brideshead*, I was hooked. The music. The lush locations. Glorious and beautiful Castle Howard. The tragic story of the Flyte family. World War II. As I progressed through the rest of the series, I became very ill - one of the few times in my life I actually had the flu. I missed school and work. All I could do was lie in bed and watch *Brideshead Revisited*. So, I did.

I didn't care that I was sick. It was incredible. That show cemented my interest in Britain's aristocratic history. It instilled my love of Britain's Stately Homes to the point where I've now visited more than I can count (and a few more than once). It also inspired me to study for a week at Oxford in a summer program and fall in love with its dreamy spires. It helped begin my appreciation for fine art and high culture. I've now watched *Brideshead* several times, read the book several times (and other Evelyn Waugh works as well), and seen the atrocious film adaptation (great cast, but you just can't tell the story in two hours). *Brideshead Revisited* painted a sad, but beautiful picture of Britain I just wanted to move into.

Now, we come to talk about pirates. But let's start with BBC America. The name sounded so alluring. The BBC, in America. What a wonderful thought! Except it was never that. At first, it kind of was, and I was desperate to watch the channel, but it was very hard to get. It was always in the "extra" tier in cable or satellite packages, so you had to pay a lot more money for it. Pondering such a cost while a college student was just not possible. Eventually, we got a good deal on satellite TV and finally got the channel in the early 2000s.

I have been disappointed with it ever since.

I'm sure they mean well at BBC America.

In the early days, they still showed a lot of British TV - classic comedy, dramas, and factual programming like *Ground Force* (a show where they renovate English Gardens), and *Location, Location,*

LOVING A LANDSCAPE

I'll never forget seeing the British landscape for the first time with my own eyes. It was one of the most important moments of my life. On my first trip to London, I did not see any landscapes. We didn't leave London. I only saw it from the air, and I remember falling in love with the beautiful patchwork quilt that was the countryside. When I finally had a chance to go into the countryside, it was seminal. I didn't really see it from the train - you don't see much when the train is going a hundred miles per hour. When we arrived in Gillingham and took a taxi through the countryside to Shaftesbury, I struggled to chat with the driver because I was so enamored with what I was seeing.

"I don't know why you'd come all the way here," he said. "Just boring old Dorset. I much prefer East Sussex."

He just didn't understand.

As we walked around the Town Hall in Shaftesbury and Gold Hill came into view. I saw the British landscape for the first real time. The cottages sloped gently down the cobbled hill, onto the infinity of the Blackmore Vale. It was March, but everything was green and beautiful, even in the gloom. Beyond Gold Hill was Melbury Hill, farms, other hills, cottages, country lanes. There's a reason that Gold Hill is one of the most photographed places in the United Kingdom. It's because it's a perfect encapsulation of the British countryside. I had spent years staring at this landscape on my wall in my teenage bedroom, and now I was there for real.

The British landscape was real, and it completely met my expectations.

A true love affair began that day.

Since that day in 2004, I've seen so much of the British landscape that I've forgotten a lot of it. If I didn't photograph it, I would struggle to name every beautiful landscape I've seen. But that's the thing - the British countryside is pretty much beautiful everywhere. One can't help but get landscape fatigue. When I visited the Lake District for the first time, I wasn't prepared to be wowed. I never understood the grand appeal - it's just a bunch of lakes. I live near a big lake, and it's not really that interesting.

I was so wrong.

Everywhere I went to in the Lake District was the most beautiful place I'd ever been. It's an incredible landscape filled with mountains, lakes, hills, farms, and sheep. Now that I've visited beautiful places in Britain since then, they all pale in comparison to the Lake District. What do you do once you've seen something beautiful? Sit there for hours and look at it? Once you've done that, you've seen it. So, what's the point? The British landscape isn't just something pretty to look at; it's a meditative state of mind. The world moves differently in the countryside. It has a different rhythm.

A majority of Briton's are city dwellers, but I guarantee you the average Briton's soul lives in the countryside. A common hobby for people in cities is to have an allotment, a piece of garden all their own in a communal area, meant to give them a taste of the countryside in their city lives. Their most famous paintings by Turner, Constable, and Gainsborough are in the countryside. Their best TV dramas and films always take place in the countryside. It's a nebulous place where the soul of every Englishman lives.

The British landscape is an artificial place. It may look green and natural, but there isn't a hectare of Britain that hasn't been altered by the people inhabiting the British Isles. From carvings in hillsides to Stonehenge, to castles and ruined abbeys, to great cities that have seen better days, to cities that are in their heyday, the British landscape is alive and ever-changing. Granted there is a movement, spearheaded by organizations like The National Trust and English Heritage to keep the British landscape in aspic. It's easy to think when you look at a timeless landscape that it's never changed, but just sitting in a spot and studying the landscape, you can see that change is the lifeblood of the English conception of the landscape. The landscape has been so shaped by humans that when it came time to consider where to shoot the film adaptations of the Lord of the Rings trilogy, it was decided Great Britain was not suitable simply because the ancient landscape of Middle Earth, which was very much inspired by the British landscape, could not be slotted into such a human-made and sculpted environment. So, they filmed it in New Zealand (which was an inspired choice).

I don't just love the British landscape because it's beautiful to look at. It's a beautiful place to *be*. It's the feeling you get from looking at it. You feel the weight and joy of British history and heritage wherever you look in the landscape. You can easily envision the great historical events happening. When you see castles, Stately Homes, ruins, villages, and town, it's easy to picture all the things that have happened there. Here in Indiana, we don't have a landscape with history. We have fields of corn. There are no villages. Only downtrodden Midwestern farm towns that have been bypassed by history. It's a hard place to love and inhabit.

I'm also starting to reject places that conform to the standard of what we expect from Britain. Castle Combe is, by every definition, one of the most beautiful places in England, but it's a caricature now. It's mobbed with tourists - no one really *lives* there anymore. Most of the houses are B&B's or holiday lets. It's not a real place; it's a fantasy place the remaining residents simply maintain. As authentic as it looks, it doesn't feel authentic anymore. Despite that, I love it there very much. I can get the last ounce of Anglophilic enjoyment out of a place no matter how awful it becomes. Nearby Bibury and Arlington Row is another very famous place in photographs. Good luck parking within a mile of the place when you try to visit in the summer. Everyone is so convinced it's the perfect place that evokes Englishness, so they flock there, destroying it in the process. The interesting thing to note is that long after it's no longer considered an English utopia, it will still be there, and people will still inhabit and still enjoy its place in the landscape.

After speaking with many British people, I've also learned I'm looking at the landscape in the wrong way. The landscape is more than a place that looks pretty. It looks pretty because it's inhabited. When I spent some time on a farm in the Lake District, the farmer was keen to point out that one of the reasons he wrote his book was because when you read about the Lake District, you read about it from outsiders and those who only saw a pretty place. There were no locals in these books. There were no people.

To him, though, the landscape could not exist without the people. Now, I look at the British countryside in a completely different context. Yes, it may be pretty, but why is it pretty? How is life for the farmer down the Blackmore Vale whose smoking chimney you always see in photographs? He maintains his farm perfectly. It's a critical part of the landscape when you see pictures of it. If it was a garbage dump, it would not look pretty in the landscape. However, it's not like the farmer purposefully maintains his farm and house to look pretty in landscape photographs. His farm just *is*.

Melbury Hill, in the background of most Gold Hill pictures, is a beautiful hill (I highly recommend climbing it for the views), but it too has been sculpted by the people who've lived there for thousands of years. You can see it subtly when you climb the hill; you're walking on the ruins of an Iron Age hill settlement. Now sheep graze it, but people have been sculpting it for thousands of years. What family history surround Melbury Hill and Shaftesbury? There's a house in Melbury Abbas at the foot of the hill with an American postbox. Why? Why is there even a settlement there to begin with? Dorset is a very rural county, and it's also one of the least populated. Why does anyone choose to live there? There are more economic opportunities elsewhere. Yet people live there, and people want to live there - just try buying a property will cost a mint!

Some British landscapes are just sad. When we visited the Scottish Highlands for the first time, it was very empty. It's easy to think that it's always been that way. Unpeopled and windswept, it just fits with what you see. But when you look closer, you see the scars of history. You see an entire people who were cast out during the Highland clearances (and settled in North America and Australia). Every time you drive by an abandoned cottage in Caithness or an empty croft farm, you are seeing the traumas of the past. You can begin to understand the resentment the Scottish have for the English and the landlords who kicked them out of their beautiful landscape. That's why so many Scottish folk songs are laments about the lost landscape.

It's a truly sad, but beautiful place.

I can't wait to go back to it.

Planting the trees in the British landscape was to be the penultimate experience of the writer's workshop. Everything we talked about, all the exercises, all the pontificating, would culminate in us planting our own tree on the land the farmer was setting aside to be reforested. This writer's wood was to be a permanent fixture on his farm and a way for us all to make our own mark on the British landscape. It's a moving thought that a tree I was going to plant in the Lake District could possibly inspire a poet in the future.

It had been a very long day, and we were all pretty shattered by this point. It was late afternoon, the end of a hot summer's day in the Lake District. I didn't think we would have time to plant the trees at all, but the organizers made it work. We were each given a tree and told to spread out.

Orders were shouted over large distances as each of us was sent to a suitable spot to plant the tree.

I'd never planted a tree before, so I had no idea what I was doing.

The air was quiet; we could only hear the sounds of the birds and the stream where all our trees were being planted. It was the perfect English summer's afternoon. A perfect day to plant a tree.

One of the organizers came over to help me put it in the ground and show me what to do. I got my hands dirty with rich English earth.

When the farmer came over to inspect the work, he said to me, "Jonathan, now you can say you have your own piece of England."

I cried a little after he walked away.

He was right. I'd never thought about it that way.

I've spent over twenty years loving Britain, and its landscape, and doing everything I could to spend as much time in it as possible, but I was always a visitor. Of course, I harbor a dream of one day living in England and owning a house there. As of now, I don't. I have connections to several places simply by visiting them often and loving them to bits. Until I planted that tree, there wasn't a place in Britain I could honestly say was mine. A place I'm physically connected to – my own bit.

It was like I'd been given a knighthood by the Queen, when that farmer told me a piece of his land now belonged to me.

"I hope that means you'll let me come visit it!" I managed to get out before the tears started.

"Of course," he said, walking away.

After we finished planting our trees, we all sat beside the stream while both authors in charge of the workshop read passages from their favorite works. There are only a few times in my life I can say are perfect moments, and that was one of the most perfect moments I've ever experienced.

Months later, chatting to the author on Instagram, I learned that, unfortunately, my tree had died a few weeks after it was planted due to the record drought that hit England in the summer of 2018. He promised to plant a new one in its place, a hearty English oak this time.

I hope he'll wait and let me plant the replacement.

I will spend the rest of my life trying to see every hectare of the British landscape. From the cliffs of Cornwall to the islands of Scotland, I want to see it all. It's remarkable simply because it exists. I love it. My soul lives in the British countryside and one day I will live out my days there, perfectly content as part of a social and political landscape that will endure for centuries after I'm gone. My story will become part of the landscape. Will anybody remember it when they see my place in it?

THE BOY WHO LIVED AND LIVED

The convention was exhausting. For many years, the highlight of my year was traveling down to Atlanta every Labor Day weekend for the massive DragonCon sci-fi, fantasy, and multimedia convention. Every year I went, it got bigger. I looked forward to it every year, but mostly I looked forward to hanging out with my best mate, as it was a bonding experience for us. We have been friends since high school, and life had taken us in different directions, but we made an effort to have "bro time" every year at DragonCon. The older we got, the more exhausting the convention got (and the way we interacted with the convention changed).

It became more of a vacation, time away from our busy (but wonderful) lives, and less of us trying to cram in as much as we could. The ABC Family Channel or whatever its name was at the time, started doing a yearly marathon of all the Harry Potter films. On Friday, they'd start with the first film and play through the entire run of films over the whole weekend. When you added in commercial breaks, it would take a whole weekend. It became the background noise of our trip.

At several points, all we did was watch the Harry Potter films even though we'd both seen them dozens of times, and almost knew them by heart. I was on vacation in another city (shout out to Atlanta, a wonderful city), and I spent most of my time chilling with my best mate in the hotel room watching Harry Potter. It's always interesting to watch the films all the way through and watch the cast age with the films because I remember aging with them. The story of Harry Potter is the story of my life, minus the witchcraft and wizardry.

I grew up with Harry Potter and so did an entire generation of Anglophiles. It's weird saying that. I'm thirty-five years old as I write this. Harry Potter still seems so new; it's hard to believe that it's now over twenty years old. You could say Harry Potter turned more Americans into Anglophiles than any other film, book, or TV show in the last twenty-five years, save for *Downton Abbey* which appeals to a completely different audience (though, Harry Potter fans were primed to embrace *Downtown* when it came out).

I remember first hearing about Harry Potter - it was in whispers, and then it was all over the news. Then, the story of J.K. Rowling, a poor, unemployed single mother being inspired to write this book made its rounds, and it became an international bestseller. When I heard that it was about an imaginary British boarding school of witchcraft and wizardry, I was immediately sold. I bought my first copy from my local Barnes and Noble bookstore when there still was one.

Once I started the book, I couldn't put it down. I read it in my classes in high school when I was supposed to be doing work. I read it during lunch. I read it at home instead of watching *Star Trek*. I became obsessed. When I finished the first book, I went and bought the second book. And then I read through that as quickly as possible. Then I read the third book. And then there were no more books to read because they hadn't come out yet. My cultural calendar for the next few years would revolve around the releases of the books.

As a confirmed Anglophile by this point in my life, the books were primed for me to love them. I loved the writing, the feel, the characters. I loved this imaginary Britain that was just slightly off what you think Britain is like. Rowling's story was engaging and fun (even with the very dark undertones). I sneered at the religious nuts who would burn the books and ban them from libraries. They were harmless fun. I imagined my own life changing drastically by going to a British boarding school. Oh, how I wanted to go - even without magic!

The Harry Potter books were selling the fantasy of Britain, and I ate up every word.

New book releases became seminal moments in a reading teenager's life in those years, and nothing since has had such an impact as Harry Potter. Instead of lining up outside a movie theater at midnight, we would line up at our local bookstore. We'd place our preorders weeks in advance, hoping we were at the front of the queue when the release time came. Our local Barnes and Noble took advantage of the events by throwing huge parties. It was the place to be seen if you were a literati nerd in the early 2000s. They were good fun. Then, once you had the book in your hands, you had to read it as quickly as possible so you could find out what happened before spoliers would leak out.

SPOILER WARNING!

When *Harry Potter and the Half-Blood Prince* came out in 2005, I'd evolved to just ordering the book on Amazon and getting it on the release day. I was in college in those days, and when I wasn't in school, I was working full-time for my family's cleaning business. I was very busy, so when the book came, I couldn't read it right away. We were in a house in upscale Ogden Dunes, cleaning the carpets, which I did quickly so I could finish and get back home to read the new book.

Other people were more fortunate than me and had already read through the book once it was released at midnight. I happened to be cleaning the carpets in a house of homeschooled kids who'd been reading all night.

"I can't believe they killed Dumbledore!" I heard one shout.

I stopped what I was doing and looked up in horror.

The seminal moment in the entire Harry Potter series had just been ruined for me simply because I didn't have time to read it fast enough.

You did not want to be around me that day.

When I got home from work, I began reading as quickly as possible, hoping that they were simply taking the piss (a British phrase I love). But they weren't, and I spent the whole book anticipating an ending I already knew. I didn't know the details, so that was fun to find out. That day I learned the true danger of spoilers. Typing this story out still makes me incandescently angry.

The films probably played an even bigger role in cementing my love of Harry Potter because it took the best bits of the books and condensed them to the big screen in a way that made the fantasy of Britain real. Not all of the films were perfect by any means, but by the time the film adaptation of *The Prisoner of Azkaban* was released, I began to prefer the films over reading the books. In fact, I haven't read the books since they were all originally released. Repeated attempts to read them to my children have failed (the disappointment burns, but I will turn them into Harry Potter fans yet).

Once the book releases faded away, I looked forward to the big events of the film releases. Instead of ordering the book in advance, I'd order the tickets in advance, and wait in line for hours until they started. It's important to stop and survey what an incredible achievement the Harry Potter films were. They managed to make a total of eight films, within the same universe, using mostly the same cast, and keeping an internal consistency that makes all the films recognizable as bits of a greater whole. It's incredible, and doesn't happen in Hollywood. Look at the C.S. Lewis adaptations that failed. It's very hard to make this work.

The films have played a big role in my travel life as we've explored Britain. When I first visited with Jackie in 2004, we made a point to visit Platform 9 ¾ at King's Cross, which at the time had been set up as a photo spot by the station (in an out of the way place to prevent crowds). I have a typical tourist snap of me trying to enter the magical platform. Harry Potter is now a much bigger draw than it was back in 2004, so now there's a line to take your picture at Platform 9 ¾, and an official gift shop next to it as well.

I was very excited when they opened up the studios where they filmed most of the films. It's advertised as the Harry Potter Studio Tour London, which is a bit of a lie. It's not in London. It's in Leavesden which is outside the M25 (the traditional border of London). There are special tourist buses running several times an hour to get the punters there in massive droves. Even to this day, you have to book your tickets weeks in advance to ensure you can get in. It's now one of the most popular tourist attractions in Britain.

I was thrilled to visit back in 2013 with my family. We'd booked the tickets weeks in advance. It was originally sold out, but I kept watching the website for new tickets to be released and was lucky one morning when I snagged some for us all. We had a rental car, so we drove to the place when we were on our way out of London and into Dorset for Christmas. We parked in the massive car park and entered the studio. From the outside, it's an unassuming metal shed, but inside, you enter the world of Harry Potter.

Sure, you can go to Universal Studios in Florida to visit a Harry Potter theme park, but I'd much rather go to London and visit the place where the films were actually made. They have all the sets on display. They have an entire experience designed to immerse you in how they made the films. They open regular exhibitions on different parts of the set. When they first started making the movies, they would film in locations around Britain to give some authenticity. But as time went on, they built an incredible series of sets. They were very wise in saving them. The first room you go into is the massive Great Hall, just as it is on screen. They now even book real feasts for people (tickets sell out very quickly).

It was incredible to walk down Diagon Alley and see all the props and places we'd seen in the films so many times. You can even try "real" butterbeer. I did not partake, see the chapter on my irrational fear of trying new food things. The skill and craftsmanship that went into making the movies is simply incredible; it made me really appreciate the films a lot more. Don't get me wrong, the films are not perfect, but they're perfect enough. Of course, you exit through the gift shop. Many Harry Potter souvenirs were purchased before we hit the road for Dorset.

Now, Harry Potter exists in the background of my Anglophilia. It's part of who I am. I'm a grown-up now. The actors have all grown up. Still, for a few years, we were all a part of the same commonality - celebrating what was great and fun about Britain. Sometimes I really wish I could have those days back, but as Harry Potter learns in the books, you have to grow up, move on, and face all your challenges with bravery (and your best mate, and a girl who knows everything).

When I browse the TV channels and come across a Harry Potter film, I have no choice but to turn it on and leave it on, even if it's only background noise. And sometimes, when you're on vacation with your best mate, there's nothing better than lying on the hotel bed, eating garbage food from the food court below and watching some Harry Potter. I can't think of a better way to spend a weekend.

Oh, and, in case you're wondering, my house is Gryffindor. How could it be any other way?

ENGLISH SILENCE

I did not grow up in a quiet place. I didn't know what quiet was. I didn't know how bad my life was without it. I'd never known silence until I'd experienced English silence. Noise is such a part of modern life you sort of tune it out, but it's always there. It's almost hard to notice it when it's not there, but it came to me in a moment in Updown Cottage; it was quiet. Not only was it quiet, when I went out onto the terrace out the back, it was quiet there too. The only sound filling the air was the occasional bird. Silence was the default. I'd never experienced it before. It was exhilarating.

I spent most of my childhood in a place called Ogden Dunes. This romantic sounding place is a village within a town in Northwest Indiana. The most notable feature is that it sits on the shore of Lake Michigan. It's a very desirable place to live. Every house is different, it's hilly, and those hills create a sort of exclusivity that's not really present in the largely flat geography of northern Indiana. On its west side, it's bordered by a National Park and a very beautiful one at that. On its east side, it's bordered by steel mills and an industrial wasteland.

As a consequence, Ogden Dunes is not a quiet nor peaceful place. It's never quiet. The steel mills next door clang, clang, clang twenty-four hours a day. When they're not clanging, there's simply a dull hum that always pervades the air (the smell that also taints the air is outside the purview of this chapter). You can stand on the shore of Lake Michigan, a great body of water, and hear the roar of industry even when the lake has high waves. When the wind blows in a different direction, and you don't hear the mills, you hear the roar of traffic down Interstate 80/94 less than a mile away.

Then there were the trains. I lived less than a mile away from a set of four separate railroad tracks. They're a major east-west corridor for the entire country, so there were constantly trains. Again, you tend to tune them out, but their horns were always there. I don't know how the people who lived literally right next to the tracks dealt with it. There was constant noise, even on a cold winter's night when all was supposed to be silent. When the ground is covered in a foot of snow, that usually quiets things a bit. But, no: clang, clang, clang. It never ceased.

America is a loud place in general. Americans are a loud

people. We listen to our TVs as loudly as possible. Our cinemas have the sounds set so loud, they make your body vibrate. We like our cars to be loud. We like our motorcycles to be even louder (though, apparently, this is a safety "feature"). Our sporting events are as loud as you would expect them coming from a loud people. Even our stealth fighter jets are loud (after they've passed).

England is the opposite. One time, when I was standing outside a pub in Southwark, talking to some business associates, it should have been loud. But it was a quiet summer's evening. There were people about, but pubs don't get loud, the conversation is usually kept at a low volume. We were near a train station, but I didn't hear the trains. The sounds of the city were not there. It was oddly discomforting. Then, I heard it.

A Harley Davidson went speeding down the street, filling the canyon of old buildings with a roar that simply did not belong. I could see my British companions cringe at the sound.

"I'm so sorry for my people," I said to much laughter.

It made me a bit sad that'd we brought some of our noise over.

If you want peace and quiet, then get up early, as the sun is rising, and go for a walk in the English countryside. My favorite place to do this is Shaftesbury as there are plenty of neat places to walk to around the town without venturing too far. You can go for a nice walk and then get your newspaper and a pastry before going to wake up the family. I love the absolute stillness of walking in the English morning. It's best on a cool winter or autumn day. If you're lucky, you can watch the sun burn away the fog over the Blackmore Vale. You might occasionally run into a person walking their dog or also going for a quiet morning stroll.

I feel most alive when I'm on one of these sojourns.

I love hearing the birds of an English morning, the crows in the distance, the owls who haven't gone back to bed. Other than the sounds of nature, there is absolute silence. It's bliss. Almost any other noise almost feels like an unwelcome intrusion. British cars can be quite loud, but I've even begun to find the sound of a diesel engine rather soothing in its own way.

There are plenty of places to walk that have a view. Everywhere you look, you see open countryside. There are roads, yes, but they are only double or single track lanes, so their sparse traffic doesn't create any noise. Britain's ubiquitous hedgerows absorb a lot of road noise. It can get quite windy in Shaftesbury, but even the wind doesn't make too much noise - unless it really gets going with gales. From the north of the town, on a clear day, you can see almost all the way to the Stourhead Estate. It's easy to spot King Alfred's Tower.

Stourhead has become one of our favorite places. It's our "local" Stately Home whenever we're in Shaftesbury. It's where you can get the complete National Trust experience of a garden, grand house, and a good National Trust Café . It's absolutely heaving with people on the weekends, but it's so vast that it never really feels crowded or busy unless you're in the car park. You've seen Stourhead before yourself; it's been used as a filming location in countless films and TV shows, most notably the 2005 adaptation of Pride and Prejudice (one of my favorite films, but, yes, I know it's a terrible adaptation).

It's every bit as beautiful as you've seen it on the screen. There's a nice, gentle walk that takes you around the humanmade lake that defines this grand view. The lake is surrounded by follies and other artifacts. All of it is artificial. You can see where Walt Disney got some of his ideas. But, it's still very real in the sense that its permanence has made it real. It's real if people come, look at it, and experience the bliss of its silence.

The gardens are sheltered from the busy roads around the estate. You feel like you're in the middle of nowhere when you're really not. Nature has been managed and fostered to give it an appearance of being a natural place. Stourhead is the definition of an English arcadia - a utopian landscape where everything is beautiful, perfect, and recalls a great history. It's as artificial as the idea, but I dare you not to walk through Stourhead and think for a moment the stewards of the Stourhead estate - the Hoare family and now the National Trust - haven't achieved that. It is a utopia of sorts. It is to me. It *is* Anglotopia.

The hardest part of visiting Stourhead is leaving, returning to the world, returning to the modern era - not that life was any better in the heyday of the estate. We watch hours of British periods dramas and read all the Jane Austen novels not just because they're good, but because they're a fantasy that we like to inhabit. We imagine ourselves in these simpler worlds without smartphones, computers, and two-hour commutes to work. They're a respite from an insane world. Visiting a place like Stourhead is to step into that world, albeit briefly (and make you admire the people who still live on the estate). We are all seeking silence. You can find some here.

The silence allows you to hear details you don't normally hear above the din of the modern world. Birds are so much better with a British accent. A babbling brook is so much better when it's not drowned out by a busy road. A walk through an ancient wood is so much better when you listen to the wind blow through the trees, creating a din of noise and language all its own. The trees are speaking to you (and I don't mean in the Tolkien sense). Will you listen?

Every year, around the same time, I read the same book: my favorite book. It's a science fiction book called *The Songs of Distant Earth* by the British author Arthur C. Clarke. It's about a long lost human colony making contact with the last survivors of a dead earth on their way to somewhere else. I've read it consistently for almost a decade, and it's still difficult to understand why I love the book so much. It's a very English conception of what a utopian society could be like. It very much takes that Arcadian ideal to the stars, albeit with key changes. It's not an exciting novel by any means, and Clarke's prose is workmanlike. Hemingway, he is not.

Yet, I return to it every year.

One year, I had the pleasure of finishing it in our favorite cottage in Dorset. We had a trip planned that ended up falling in the middle of my annual reread, so I brought along my special hardcover copy to finish it. I read it in bed in the blue room, late at night. I read it in the sitting room, but one afternoon, as our trip came to an end, I sat in the piano room with the warm golden winter sun streaming in, and read a huge chunk of the book. It was very special to read such a special book in a special place. Once again, it was the silence I remember the most. I was completely engrossed in the book. Nothing could bring me out of it because there was nothing to create a distraction. I was being cocooned in English silence.

My fond memories of that reading are perhaps why I've struggled to begin the book again this year. How can I replace such a wonderful memory? Reading *The Songs of Distant Earth* in such a quiet and beautiful place will be hard to replicate, even at home.

One afternoon, I was finally decompressing in the cottage sitting room after the exhausting trip to get there. The TV was off. Jackie was out getting a much-needed massage. It was a weekend, so my email inbox did not need to be attended to, and our children were well cared for - there was no one to call or text. I was an island of contentment. I closed my eyes and reveled in the silence. The only sound was the occasional person walking down Gold Hill outside, shoes clopping on the cobbles. Or the occasional bird - crow, blue tit, or owl. That was it. Silence insulated by the ancient stone wall opposite the cottage. I nodded off into a light twilight sleep, perfectly content in my cocoon of English silence.

Now, of course, if you want this experience as well, I recommend going to stay somewhere in the English countryside, far away from a motorway. But if you would like to have this experience at home, I have a solution for you. Turn on the 2005 Pride and Prejudice, but only the last few minutes. The bit at the end where the camera lingers on the foggy sun coming up in the countryside, where Darcy and Elizabeth finally get together. That film perfectly captures the feeling and the sound of an English morning. It's the best part of the movie. There's also a plot going on, but I'm just there for the scenery and the sounds.

A LOVE LETTER TO THE TUBE

The Tube Station at Heathrow Terminal Five is relatively new when you consider the overall age of the London Underground. This is often your first introduction to the Tube, and that's fine. Better a brand new station than an old one. When presented with the options of getting from well-connected Heathrow into central London, you realize you perhaps didn't bring enough money with you on your trip. A taxi is almost a hundred dollars. The Heathrow Express, the other train to Paddington, is £25 one way. It's the most expensive rail journey in Britain by track length versus cost. A bus does not appeal. So, you opt for the Tube - the cheapest option.

It's a deceiving ride at the start because the train is practically empty. You get comfortable, thinking that you'll have it to yourself. Buckle in and get ready, because this is the longest way into central London and will take at least forty-five minutes. As you leave the tunnels of Heathrow, the train fills with the warmth of that English sun for which you came all this way. It's slightly disorienting - you thought the Tube was all underground? Well, it's not. Out in the suburbs, or the outer zones, the Tube is mostly above ground. It only goes underground when it gets more toward central London.

From this vantage point - you get a strange view of London you weren't expecting and the guidebooks don't tell you about. You're seeing what London is really like for the people who live there. It's the back garden tour of London. Some back gardens are nicer than others. You see the uniformity in London's architecture that varies from Victorian to Edwardian, to post-war Modernist, to modern glass box tower blocks. You can't help but think large parts of this area of London look slightly shabby. You're not wrong in thinking this. London is not a gleaming, perfect city - even in its tourist heart.

You're tired after your transatlantic flight. It's early. The sun is nice, but you can't help nodding off a bit as the train rocks back and forth as it speeds towards central London. But you never fall asleep, because the train is always coming to a gentle stop, thanks to the skill of your Tube driver to pick up more passengers. It's not safe to fall asleep anyway. You hold your bag closer and closer as more people get on. You begin to think about the end of your journey; it's still pretty early, and you know your hotel won't be ready until the afternoon. All you want to do is sleep, but you can't.

You're in London, how could you sleep?

No one talks to you. Everyone minds their own business on the Tube. People read books, listen to music (some a bit too loud, you tut), read the free *Metro* newspaper, or just zone off into space, knowing they'll be at work soon. You're not at work.

You're in London for fun, which the locals may find a bit odd.

This is all a novelty for you, but it's not for them. They don't really even care that you're there, except they're slightly annoyed when they see your luggage taking up so much space on the train. Your bag is probably too big, but packing for London is always a challenge. No matter how hard you try, you can't fit everything into a single carry-on bag. You did your best. Best to just ignore the glares. They will get worse the closer you get to central London.

"Please mind the gap," the announcer occasionally says as the train stops at stations with the most London-y names you can imagine.

Uxbridge.

Sudbury Hill.

Park Royal.

North Ealing.

Hammersmith.

The places sound like magical, fantasy names in a Tolkien book. You wonder what exciting things there are in these places. In all honesty, there isn't much of interest there for you, the tourist. These are places Londoners live. They're delightfully banal. Streets are filled with rows of houses that look similar. High streets are filled with charity shops, fried chicken shops, fish and chip shops, and other fast food chains. And the bookmakers, taking bets on everything. A lot of the time, they're not very nice places. You can understand why you keep hearing about the "death of the high street," because even the people who live there don't really want to visit them. Not everyone can live in a twee village with a posh high street.

"Please mind the gap." It's a soothing phrase. You don't remember hearing anyone tell you to be careful on your public transport system back home.

Then, the light of London's sun is gone.

You go underground somewhere near or around Earl's Court.

You really begin to wonder about these place names. Who is

Earl? And what's in his court? Do they mean Earl in the titled Earl of Grantham sense or Earl as in the bloke's name was Earl? Was there a palace where Earl held court? Or is it a tennis court? You've heard it's a cheap neighborhood near central London,. but you've also been warned away from there by several people. So, you picked somewhere else to stay. This is where you go back underground.

The train seems to go faster when it goes through the dark tunnels. The warm London sunlight is banished by the darkness of the tunnels, and now you have artificial lighting to bear down on you. Now, there's only room to stand. You cannot get your bag any closer to you. You hope the Londoners don't hate you right now. Most probably aren't even paying attention to you at all - just another tourist in the way. It's a shame transatlantic flight arrivals coincide with rush hour on the Tube. Even though the train is packed, you could almost hear a pin drop, save for the noise of the train and the tunnels outside.

People start to get off the train, but it seems even more people get back on.

Your stop is close; you can feel it. You've been watching the map above the door for almost the whole journey. It gave you something to look it, so you didn't look with too much curiosity at the Londoners around you. You start to hear names you've heard in your dreams of London.

South Kensington. Diana lived there.

Knightsbridge. That's where Harrods is.

Hyde Park Corner. That's where you can scream crazy ideas at anyone who will listen.

Green Park. That's by Buckingham Palace, where the Queen lives.

Piccadilly Circus. That's where the famous billboards are.

Leicester Square. That's where the theaters and cinemas are.

Covent Garden. That's where the famous market is.

Holborn. You don't know what's there. You can't place it.

Then, you get to Russell Square. It's your stop!

Stand up!

Wake up!

You're in London!

The train comes to a stop. You push your way out with your bags and everyone makes way – just another tourist arriving in London.

You step out onto the platform, a beautiful circular space, with green tiling all around. An old clock hangs above the platform. There are giant ads opposite the platform, adverting things Londoners should be interested in or buying. You see one for the movie you hoped to see while in London; it won't open back home for months. You stand for a brief second, searching for the black and yellow "Way Out" sign. As you begin your walk along the platform, the train accelerates out of the station, and it makes the most wonderful sound.

It takes a gush of wind with it and fills your nose with the smell of London's grime, cleaners, and detritus. It's the most wonderful smell, not like that urine and cigarette smell you get on the Paris Metro. You've arrived in London. You follow the signs to the exit and arrive at the lift. It feels like it takes ages to get there, then ages to get you to the surface. You wonder just how far underground you are.

The elevator deposits you into the ticket hall and the gate line ahead of you. It's the most wonderfully old space, almost exactly as it was over a hundred years ago when it was opened for the first time. As you tap your Oyster card (because you're a tourist who comes prepared) and exit the station, you turn around and admire the beautiful crimson station tiles. This has to be one of the most beautifully designed stations on the network.

You turn right thinking that's the way to your hotel, but as you go a few blocks and check your map again, you realize it was left, so you immediately turn around and head back towards the station, passing it again.

You enter Russell Square, a beautiful leafy green space in the middle of the city, and soon find your hotel. As you suspected, it's too early to check in, but you're able to leave your bags with the concierge. You leave the hotel and find a café; time for a quick breakfast and a cup of tea to get you going. You find a hole in the wall, a place where local workers gather - not the kind of place tourists swamp. The food is hearty, greasy, and delicious. The two cups of tea you down wake you up and prepare you to make the most of your first day in London.

You get up and walk back to the Tube station, tap in, and go down to the platforms - this time awake and aware of where you are.

You're in London properly. Finally!

You look at the map between the platforms; you're not sure where you want to go. There are so many possibilities — so many favorites. You immediately think, "All right, if I go to Covent Garden, I can get a Ben's cookie, then see the market, then walk down Long

Acre towards Trafalgar Square to see some art at the National Gallery."
Already, that's the perfect start to any trip to London.

You turn right towards the platform. It's relatively empty
now. It's late morning. Londoners are at work. The Tube is now for
the tourists, and you can take it anywhere in London. It's now *your*
London. The dot matrix sign above the platform indicates there's a
train approaching in two minutes. You wonder how accurate that it is.
When the train arrives in two minutes, you realize it's very accurate.
You hop on the train.

"Please mind the gap," the voice tells you again.

And you're off. Next Stop Covent Garden. Next stop your
London trip you've waited so long for, your London dream.

Your trip to London has finally begun properly. No more airports,
no more shuffling. The Tube will take you everywhere you want to go
now. It will hold you, it will keep you safe, and it will transport you.
When you leave London a few days later, you'll miss it. You'll miss
that rocking feeling and holding the railings for dear life. You'll miss
the free newspapers in the late afternoon, handed out at each station.
You'll miss the smells as the Tube comes into the station and you're
hit with that gust of wind. You'll miss watching the platform, hoping to
see the station mice scurry about. You'll miss watching the darkness of
the tunnel ahead in anticipation of the lights announcing the arrival of
your train. Most of all, you'll miss the sense of exploration. You'll miss
stepping onto a platform, open to the possibility of traveling anywhere
on the almost 400-station network. London is all yours to see and
explore.

Most of all, you'll miss just being there and inhabiting the
place.

"Please mind the gap."

You wonder if you can bottle the sounds, the smells, and the
feelings to take home with you.

You can't.

But you always have a reason to come back, again and again.

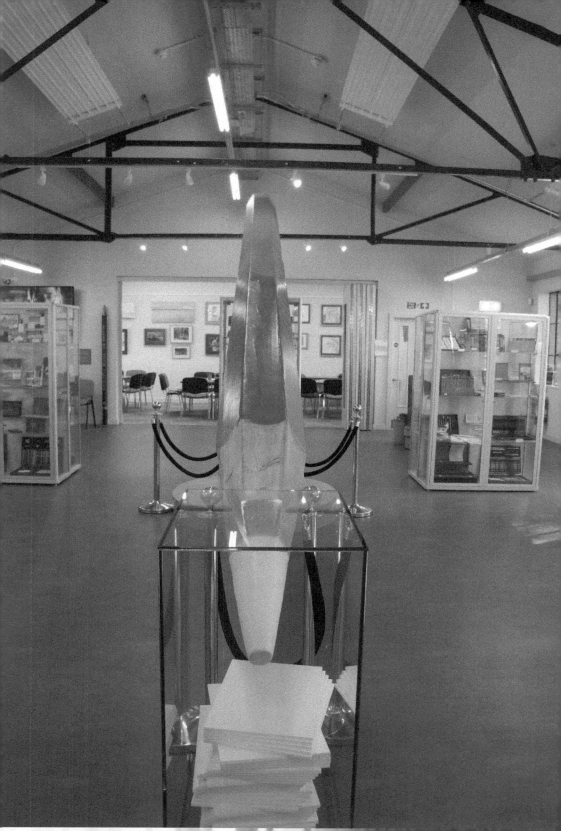

PROVINCIAL MUSEUMS

The National Gallery. The British Museum. The Imperial War Museum. I could go on. London is not only home to amazing museums, they're world-class as well. I have been to London twenty times, and I still haven't been to all the museums on offer. It's amazing, but as any small-minded English person will tell you, when you say you've been to London several times, there's more to Britain than London. That means there are so many museums outside of London to see. The problem is that there are also a ton of terrible museums outside of London, and guidebooks convince you otherwise. They have a charm of their own, however. They're Britain's provincial museums.

And they multiply like rabbits.

I will not identify the places I write about in this chapter to protect the innocent (or guilty depending on how you want to look at it).

If an economically depressed area wants to attract visitors and investment, one of the first things proposed is a glossy new museum. Britain's northern cities are guilty of this. Billions of pounds were poured into Britain's economically challenged cities in the 1990s and 2000s. Starchitects were called in. Giant white elephants were constructed. I'm sure the people behind these museums learned something along the way. These museums outside of London don't attract very many foreign tourists. They only really attract domestic tourists and school groups. I'm sorry, Newcastle and Birmingham. No matter how lovely you are, you are not on the American tourist itinerary.

No swanky new branch of the V&A or Imperial War Museum is going to change that. But, it makes for pretty skyline pictures, and makes it look like Britain's cities with a poor reputation have been dragged into the future.

It's the niche museums that trap you. They're usually on one specific topic, large enough to get a mention in a guidebook, but not so large that it's ever really overrun with tourists. If something exists, and I mean anything, there is a museum for it in Britain. Just like the propensity for the British to catalog their islands via the Ordnance Survey, there is a propensity to create a museum for topics as anodyne as pencils and lawn mowers. Many even manage to get Heritage Lottery

Funding (basically welfare for Britain's cultural institutions, funded by the National Lottery).

When I arrived at the Interesting Topic Museum in a beautiful Georgian City, it had just opened. It was reached by a staircase, which felt rather like going into a Soho strip club, except there were no exotic dancers inside — just an entire museum dedicated to the Interesting Topic. When I approached the admissions desk, there was no one there other than the chap working the till.

He seemed alarmed that he had a punter, or patron in British speak.

As we began our transaction so I could buy an admission ticket, it became immediately clear my mere presence had made the man's day. He told me I had been his first visitor in days.

In days.

Mind you, this museum is hard to miss, and it's in one of the most popular places to visit in Britain.

Because I was this poor man's only human contact that day, I had to stand there and get a history lesson. He knew his subject, the Interesting Topic, deeply, and provided a complete overview of what I could expect in the museum if he ever let me beyond the till to see it. His knowledge was impressive, and I was genuinely interested in the Interesting Topic. But, then, well, it's clear he was an amateur historian. Detecting I was an American, he surmised that I knew nothing about anything and began going through a detailed history of Georgian and Victorian Britain as it related to the Interesting Topic.

I didn't have the heart to tell him he was wasting his time - I knew all of this.

As I stood there, occasionally making eye contact with the excited man, I looked around the entryway, looking longingly at the turnstile to the rest of the museum. There was plenty of souvenirs related to the Interesting Topic, but a lot of it was stuff I wasn't interested in. I was sure to buy the museum guidebook. I always get the museum guidebook. I'm a travel writer; it's necessary. My feet were beginning to get very sore from standing there for so long.

At one point, I pondered chewing off my own arm to escape the history lesson. I have to applaud the man's passion. Eventually, the man either tired of talking or the phone rang, and I made my escape. The museum itself was interesting, but it was small. It was just one large room. There were plenty of artifacts related to the Interesting

Topic, some of which you can only see there, so that's a treat. The museum has done it's best to be relevant to the modern era, and there are interactive displays and ample computer screens. However, my visit was at a heightened anxiety because I was afraid the man would follow me into the museum to tell me more history I already knew. I carefully timed my exit so he wasn't at the till when I left.

Whew.

I'm not identifying the museum where this experience took place because it's an experience you can have at pretty much any small English museum outside of London.

***

Last year, when I learned I was in the same geographic area as the world's largest pencil, I knew I had to visit. I was the first to arrive at the Derwent Pencil Museum. Yes, I know I have a tendency to arrive at these places right when they open. That's how you avoid crowds and people in your pictures. It was 9:30 a.m. I'm an early riser, but the problem with that when you travel around Britain is tourist attractions don't usually open until after 10:00 or 11:00 a.m. I decided to go to the Derwent Pencil Museum simply because it opened at 9:30, and I could do it to kill time on my way to do something else.

"Just mind your head when you go through," said the cashier after she took my £4.95 and handed me my ticket, cleverly a pencil made by Derwent, which is now one of my most cherished writing instruments. "The ceiling can get quite low as you go through."

Oh, how exciting, I thought, looking at the portal ahead. A representation of what a graphite mine would have been like.

I made my way through.

Then, I hit my head on the ceiling.

Well, she did warn me.

When I finally came out the other side, there it was.

The world's largest pencil.

I guess I was supposed to be impressed by it. It takes up a large portion of the room. The Museum consists of a single room, dominated by the pencil in the middle, surrounded by artifacts from the history of Derwent Pencil production. It felt less like a museum and more like a side room with pencil related artifacts next to a shop selling overpriced pencils. I have now seen more novelty pencil sharpeners than a person ever really needs to see.

The pencil was large, but was it a real pencil? Could you take it out to the parking lot and draw with it? I don't know. No, the most impressive thing in the room was the diamond encrusted pencil they made especially for the

Queen, which was off to the side.

I'm a sucker for these provincial museums. They're often a terrible waste of time, but being a completist, I can't not visit them. Some museums I've tried to visit over and over, and have been stymied — for example, there's a museum at the top of Gold Hill, in Shaftesbury. My most favorite place on Earth has a museum dedicated to it.

I've never been to the museum.

Why?

Usually, when I'm there, it's closed.

We're usually in Shaftesbury in winter, when it's closed. Or in autumn, when it's closed.

There was one time I was in Shaftesbury in the summer, and it was the one thing we didn't have time to do.

During our longest trip to Britain in 2013, in which we were there for five weeks, the fifth week we spent holed up in a cottage in the Cotswolds. And I mean holed up. The weather was generally terrible, and we were broke, so we couldn't really afford to do much. We were all going a bit cabin crazy and our son had recently been ill.

So, looking at the stack of brochures helpfully left by the cottage owner, we discovered that a museum nearby was dedicated to an assortment of things. Called Oakham Treasures, it was advertised as a museum dedicated to advertising and nostalgic Britishness.

Sure, why not?

We went primarily for the tractors. My son, who was almost three at the time, was obsessed with tractors. We would learn years later that his obsessions were actually a mild form of autism. So, knowing he was having a hard time traveling and quite ready to go home, we did the one thing we knew he would love, took him to see the "tractor show" as he called it. He's eight now and still remembers this.

So, we all piled into the hire car and drove almost an hour around the Bristol suburbs until we found the place. It was an odd museum. It was literally the collection of a rich person with too much time on their hands. Don't get me wrong; it was an amazingly cool collection of a rich person with too much time on their hands. It had a family friendly café out front which fed us all. We wandered around the museum itself and practically had it to ourselves. It was basically a metal shed filled with the history of Britain's brands and imperial holdings. I quite liked the old post boxes all lined up in a row.

When my son saw all the tractors, he was blissfully happy.

We spent pretty much all our time in the room as he admired them. Not only were they tractors, but they were *British* tractors, which he'd never seen before. It was hard for him to understand why he couldn't climb onto each one, but we helpfully explained that he couldn't go beyond the steel chains protecting the tractors from wayward hands.

So, the lesson here is that while provincial museum can easily be borderline boring and a waste of time, they can also provide a welcome respite to a travel-weary family with a child obsessed with the topic on display.

On a trip to Cornwall, we happened upon another museum dedicated to another Interesting Topic. The problem was it wasn't on our itinerary, and we weren't the ones driving. We were quite sure our hosts did not want to go into the museum. So, they offered to wait in the car while we ran through it quickly. This was all well and good until we waited in the admission line for almost fifteen minutes.

Sometimes, you get helped by the person who has the least training. Apparently, it wasn't her day to shine.

The transaction is pretty straightforward, take the admission money and give the patron a ticket.

This was entirely too much for the person working the till that day. The credit card machine wouldn't cooperate, but she didn't have a key to take cash. While the transaction problems were going on, she also wanted to talk the ear off of the people who just wanted to get into the museum.

And, I should add, we were *behind* these people.

We looked at our phones nervously, this was not quick, and there were people waiting for us in the car. Still, we were genuinely interested in seeing the museum.

So, we had to hear all about the museum's membership program. The local walking paths.

The café on offer.

We had to hear about it all as she explained it to the people in front of us.

Then, finally, it was our turn, and we had to go through the whole process again.

At one point, she actually apologized for it taking so long. The sentiment was nice, but begged the question of why she was taking so long in the first place. Still, the poor woman was just doing her job.

There was no malice here; she was perfectly nice. But it's a good example, especially outside of London, of no one in the English countryside ever really being in a particular hurry. This includes the, often, elderly people working the tills at provincial museums.

Britain's provincial museums are fascinating places, not least because of the topics they're about. They're a fascinating microcosm of British society. You can get a good idea about a society, its history, and its culture by seeing what they decide to dedicate an entire museum too. They're unique. They're quirky. They're infuriating.

I will visit every single one before I die.

TUT-TUTTING AND TAKING THE PISS

As much as I love the place, and if we ever do get to move there, I'll never *be* British. Even if you immigrate, assimilate, and get citizenship, you'll still always be an outsider (but your children will be as British as Marmite). That doesn't stop me from acquiring British tendencies and having them become part of my personality (or they were always there and I didn't realize they were particularly British). One of those elements is the art of tut-tutting.

This is one of those things that's a physical act as well as a mental one. The raw definition of tutting is to simply show your disproval for something, but usually in a way that involves uttering an audible tut. It's so much more than saying, "Tut." It's an attitude. No one but the English can express disapproval with saying or doing so little.

In the early years of our travels to Britain, I was oblivious to it, which makes it much worse when you look back at all the situations you may have caused someone to tut in your general direction. It's a bit rich of us to tut towards our fellow tourists because we've been clueless tourists (and, admittedly, probably are still more clueless than clued in).

Sometimes, you just can't help yourself. After twenty years of traveling in Britain, we've begun to tut ourselves. It's almost unconscious. We are now just as disappointed when a British person doesn't do something properly, or a way we expect — tut, tut. It's something you do privately; it's a very English way of doing nothing about something that's bothering you. If the person did hear you tut, you would be horribly embarrassed.

Recently, we visited Durham Cathedral, one of the finest examples of Norman architecture. We were dismayed, though, when we arrived and learned that photography was not allowed inside. As someone who needs these images for the website, or our print magazine, it's always a frustration when places don't allow photography. However, we respectfully follow the rules.

Most of the tourists there did not. There were plenty still sneaking pictures with their phones, only to be told off by one of the cathedral staff. This is perfectly fine.

Later on during our visit, in one of the altar areas, I came across someone standing in the pulpit, beyond a velvet rope, holding up their camera for a selfie. Then, when she wasn't satisfied with it, had a friend help her take the perfect picture - in a roped off place of worship. In a place where photography isn't allowed.

There was much tut-tutting once we left the cathedral; we couldn't believe it.

The whole rest of that trip, we flexed our new tutting muscle.

It felt great.

America doesn't really have an equivalent other than to judge someone poorly and just assume that they're trash. It's a very cruel way of thinking. It's not really cold disapproval, as the British manage. It's more of a steaming hatred because you simply cannot believe someone would do that. Whenever I see someone drive through town in a giant pick-up truck, belching black exhaust with American and Confederate flags flying (which doesn't make any sense), I don't just stand they're dismayed like a British person would and tut. I just get angry and immediately judge that person's entire life of poor choices.

We've come to expect different standards when we travel. We have lots of British friends, and when we tell them about various things related to our trip that didn't go right, that a British person was responsible for, they tut (sometimes audibly). When our accommodation isn't up to standard, tut, when our rental car has scratches that they try to blame on us, tut, when our service in a restaurant isn't great. Tut, tut. Being served tea at a National Trust property in a foam cup, tut, tut. Watching someone take a book from the honesty bookshop and not put a pound in the lockbox, tut, tut.

Most British people will wave or acknowledge you when you let them pass from the opposite direction while driving on narrow lanes - or at least give you the lazy single finger wave where they lift their index finger off the wheel slightly. When they don't, tut, tut.

Tutting is a versatile skill to have. It comes in handy.

If anything, it makes you feel better when something doesn't go the way it's supposed to, and it's not your fault. And if it is your fault, tut, tut! Then, there is the next stage of British disapproval that goes beyond tut-tutting: taking the piss. When a tut won't do, it's time to bring someone down a few levels by showing them how wrong they were to begin with. It's a strand of British humor I struggled with at the start of my Anglophilia but now have a stronger understanding of it, mostly through personal experience.

I love British humor, but I've only been exposed to it second hand, through entertainment since I was a teenager. Since I was not raised within from birth, this means I will never truly understand British humor, which is a shame, because I bloody love it. I love wicked wit and cutting sarcasm, and finding humor in the bleakest of circumstances. Even after watching hundreds of hours of British TV and seeing countless films, I can never shake the feeling that I'm missing something. I feel it most when I interact with British people. They know that, and many use this weakness as a source for their own amusement. Taking the piss is a national British pastime.

This is a difficult concept to define, and it's not a phrase we use here in the USA. In fact, it would be considered quite rude - but that's not the case in Britain. It's a common term, and everyone knows what it means.

Essentially, it's making a joke at the expense of others. The joke is even better if the person doesn't get it.

I'll never forget meeting British people for the first time. It was the summer of 1996, and I was sent to Boy Scout summer camp. It was exactly the kind of summer camp you see in American TV and movies - located somewhere remote, with a lake, cabins, tents, and a surly staff sick of dealing with other people's kids (and don't you dare ask for a spoon when nothing with a spoon is being served at mealtime). It was all suitably terrible. The bathroom blocks were open to the air and filled with daddy long-legs (that's a spider to my British readers who have a different definition). You had to pull the big ones out and do your business before they crawled back around you. Someone, who will forever remain anonymous, did a big poo in the middle of the shower block. It was hot, and the mosquitos were relentless.

This was the first time I met British people, and I was very excited about that. I'd never met a foreigner. The most exciting person I'd ever met was a fellow classmate's mother who came to talk to our elementary school about her glamorous job as a flight attendant. She'd been all over the world. It was unbelievable! I had a lot more respect for said classmate when I learned her mother had such a cool job. I also felt bad for her because her mother was gone all the time. But they lived in a big house, so maybe it wasn't so bad?

Our Boy Scout summer camp wasn't a big jamboree per se; it was more of a summer gathering where troops from all over the country and a few from outside the country would gather for a few weeks in the summer. When our Scoutmaster told us we would be hosting guests from England, I was thrilled. I couldn't wait to meet them!

These boys were from England - who knows where. I certainly don't remember. They could sense our ignorance as soon as they stepped into our camp. The only things I knew about England were from movies, TV shows, and the bits we'd learned in history class. I knew America used to be British, but we liked to forget that because AMERICA magically sprang into existence in 1776. *The Simpsons*, the hit animated show that miraculously is still on TV, told me that we'd saved their asses in World War II (which is not true, by the way, never say this to a British person), but I had no context. I was genuinely interested in knowing these things, but hadn't been taught them yet. It was a weakness I would spend my entire life trying to reconcile. That's why there are 2,000 books in my home library.

They acted like they lived in a primitive country, and we didn't know any better, so we believed them at face value. When they saw a Gameboy, they pretended to have never seen one before and thought it was some kind of magical device. Then, they couldn't believe we had running water in our campsite!

Why, their village only has the one well everyone shared!

"When we want to watch TV, we gather all around the one cottage in the village that has a TV and watch it together," one of them confidently told us. We believed him. We had no reason not to. British humor loves to destroy the face value.

We heard stories about the village bicycle they all shared. It was all slightly unbelievable, but being of about the same age, and being Boy Scouts, we took them at their word. It was only later we realized they were taking the piss out of us the whole time.

You could almost hear them mutter, "ignorant Americans," when they walked away.

Once they got done making fun of us, they were lovely, friendly chaps. I loved their accents and listening to them talk, even if it was all bullshit. We marveled at their Scout cards, which had a different oath and national anthem (*God Save the Queen*). I'd never particularly liked having to say our Scout oath, or swear to God, because I was in the existential atheist phase of my life at that point. It was amazing to see that we all adhered somewhat to the same Boy Scout values, but they were a bit different. I didn't even know the British actually invented the Boy Scout movement. I'd just assumed it was an American creation.

The English love to sense weakness and pull away at those threads, and that was a lesson I learned that day meeting those kids from England. Afterward, I was left with the impression that English people were jerks and I didn't really like them. But, I also did. I wanted to meet more! Maybe they would be nicer to me now that they had gotten the initial piss-taking out of the way. I've noticed in the years since that the more you get to know a British person, they less they take the piss out of you. It's almost like a requirement to be friends with them. It must be a holdover from their imperial days when they wandered around the world feeling superior to everyone. Now, they can only feel superior to themselves and those they meet.

When I visited London for the first time, I hated it. The British were so cold, and the people we interacted with didn't really like Americans (this was before 9/11 and the Iraq War, so I'm not sure why there was any animosity at that stage).

After a day of exploring London, we decided to eat in the overpriced hotel restaurant simply because it was easy and there.

The young man, whose accent indicated he was from Eastern Europe, was doing double duty as the host and the waiter. He was friendly enough.

I asked him if I could buy a newspaper.

"That'll be fifty quid," he said with a smirk.

"Oh, OK," I said starting to dig through my pockets.

He looked at me with a look of sadness. I hadn't gotten the joke.

"Mate, fifty quid is fifty pounds. I'm joking. The newspaper is 50p."

"Oh, right," I said very confusedly, I didn't know the difference yet.

Even the foreigners who've lived in England for a while had learned how to take the piss out of Americans, but it provided a valuable lesson and I quickly learned what quid meant. So, thanks, random foreigner, for making fun of me.

The more and more you interact with British people along with the more time you spend there, you begin to internalize their humor and way of doing things. Having spent a childhood being made fun of for the dumbest things, I really don't like it when it happens to me when I'm traveling. So, I try to go out of my way to learn social cues and the correct ways to do things - more so than most people when they travel. Most people would rather stay clueless. Cluelessness to me is terrible. I have to be in the know.

Once, when I was sitting with two British men at a pub next to the Thames, finishing a lunch and job interview, they finished by offering me the job.

My first thought was, "You're taking the piss, aren't you?"

Training had taught me to be skeptical of anything the British say; it usually isn't actually what they mean.

They weren't, though, I'd gotten the job (though had to later turn it down).

Sometimes, you just have to look at a British person and ask, "Are you taking the piss?"

They generally won't be offended if you do, and if they are, just explain that you're an American and you don't understand. Then, wait for them to do it again because they will. Then, when you walk away, you can silently tut to yourself.

ENGLISH SUMMERS ARE BETTER THAN ALL OTHER POSSIBLE SUMMERS

When I had the chance to study at Oxford for a week in the summer, it was a truly wonderful time to be there. It was between term time, so the city had a different vibe. The environment wasn't as studious; the proper students simply weren't around. My rooms in the old Oxford college were actually somewhat new, so I didn't boil as much as I thought I would. It also rained a few times, which brought a wonderful coolness to the air. Of course, during the day, the city was mobbed with tour groups - some ruder than others. I'll never forget our tour guide telling off another tour guide for being too loud (they were using loudspeakers - LOUDSPEAKERS). But after about 4:00 p.m., the center of Oxford emptied out as the tour buses left. Then, the ancient stone university came alive in the late afternoon sunlight that seemed to last all the way until sunset.

Britain often saves it's major events for the summer months because they know the weather will be better. The Queen's real birthday is in April, but her "official" birthday is in June because the weather is better and it's much more conducive for grand state celebrations. Both Royal Weddings I've been to took place in the beginning of summertime. I can't imagine them taking place in November or February - that would have been awful. Instead, both Prince William and Prince Harry had gloriously warm and sunny clear skies for their weddings.

English summers are even wonderful when it rains. The rain is inevitable. The British expect it every day at any time. That's why everyone always has an umbrella with them or keeps a warm jacket in their cars. Even after all my travels in Britain, I've still been caught out by the rain. When I visited Oxford, I finished my stay there by venturing over to Blenheim Palace for a Battle Proms concert. The Battle Proms is a series of concerts every summer that is basically a facsimile of The Last Night of the Proms but with a Spitfire flyby and canons. It sounded like a gloriously British evening when I booked it.

When I arrived in Woodstock, the town next to Blenheim Palace, it was raining. The rain didn't stop. I was really surprised that the concert wasn't canceled. I pondered not going, but it was the whole reason I was there. Blenheim is a wonderful place to visit, but I'd already been there before. I gathered my bag, the foldable chair I'd brought, snacks, my zip-up hoodie, and my umbrella and figured I just needed to be British about it.

I walked from Woodstock all the way up the drive to Blenheim in the rain. I was relieved to see I was not alone in doing this. I waited at the free shuttle stop with everyone else as the rain increased in its intensity. I managed to stay dry under the umbrella. I relished the heated and dry bus as it took us to the pitch on the estate where the concert was being held. The rain continued. I found a spot not too far from the stage, and was shocked to see how much earlier other people had arrived. I was also shocked at how prepared they were. They had small tents, blankets, and many people were in proper winter coats. In July.

Clearly, I didn't get the memo.

It was still a few hours before the concert, and I basically sat there, in the rain, huddled under my umbrella, trying to stay dry while I waited for the concert to begin. I did stay somewhat dry, but my bag did not, and my back did not. Eventually, it became clear I was not going to survive the night without getting soaked. The hosts of the concert tried to keep it fun and light and to keep us entertained. The orchestra practiced, which was strange because it was like a pre-concert. Then, we got word that the Spitfire was canceled. There was no way it could fly in the cloudy weather, or that we could even see it if it was. By that point, I was really only there for the Spitfire.

It was fun to watch the Brits around me making the most of it. They'd brought picnics and vats of tea. And beer. They were staying warm, and they were having fun. But as night began to fall, the temperature dropped, the rain persisted. I looked at my phone, and it told me that it was in the 40s (Fahrenheit). In July. The concert started, and it was lovely. At intermission, I could not stop shivering, and I was soaked. I threw in the towel, packed up my gear, and made a lonely walk back to the bus stop that would ferry me back to the entrance so I could walk the rest of the way back to my hotel in the rain.

It was only me and two other people on the bus. We felt like the defeated cavalry in a war. We weren't prepared and couldn't survive a single English summer concert. Still, there was nothing more glorious than sitting on the front lawn of Blenheim Palace, enjoying the festive atmosphere of the Battle Proms concert, even in the rain. English summers are glorious, even when they let you down. The show must go on. Try not to be disappointed. The British are used to this, and they weren't disappointed. Mustn't grumble. Just a bit of rain - but you can bet I'll be better prepared next time!

I'm a broken record: we don't travel to Britain for the weather. When the weather is wonderful, Britain is wonderful. Case in point, British summers are better than all other possible summers. Summers are much milder in Britain than we're used to in North America, but they're still hot. The British are so used to moaning about their terrible weather, they're deliriously happy for a few months in the summer when it's nice. Summer in Britain is Britain at its societal best.

I did not experience my first British summer until 2010 when we visited on business trip for a week in July. It was a shock to our systems. We were woefully unprepared for it. I had packed for business, so I roasted in all my clothing. The flat we were staying in was a 300-year-old Georgian building with grand windows. It faced the sun directly. There was no air conditioning or ventilation. It wasn't so bad during the day, but the day was deceiving because those 300-year-old bricks were soaking in all that glorious summer heat, which means we roasted in our bed at night. And, let me tell you, Jackie was pregnant with our firstborn at the time and she was not happy.

The summer heat in Britain is much different than the humid heat we get in Northwest Indiana in the summer, or the dry heat I experienced growing up in Texas. Because of Britain's position on the globe, the direction of the sunlight is simply different, so it feels much different. It's not as stifling as a humid heat, and it's not as horrible as the "I want to die" heat in the desert. It's much more pleasant - except when it's not. Because Britain doesn't get that hot (again this is comparative, Brits will disagree with everything I'm writing in this chapter), the country is not designed to be hot.

Most modern buildings will have air conditioners (or air-con as the British call it), but most buildings in Britain are not new. Even a lot of new ones don't have air-con because why pay for it when you don't need it that much? So, while the heat is more gentle and pleasant, you simply never get a break from it. You never have a chance to cool down, so you spend all day sweating profusely. Then, you don't cool down at night because of the warm stone buildings. Though when you're boiling, a cool summer breeze at night through your windows is heavenly.

The old stone buildings tend to stay cool during the day, but at night, they stop being cool and become ovens. This is particularly fun when you are traveling with a six-month-old baby. We were staying in a very nice hotel in the Cotswolds, and it had been modernized to a comfortable standard. But there was no aircon (so, not that modern, then), and the building was made of stone. Our six-month-old son was a very difficult baby (well, eight years later, he's still very difficult, but I digress), and we had a huge problem trying to get him to sleep (well, we still do).

We were jet lagged, it was late, and he simply would not stop crying We tried everything. Nothing would make him happy. It was the heat combined with baby jet lag, combined with an indescribable pain that manifested itself in torture for his parents. Finally, it got to the point where we grabbed the stroller, forgoing our shoes and still wearing our pajamas, and went for a stroll through the grounds of the hotel at night. It was so very cool outside the room. It was lovely. Almost chilly. The background noise of the hotel was the River Windrush roaring in the distance. We walked our son until he fell asleep. At one point, we stopped and walked into the dewy grass with our bare feet, and it was the most wonderful feeling.

I was actually grateful for my son being so difficult as Jackie and I got to share a magical moment together in the Cotswold night.

The British as a people are so grateful for any semblance of summer, they can hardly contain their glee. The summer headlines in the British newspapers are always hilarious when they celebrate wonderful summer weather. My favorite is one from long ago that proclaimed it was "too hot for tops," and presented several pictures of women sunbathing like the French. In the summer, the British become a seaside people. As an island race, they look for any excuse to go to the seaside - and most Brits do not live far from it. No part of England is more than 82 miles from the coast. When the weather is wonderful, you cannot find a place to lay down on the beaches of Britain.

Even if the weather is not wonderful, the British are not going to let that ruin a chance to go to the seaside. When we recently traveled in Cornwall in September, it was still very summer-like (summer lasts longer that far north). The weather was fair; we had clear blue skies our whole trip. But it was still rather cool. When we visited St. Ives, the beaches were still packed. Despite the wind, people had mobbed the beach. They simply came prepared. They brought along portable wind barriers that blocked the blowing sand and gravel. Leave it to the

British to create inventions that allow them to enjoy the beach in the sun, even if it's windy. People were still swimming despite the water being rather cold. There were plenty of wetsuits. We struggled to get a table at restaurants along the shore.

The entire English aristocratic social calendar revolves around the summer weather. While the season sort of starts in April with the Oxford-Cambridge boat race, it doesn't kick into full gear until May; then once Wimbledon arrives, it's officially high summer in Britain, and it's time to break out the big hats and the strawberries and cream. This is a nation that has an entire opera festival that takes place outdoors called Glyndebourne. And then there are the garden shows, which allow Brits to show off that they're truly the most "green-fingered" of all the countries. It's such an important event; the Queen even attends - even at her advanced age.

Britain being wonderful in the summer is no grand secret - that's why it's the most popular time for tourists to visit. It can be a bit exhausting, navigating a country under siege by tourists. You have to rethink your trip to avoid them. You may want to visit a place like Bibury and photograph Arlington Row, but every tourist in the world also wants to do that. If you try to go in July, as I did, you simply won't be able to find a place to park within a couple miles of this charming little village. The same goes for Castle Combe. Some people just drive up, pop out of their cars, take their selfies, pop back in, and drive off, not even bothering to stop and enjoy the place (which is wonderful).

Whether you're exploring London, attending an outdoor concert, or climbing a fell in the Lake District, if you do it in the summer, it will automatically be better. You just have to be prepared. Uncertainty is exactly what makes British summers so wonderful. You just have to plan for all scenarios, which is hard to do with airline luggage restrictions. Having to quit an outdoor concert halfway through to prevent hypothermia makes for a funny story, but I really wish I could have stayed to the end of the that concert. And I really, really, wish there had been a Spitfire. I'll be back for the Great British summer, and I'll go to a Battle Proms concert again. I'll need to bring a separate suitcase for all the gear required to be properly prepared .

THE AGE OF THINGS

The small town in Indiana where I live, LaPorte, was founded in 1832. Where I come from, that qualifies as old. My favorite town in England, Shaftesbury, doesn't have a firm founding date. It's generally accepted to be sometime in the 8th century, but it was put on the map when the local abbey was founded by Alfred The Great in 880 AD. Comparing these two facts always blows my mind. One of the things I love about Britain is just how old it is. Everywhere you step, you're stepping on recorded history. The average age of a house in Shaftesbury is several hundred years old. In LaPorte, its decades. I don't mean to say this is better or even preferable. I'm just really fascinated by it, and I love it.

It's often said that in America, one hundred years is a long time, and in England, one hundred miles is a long way. Americans have no sense of history, other than the myths they're taught about their founding fathers (and subsequent Manifest Destiny related "greatness"). Our closest major city is Chicago, and history has all but been obliterated there. It's a city of brand new gleaming skyscrapers. They practically invented the concept, after all. Skyscrapers have been there for so long that enough time has passed for old ones to be torn down and replaced with new ones. Chicago has been a thriving city for over 150 years, but if you go downtown and search for any of this history in physical form, you won't find it unless you go the historical society and look at pictures. Chicago spends a lot of time waxing on about the World's Fair, but good luck finding many traces of it (other than the Museum of Science and Industry and the park that surrounds it).

In London, you can't walk three feet without running into some bit of interesting history. Oh, look! Over there is a bit of Roman Wall. Over there is a bit of Old St. Paul's. Oh, and over there is London Bridge, no not the one falling down, the Tower one. It's everywhere you look, and it's glorious. Not only that, there is a huge sense of history that is protected. Long ago Britons understood that in their long history any ownership you have over a building or property is simply temporary, one in a long line. You may own that beautiful 400-year-old cottage now, but you're probably the 20th person to own it and won't be the last. You have a duty to maintain and leave that building either

219

as you found it or in better condition.

When you observe the London skyline, it looks rather odd and nothing like an American skyline. Chicago, for example, is a single massive jumble of skyscrapers. It's so big; you can see it from fifty miles away across Lake Michigan. London, at first glance, doesn't appear to have many skyscrapers and they appear to exist in two separate places, mostly in the City of London (the ancient square mile of the original London settlement) and in Canary Wharf. The rest of London is pretty low-rise by skyline standards. This is by design. London has very restrictive planning regulations in place.

Some seem rather odd to an American where one's ability to do whatever they want with their property is sacrosanct. For example, St. Paul's Cathedral is an iconic and beautiful building in London. Not only is new building around it restricted, the very placement and view of it in London's skyline are protected. Nothing is allowed to block the sight-lines of St. Paul's, or crowd around it. Try looking at the Chicago skyline and picking out the biggest cathedral, you won't find it. In recent years, it seems regulations have been relaxed, and, let's face it, this really depends on the mayor in charge. The mayor of London has the final say in big building projects.

That's why the Shard ended up where it did, on the south side of the Thames where no one really objected. But that strange slanted shape it has? That's so it doesn't block the sight-lines to St. Paul's. There is always a new tower block under construction in the City of London; this is mostly because the Luftwaffe cleared large sections of the city during the war, so there were plenty of empty spaces to build. Dozens of ugly concrete tower blocks went up after the war. Now, the real estate is so valuable, they're being torn down and replaced with gleaming new glass skyscrapers. Canary Wharf houses the other cluster of skyscrapers in London. It's built upon the old docklands - this is the area depicted in *Call the Midwife*.

When containerization took over the shipping industry in the 1960s and 1970s, the docks were redundant. Large swatches of real estate in London were simply derelict. It was a huge problem. So, the British government did something remarkably sensible for the 1980s; they set up a special economic zone and earmarked it to be a rival to the City of London. It took a bit to get going, but now Canary Wharf is as synonymous with corporate finance as "the City" is. London is a strange amalgamation of places, but this means beautiful places like

Westminster, Nothing Hill, Hyde Park, and Knightsbridge will never be built upon and London's neighborhoods maintain their village-like charm.

In the town next to me is a mall. Well, actually there are two malls, but that's beside the point. It's called Lighthouse Place. It was a regeneration project back in the '90s. The goal was to turn a former industrial site into an outlet mall. It was a huge success. Surprisingly, the developers were very forward thinking; they wanted to preserve some of the industrial heritage of the site instead of just sweeping it all away. You see, the area was a former Pullman Car factory – yes, those Pullman cars. Pullman train cars are still considered the standard for luxury rail travel, even in a day where rail travel is no longer commonplace.

Large sections of the industrial areas were cleared to make way for the mall, but they preserved one giant factory building, restored it, and converted it for use as shops in the new mall. They called it The Works. It was a remarkable thing for the developers to have done. The place looked fantastic when it was done. There were tons of great shops in it. I discovered my love of bookstores because of the bookshop located on the first floor. Inside the building were images of its former life as a factory and artifacts from its heyday - like giant railroad wheels. It was fantastic.

As the years wore on, the anchor tenants left one by one. Most of the place ended up empty. When the final places closed, the owner of the mall, which had changed hands several times, had no loyalty to the idea of the place. It became a cost sink for them. When the tax write-off for the empty building became uneconomical, unceremoniously and practically under the cover of darkness, the building disappeared. The final link to the area's industrial heritage was wiped away. The land was cleared, along with an adjacent church that had been there for over a hundred years. I suspect the plan was to create more shops like the rest of the mall.

It's been over a decade, and the land is still an empty patch of grass.

Such a waste. Such a loss.

The irony is that the vacancy rate in the mall is at an all-time high right now and there's one reason for that: the internet. Eventually, that entire mall will be abandoned, just like the factory was, just like the other mall in Michigan City which also sits empty.

In Britain, something like that never would have happened. The building would have been listed and protected. It would have found a use - an art gallery, museum, or something to keep the building alive and as a monument to our past. Various government departments would have had a duty of care to protect the building, because, after all, the owners were simply stewards until it passed into the next hands. In America, there is no continuity like this. There have been situations where a listed building in Britain was torn down without permission. Recently, the Carlton Tavern in Maida Vale was torn down by property developers. The problem was the building was listed and thus protected. It was considered a pub of historical and architectural importance. Yet, it was just town down without permission. The developers were sanctioned with criminal charges and ordered to reconstruct the building exactly as it was with the materials they'd thrown away - like a giant Lego set. The British don't mess around with heritage.

When you drive around Britain, which to me is the best way to see the country, you can't drive one mile without coming across something of historical importance. I was exploring Kent and Sussex one summer and searched around for things to do until the "big" attractions like Hever Castle opened. Driving down a country lane, I saw signs for a ruined abbey. When I see signs for a ruined abbey, I have to stop. I was still very early, so it hadn't opened yet. I walked around the grounds outside and spotted a Stately Home off in the distance. I took pictures . Later, I learned it was still a private home, one of the many Stately Homes in Britain that still aren't publicly accessible.

Old Bayham Abbey was a delightful little diversion on my way to something else. When it opened up, I raced the rain, trying to have a look around. It was a weird place. Old Bayham Abbey used to be a grand Stately Home until it was demolished in the Dissolution of the Monasteries, then it became a garden ornament for the great house, the new one built a short distance away. Then, it became a garden ornament for the Dowager House, which also fell derelict and was recently restored. There is a lot of history to unpack here.

The abbey was old, and unlike a lot of the bigger derelict abbeys, there wasn't much left of it. But there was something very cool in the old nave. I found a tree growing out of the wall. The tree itself looked hundreds of years old, and it formed a perfect cocoon of life around the wall it grew in, simultaneously becoming a part of the wall, and the wall becoming part of it. It looked like something you'd see in Angor Wat in Cambodia. It was truly remarkable. That's England to me - permanence and fortitude.

My house in Indiana is just over 40 years old. That is considered old around here. We got a great deal on the house because it sat on the market for a long time; many other homebuyers considered it "dated." My favorite cottage in England where we always stay is over 400 years old. That's considered relatively new in British terms. There are buildings all over Britain much older that are still lived in, and this always amazes me. It's just baffling that something 1,000 years old can still be a place suitable for habitation (obviously with modern improvements). I grew up in a place where it's not uncommon for someone to buy a million dollar house only to tear it down and build a completely new three million dollar house. Was the house architecturally significant in some way? Doesn't matter.

When you enter a Stately Home that's several hundred years old, it has the most wonderful smell. The British would say that it's the damp (what they call mold), but it's so much more than that. It's the smell of old leather and old furnishings, slightly moth-eaten. It's the glorious smell of old books, of peeling wallpaper. Of old wood stain and paint (probably lead paint, let's be honest). It all combines into making the most perfect symphony of smells. I suspect the National Trust knows this smell triggers the addiction part of your brain because once you smell it, you want to visit as many Stately Homes as possible. Perhaps they even manufacture the smell, if you'll allow me to put on my tin foil hat for a moment.

Some things look older than others. Some things are built simply to look older. Tower Bridge in London, for example, is only just over 130 years old, but it looks much older than that, which is by design. If you peel away the layers, you will find a steel frame, but it looks like it was built by William the Conqueror just like the Tower of London nearby. The House of Parliament looks like a glorious gothic cathedral, but it was built in the mid-1800s when neo-gothic architecture was all the rage. This goes on, even today. Prince Charles has very strong views about architecture and how buildings look. So much so, he commissioned an entirely new town based on his philosophies in Poundbury, Dorset. Driving through this town looks very much like all the other towns in Dorset, except every building is brand new and follows strict designs to look like the vernacular architecture of Dorset and the surrounding areas. It's false history. Many architects scoff at it, but you know what? The place has not had a problem selling all the houses and flats. People want to live there.

The British love looking to their past so much, they even want the new stuff to look like the past. There's even been a strange inversion to this. After World War II, many concrete tower blocks and buildings were thrown up in the heyday of Brutalist architecture. Many of these buildings were hated and thus not taken care of, so many ended up being demolished. But the same movement that protects ancient ruins and old cottages took pause and realized that, hey, some of these ugly buildings we all hate also have architectural merit. So, now, even some of these concrete monstrosities have been given protected status. Undoubtedly, there will be a neo-Brutalist revival one day. Time is a closed circle.

Permanence. Britain is permanence, even in a world where it seems like holding on to the permanence is a handicap of a sort. In the hills of Dorset, a naked man with a rather large phallus has been carved into the chalk hills. No one knows for sure when the Cerne Abbas Giant was carved into the hillside. When you think of England, most consider it to be a rather prudish country (the older generations might be, but younger generations, no - they have a TV show where people go on first dates naked), so it's a bit odd to see a man with a giant penis carved in the hillside. Children might see it!

But it's there.

And it's always been there.

Archeologists think it's been there for thousands of years.

The odd thing, though, is that it had to have been maintained for all this time. If people hadn't regularly gone to refresh the chalk and cut the grass around it, the hills would have swallowed it up ages ago. Yet, it has survived, and people have tended to it for thousands of years. No one is paid to do this. No one benefits from this other than that it's an important part of the Dorset Landscape.

Now, it's a fun weekend out to volunteer to re-chalk the hill and make sure that it stays there for another few years. Now, it's gained a life of its own. Many think it's a sign of fertility. If a woman is seeking to get pregnant, it doesn't hurt to go sit on the carving's literal representation for good luck in conceiving.

Don't ever tell me that Britain isn't a fascinating place. People literally go sit on a giant chalk penis for good luck whey they want to have a baby. As visitors, it's a strange experience to round the bend and see a giant naked man on the horizon. It's even stranger to see a line of people waiting to sit on the giant penis. Britain is such a fascinating place, and they don't even know it.

Places aren't the only things that have endured history's ravages. Business has too. One of the oldest businesses in Britain is Lock Hatters, located in Piccadilly. They were founded in 1676. 1676! The same company, run by the same family. Since 1676. There were barely any colonies in American in 1676. And it's still around, selling hats to the Royal Family, as they have always done. Even Winston Churchill got his iconic bowler hats from there. The oldest bookstore in London is Hatchards, and it dates back to 1797, when America, as an independent country, was only a few years old. The great explorers in British history and the imperialists would buy their books there. And it's still around in its stately premises in Piccadilly. My favorite bookstore around here is only a decade old. Remarkable.

In America, we want history so desperately, we simply imitate what the British have already done. Walk on the campus of any older university in America, and it begins to look slightly familiar because they're all modeled on Oxford or Cambridge, right down to the architecture and the language (quads and dorms). The University of Chicago, probably the oldest university around here, looks very much like Oxford, even down to the ivy growing up the buildings. Oxford has set the standard of what a university should look like, so most look like it. Notre Dame, another nearby school, is modeled to look like it's from France (despite the school being heavily connected to the Irish community).

Our attempts at history and heritage may be imitations, but that's doing America a disservice as there is genuinely plenty of history here worth admiring, preserving, and learning about only if we can stop and prevent ourselves from sweeping it all away to build a new skyscraper or freeway. Every time I see the empty space where The Works used to be, I feel a pang of sadness. It didn't have to be this way. In Britain, the Age of Things is in the everyday mind of an English person; they live in the ruins of a dozen former civilizations and empires. It surrounds them; it encompasses them. It lives in their minds. They are their history. It's a terrible burden to bear but also an incredible gift. We would do well to learn lessons from that as we progress as a culture.

THE LAKE DISTRICT

After arriving in the Lake District, after an eight-hour transatlantic flight and a two-hour drive from Manchester, I was exhausted. But it was still only midday; it felt like a terrible waste to do nothing for the rest of the day. So, I took a nap, recouped and went out to see a waterfall.

It was late afternoon by this point, but it still felt early; being so far north, English summers last a ridiculously long time. It wouldn't get dark until almost 11:00 p.m. and then after that it never got fully dark. So, the sun was still shining, the sky was clear and blue, and it wasn't too hot. It was a perfect English summer day.

Aira Force sounds made up. Who would name a waterfall something that sounds like the Air Force? And why didn't they go for the full-throttled name of Royal Aira Force? The name intrigued me enough to get me dressed and back out when all my body wanted to do was lay down and do nothing. The walk would do me good, and it wasn't far. The car could take me most of the way. Besides, it was owned by the National Trust, so that meant there would be a National Trust Café nearby, which meant tea and cake.

So, when I say I went to see a waterfall, I really used the waterfall as an excuse to get some cake. I parked in the car park and headed towards the visitors' center. It was located in a suitable shed that blended in with the landscape. The woman behind the counter was very helpful, and I got a map (which was £3 but helpfully waterproof), and instructions on how to get to the waterfall. Map and camera in hand, I headed off. It was supposed to be a short, circular walk of about a mile. I told myself there would be cake at the end. I pretty much had the path to myself, which gave me the feeling of exploring a small corner of England not many people knew about (this was a wrong supposition, I'd just come when it wasn't busy).

Now, for the name. Aira Force is named for the Aira Beck, which is the river that flows through the Lake District and comes through Matterdale on its way to draining into Ullswater (spoiler: the prettiest lake in Cumbria). It drops almost sixty-five feet at the spot that has been immortalized by the National Trust. The name is, disappointingly, only linguistically similar to Air Force. Aira is of Greek origin, something to do with long grasses. A force is simply a drop. It's a ridiculously descriptive name.

The path is pretty even, but there is much climbing uphill and then downhill. The path leads you through a beautiful wood, which gives you plenty of cover from the summer sun. It all seems remarkably beautiful and natural, except the forest is not natural - at least according to the map. It was, in fact, planted by the family who owned the land - a great example of how England's landscape has been continually shaped by the people who've lived in it. Pleasing landscapes like England's don't just happen by accident. Apparently, there is a money tree, where people insert coins into a fallen tree for good luck. I missed it because I didn't know to look for it.

The closer you get to the waterfall, the louder it becomes. The area around Ullswater is relatively quiet. Throughout the walk, the loudest sound you'll hear is the local Hardwick sheep bleating as they graze the hills around the waterfall. Eventually, you round a corner, and there it is - the grand show. It really is remarkable. I stood there and watched the waterfall roar endlessly down the drop. You can feel the mist of the waterfall. It's probably the biggest waterfall I've ever seen. Above the waterfall is a beautiful old stone bridge. It really makes the perfect scene. On the bank opposite, I watched another photographer struggle up and down the precipitous cliff, trying to get the perfect shot. I kept expecting him to slip and fall. I doubt he would have been gravely injured, but his expensive camera with a giant lens surely would not have survived.

I descended the stairs, which were a little scary. There were a total of 104 steps, which seemed to have been built when Queen Victoria was still on the throne. There was another stone bridge, providing another viewpoint to admire the scenery. This one was newly built to honor a gentleman named Cecil Spring Rice, who was apparently the ambassador for the United States during the "Great War. So, that was a strange American connection to run across in a very British place such as Aira Force.

There were those beautiful flowers all around, growing from rocks and overhands and near trees. They were this most beautiful purple color, and I would learn later that they were called foxgloves. This place is also famous for daffodils, which didn't grow that time of year. It was almost two hundred years ago when Dorothy Wordsworth took a stroll through here and took note of the beautiful daffodils in

February. She told her brother about them, and that led to the inspiration for one of the finest poems ever written in English literature.

I followed the path away from the waterfall, and the roar receded to the point where it was a whisper. The silence of the forest returned to me. I looked at my phone for the time; it was getting late. I rushed back to the car park and the café. I lingered too long at the waterfall. The café was closing, and they were out of cake.

There was no cake that day, but at least my disappointment was dissipated by seeing Aira Force, one of the most beautiful things I've ever seen. Anywhere.

The Lake District is one of the most enchanting places I've been in England; it has such a different vibe than anywhere else I've been. It's a combination of leisure with a beautiful landscape. The best place that illustrates this is the hotel where I stayed for a week. When I arrived at my Lake District hotel earlier in the day, it appeared to be closed. There were no cars in the parking lot out front. The doors were locked, and the lights were off inside. On a Wednesday afternoon, in the summer.

I rang the doorbell and eventually a woman came running down the stairs and opened the door.

"Can I help you?" she said, surprised at my presence, and surprised at the very idea that someone would be staying in her hotel.

"I'm checking in," I said.

"Check-in's not until 3 p.m.," she said matter-of-factly, but moving aside to let me in. "It's so early. I don't even have me keys!" she added, running off back upstairs to find them.

After filling in the paperwork, and paying the bill (which, since I booked through *Hotels.com*, I wasn't supposed to have paid until I left, but I wasn't going to quibble), she handed me a small key on a keychain made out of slate that had room number four on it.

"Upstairs and to the right," she said.

She disappeared as I grabbed my bags from my car and went up to my room for the first time.

I'd picked the hotel out of necessity. I needed to stay for an entire week in the Lake District for a writer's retreat. I was Johnny-on-the-spot about booking and booked the hotel as soon as I was accepted into the program. But despite being quick about it, it was a struggle to find somewhere I could stay for the whole week. Many of the hotels near the retreat were booked because it fell over a busy weekend in the summer.

After much searching, I found a lovely looking hotel just off the A66, on the northern edge of the Lake District, and, crucially, only a few miles away from the writer's retreat. It was a pub, inn, and self-catering establishment - very common these days in tourist hotspots. The hotel only had seven rooms, and, thankfully, I managed to get one for the entire week. I would later learn my fellow classmates would not be so lucky and quite a few had to shuttle between different hotels with different availability throughout the week.

It would become my temporary home in the Lake District. It was big enough to be a hotel but small enough to feel like I was staying in someone's home. The staff were very warm and welcoming, and did their best to accommodate my weird guest habits (ordering the same thing for breakfast every day and the same dinner). When the door was locked at night, I felt like I was returning to my own home in the lakes.

I found it all quite beguiling. It was not a Motel 8 along the side of a freeway. It was an old Victorian pub next to a busy road in the Lakes. When there wasn't traffic, the only sound was the bleating of sheep and the occasional clinks of glasses down in the pub. I'm always amazed that when you stay in one of these pubs, you don't really hear the pub. You expect it to be loud. It is not loud. Ensconced in my comfortable room, you couldn't even tell I was in a busy Lakes pub.

On my second night in the hotel, there was a drinks party (or a "do" as the British would say) for the writer's workshop. I met all the other classmates and mingled with the hosts. It was a prelude to dinner. I got to speaking with a fellow writer who was also staying in the hotel. I commented that it was rather nice.

She responded, and I'll never forget it, "Oh, yes, it's very Lakesy."

I took pause to that and spent the rest of the trip trying to define what exactly she meant. It was a phrase I lacked context for - I'd never been to the Lake District. She was from Northern England and had undoubtedly spent lots of time there. There was an entire life of context I didn't have. It became a puzzle I could unpack as I stayed there.

I feel like one needs a "quaint" scale to be able to define "Lakesy." By the end of my stay, I think I had a good definition of what it meant. I took Lakesy to mean a hotel, situated just on the edge of the Lake District, but can still say it's in the Lake District. It's a family run pub with a friendly publican couple running it. There's a friendly, fat, and slow-moving dog wandering around, hoping for table scraps. The place is slightly shabby as if its best days are behind it, but there's a touch of modernism around because the publicans have just taken over, and they have a multi-year improvement plan. The rooms are adequate for their age but could use some updating. The food served is good, hearty pub fare that will not win any Michelin stars. Service will bounce between good and adequate. It will be quiet, despite the continuous stream of people coming and going during the beautiful Lake District summer season.

The pub is old and built of stone with big old windows. This creates its own microclimate in the interior and in the summer that microclimate is hot. It cools off at night - and you would do well to keep the windows open to get the breeze from the north. But during the day, it's hot, and for most of the evening, it's hot. There will not be air conditioning in the place. It's 300 years old, how can you expect there to be central air? Thinking the Lakes would be cooler than I'm used to in English summer, I didn't think heat would be a problem.

The drought that greeted me on arrival had other plans.

This pathetic American has been in this situation before. I know how to deal with the mild English heat. Let's face it, it's mild. While I was there, it was around a hundred degrees back home, and that's *hot*. It never topped eighty-five in the Lakes, but there's never a chance to cool down. So, what's the first thing I did upon realizing I was going to need some kind of way to cool down at the end of my days? I drove over to Penrith and visited a hardware store and bought the biggest fans I could find for a tenner (that's what British people call their ten pound note). Luckily, I need white noise to sleep anyway.

The heat didn't bother me after that.

A few days later, the pub mistress asked me how I was handling the heat and the weather, and I said it was fine and sheepishly admitted I bought a fan.

"Oh, we know," she said. "We all saw you bring it in."

I don't know why, but this slightly embarrassed me. I'm sure the "pathetic American" conversation was had at some point during my stay.

The heat didn't really lessen at night. And I use the word night loosely because the sun never really sets in July in the Lake District. It's at the same longitude as Denmark and Sweden, so it has similar long summer days and short winter days. When I planned the trip, I was looking forward to doing some proper stargazing and amateur astronomy in the dark skies of the Lake District. I never got the chance because it doesn't get dark enough.

When I returned from one of the retreat's events, it was very late at night - almost midnight. When I pulled into the parking lot of the pub, there was still a dim twilight. The sky was a beautiful dark blue and purple. The only stars you could see on the horizon were Venus to the north and Mars to the south. You could still see the ghostly figures of the mountains around you like stately Blencathra. On late nights like that, I was grateful there were big, thick drapes in the bedroom so I could create some kind of darkness. When I awoke early in the morning, the sun was already out. I would learn from the farmer hosting our retreat that that's when he did his proper farming work before the group of writers showed up.

At the Lakes hotel, you really do get the sense that sometimes you're intruding in on someone's home. The publicans had a little girl, about my daughter's age (six or seven at least, school age). She wandered around the place as she if owned it (which, well, she did). The guests didn't scare her in the least. She would run around singing or having some imaginary adventure with herself, and we weren't invited. When she wasn't questing, she sat at one of the tables with her parents, working on homework between them pulling pints. At one point, during a dinner party, she noticed we were all dressed up for a nice dinner. A little later, she appeared again in her nicest costume princess dress, dressed for the apparent occasion, wandering around again like she was a guest at the party. It was irredeemably charming.

On my final night in the hotel, I was done with my writer's retreat and done with my Lakes adventure; I was exhausted, mentally as well as physically. I arrived shattered back at the hotel and barely managed to mutter that I wanted dinner.

"The usual?" said the hostess.

I nodded.

I sat in the main pub room and soaked the place in. It really was lovely, and a good base for my stay that week. There was American music playing on the overhead audio system, which I found rather odd but quaint, fitting into the idea of America these people probably have in their heads. It would be like me playing only British Invasion music in a British themed pub in America. The late afternoon sun was still shining brightly in the window, but its position on the horizon had turned it into a lovely golden glow you only get in England in the afternoon. It was finally starting to cool off. Cool winds were blowing in from the Irish sea, just a few miles away.

It was the end of a Lakes weekend, not just for me but for everyone who was staying there. I'd not seen the guests much during my stay, because when I wasn't in my room, I was at the retreat. When I did eat in the restaurant for breakfast or dinner, I was always early, before most people usually eat. You could tell that the publicans were ready for the weekend to be over. There were still a few guests lingering. It was easy to make judgements. One couple sat in front of the fireplace in cheap IKEA chairs (the finish was rubbing off the faux leather), arguing with each other about something with distinctly southern and cockney accents. Their clothes were cheap and the kind of thing you would expect to see at a pub in the East End of London. They were recognizably English but looked completely out of place.

"They must have went to kill yours," the gentleman bellowed at me at one point when he noticed my gaze. I noticed I had been waiting for quite some time for my steak.

I laughed. He was right.

It was while I was waiting for my dinner, utterly shattered, that I finally grasped what "Lakesy" meant. It meant this strange couple of a different class staying at this hotel without a care in the world. It meant shabby, faded carpets in the pub's main room. It meant old wine and whisky bottles lining shelves at the top of the rooms (which had very tall ceilings). It meant red, faux Victorian wallpaper, faded and peeling slightly off the walls. It meant quiet, inside voices as everyone tried to enjoy their pints in peace. It was the family of four, who had come in after a long walk in the Lakes, famished and arguing over who was going to eat what.

"Oh, lovely, they have fish and chips," said one, which is an odd thing to say in a pub since every pub has fish and chips.

The furniture is a mixture of make do and mend, from new chairs to old church pews, providing the backings for larger tables. There is not a TV to be found in the place, anywhere. There is artwork on the walls, tastefully chosen to evoke the Lakes and the local farming heritage - all for sale for £45 and above (one of the many new lines of business modern pubs have to do to make ends meet). After waiting far too long for your dinner, you eat it, and become full of the locally sourced beef and potatoes. You wander back up to your room, full and exhausted, spend too much time on Twitter connecting with your classmates, and geeking out about your retreat.

Then, you sleep, wake up, and leave, a piece of yourself still in the Lakes hotel.

Leaving a piece of yourself in the Lakes Hotel.

You'll be back one day.

Climbing the Cumbrian fell almost killed me.

I do not hike, and I do not climb. There are lots of reasons for this. The important one is that I'm lazy. I much prefer sitting in my office, working and not going anywhere. When I do go somewhere, it's usually to Britain, and that's when I become my most physically active. I walk more in Britain than I do anywhere else, mostly because I like walking there. Pretty much every landscape in Britain is prettier to walk in than any landscape I have at home. Beauty is motivation enough to walk long distances in England.

My laziness is a real problem for me. My chosen career does not help. As a writer, I spend my days in my office in front of a computer. I don't exercise. I love walking in the English countryside, but I don't walk or hike at home. There isn't anywhere nearby to do it, and I don't have time anyway. I walk in England all the time, so I didn't think twice about climbing the fell. I've climbed English hills before, and while they were a challenge, such things didn't do me any lasting harm.

But a fell is not a hill, and

I've never climbed an English hill in the summer.

The fell was located on the farm of the writer that was hosting our writer's retreat. He owned his own mountain, basically as much as you can own a piece of England that has been there long before you and will be there long after you.

The hill is right above his farm. There are tracks and public footpaths all the way to the top. The hill was a great source of inspiration for him - his family had farmed it for generations. He wanted to take us to the top to show us what a fell was like, and read from some of the works that inspired him.

So, a group of about twenty of us, all in various stages of age and fitness, started climbing the fell. We all figured that the farmer would go easy on us. He may have, but the fell did not.

The walk started off gentle enough as we followed the old track along the hill, then over a fence onto a footpath that began the climb. The sun was shining brightly in a cloudless sky. It was dry and hot, but it was beautiful. It was exactly the kind of day Wordsworth wrote about in his poems. The only sound on the hill was the sound of sheep and the still air as we climbed.

Soon, I had labored breathing as I struggled with the climb. I'm probably fifty pounds overweight, but I thought I could do it. I climbed. The farmer bounded up the fell like his sheep, seemingly with no effort. He was even carrying a pile of books he planned to read at the top. He was so excited to share the view and the words with us, I don't think anything could have stopped him.

We stopped halfway up the hill and sat in a small wooded spot. I was grateful I'd brought along a portable stool to sit on. We had a nice rest while we listened to him read us passages. I drank water to rehydrate. Others walked past us on the public path on the hill. I pondered ending the walk there. Despite it being a safe and welcoming group environment, I didn't want to be the person who turned back. If the ladies who were thirty years older than me didn't turn back, I really had no excuse.

At this point, my entire body was screaming. Despite sitting for a few minutes, I was still woefully out of breath and ridiculously thirsty.

Then, it was time to continue our climb.

"It gets easier from here, it's not as steep," he told us.

We believed him.

He was wrong.

At one point, it seemed like we would never get to the top. While the angle of ascent did lessen, I had to think about every step I took to make sure my uncooperative body could do it. It was a truly pathetic display. At the time I was only thirty-four years old, it should not have been difficult for me, but it was because it was outside the realm of my normal experience.

As we got higher above the tree line, I started to turn around and look at the view.

And, my God.

We were up so high; we were above the world. All the cottages and farms were well below us. All that surrounded us were the verdant green hills of the Lake District fells. The landscape had a language, which the farmer carefully translated for us. For the ignorant observer, we just saw a bunch of houses, sheep, and valleys. But when he explained it, we saw heritage, family history, livelihoods. We saw a living, working landscape that wasn't just there to look pretty.

I took hundreds of pictures on the climb up.

As we got closer to the top, we came across a herd of horses, grazing in the woods . They got out of our way when they saw this group of writers approaching. No tree at the top of the hill was straight - all bared the shape of structures withstanding the wind for hundreds of years. They were all just a bit askew, sentries against the endless winds at the top of the fell. We took a break when we reached the top, and sat under the trees while the farmer read to us some more.

What struck me most about the top of that hill was the silence, peace, and contentment. I'd physically made it to the top of the hill. I did not die. My whole body hurt, and I was dying of thirst after my water ran out. The struggle, and it was a struggle for me, was so worth it to sit there on top of that hill, feel the warm breeze, listen to the sounds of the English summer on the fell, and listen to the words that inspired one of Britain's greatest living writers.

It was, in that moment, a paradise.

The climb down was substantially easier than the climb up, though a few of us did the trip on our way down; it was quite steep. When we reached the bottom and the comfort of the cool workshop room, we all relaxed while we waited for the next lecture. I felt like I'd accomplished something wonderful. I'd only climbed a hill, but I did something I wouldn't normally do. I pushed myself to finish and was rewarded with an experience that can never be taken away.

A few days later, I realized after the fact how pathetic the whole performance was. I was watching *Countryfile*, a British country affairs TV program, and saw a story of an 82-year-old man who runs the fells around his farm with seemingly little effort. The man looked like he could barely stand up straight and he would literally run and bound to the top of the fells in the Lake District. He would even compete! I imagine that is how the farmer will turn out, still bounding up his fell, even when he's a hundred years old. It was really pathetic that I, a

34-year-old man, struggled so much with it.

Climbing the fell did not kill me. I experienced no lasting physical effects by forcing myself to do it. When I laid in bed that night, watching the endless twilight of a Lake District summer, I was in pain. I took Aleve and then a shower. Then, I ate something unhealthy to reward myself for doing what I'd done (delicious chocolate Kipling Cakes). The soreness only lasted a day. I survived with no lasting ill effects.

This meant only one thing: I needed to do it again. And again. And again. I have more fells to climb, more walks to take, more challenges to overcome. I know perfectly well I can do it, I just need to summon up the willpower . In the end, it'll be worth it, just to sit at the top of a fell like that and watch the English summer for hours on end. The pain of the climb gives way to the reward being in my most favorite place in the world: the English landscape.

THE STATELY HOME

Your journey to the Stately Home starts with a long driveway that takes you far away from the local village with the same name. The driveway is a single track lane, possibly in need of maintenance. Occasionally, another car comes in the opposite direction, and you both have to drive off the road slightly into the grass to let each other pass. There is no sign indicating a Stately Home nearby. There are fallen trees on the grounds; later you learn this is part of their conservation management of the land. There might even be deer milling about, occasionally crossing the road and forcing your wife to shout, "Deer."

Then, you round a bend. There it is, sitting perfectly in the landscape as if it was planned, which of course it was. Green hills surround it. There's a fine grass lawn leading practically right up to the door with a small tan gravel driveway that will crunch under your feet when you walk on it. You pause to admire the view, hoping no one honks at you from behind. You may even pull the camera out and snap the perfect picture of the grand old house sitting in the landscape.

The house is Palladian, obviously. Maybe neo-gothic or possibly a mishmash of many architectural styles, but probably Palladian, the minimalist classical architecture imported from Europe. The house is at least 300 years old, in its current form at least. The Palladian facade hides elements that are far older. Some say the house dates back to before William the Conqueror. You have trouble believing that anything can stand for over a thousand years, but this is England. There are plenty of things that have stood for much longer.

You continue along the drive until you get to the car park. It's what the British would call a "bodge job." Basically, a muddy area that was once grass but has been worn away by the legions of visitors who have come to see this very famous house. Thankfully, you brought your wellies with you, and your umbrella because it's raining. You park the car. Shockingly, you have to pay to park the car, but you brush it off, thinking every bit helps keep the house in order.

The walk from the car park takes you on a circuitous route, and you begin to think that you're being led astray. Eventually, you arrive at the swanky visitor's center, newly constructed using Heritage Lottery money and designed to blend into the landscape so it doesn't detract from the grandeur of the very famous house. You pay your admission, grateful you got a slight discount for some reason because the full admission price for a family of four was almost £100.

But you brush it off again, thinking it all goes to a good cause.

You're let past the gate, and into the gardens. The gardens are what the place is really famous for, but you're not there to see the gardens, you want to see the house! Still, the gardens suck you in with their sublime beauty. It's raining, but the garden is still in full bloom. Vibrant colors surround you. You follow the path and come to a lake, man-made by the famous landscape architect with a name that sounds made up. They had to dam an entire river to make this view.

Arcadian.

That's what the guidebook says, and you don't quite know what that means, but you soon learn that arcadian means exactly what's in front of you: a manmade lake in a manmade landscape with manmade follies designed to look like Greek and Roman temples, filled with fake statues of gods and goddesses. But it all works together. It all looks vaguely familiar because of all the famous films and TV shows that have been filmed there, seeking the perfect Arcadia for lush, romantic period pieces.

You follow the path around the lake, desperately seeking the house. You catch a chill. Conveniently, one of the follies has been turned into a café offering cheap cups of tea and biscuits. It's enough to warm your cockles on this cold and rainy summer day. Or spring. Or autumn. But not winter because the house and gardens are closed then. You sip your tea and admire the view again.

What time is it?

It suddenly doesn't matter because you're in an artificially timeless landscape and you don't want to leave.

You look to your left and see the famous temple from that scene in that movie with the rain. Or you turn to your right and see the lake with the sexy man who comes out of the water. You look up and imagine an alien invasion coming from the sky. Hollywood movies sure find some creative uses for grand old Stately Home gardens. Most of all you remember that feeling you had watching that "Perfect British Drama" for the first time. You sigh, content that the place you watched was real, and you're there to share it with your loved ones or family.

You've had enough of the garden and the rain. The sun comes out as you make your way to the house. The house is famous all around the world. It was on that one TV Show everyone was talking about. When you round a corner, leaving the gardens, there it is. And you pause. Then you remember you have to return to the concept of time because your tickets to the house are on a timed entry system to control the flow of all the people who've come from all over the world to simply look at the place. Thankfully, you're bang on time.

As you approach the house, all the scenes in all the movies and TV shows you've seen with the house begin playing in your head. Perhaps you start humming the iconic theme song. You enter the house and enter into an immediately disappointing entryway. It's not grand like on the TV show, and then you realize, thanks to the information in the pamphlet included with your ticket, that most of the interiors were filmed elsewhere, on a soundstage. But that doesn't matter. You're still there, and it looks vaguely familiar. There's a fire roaring in the entryway. You suspect that fire is roaring the entire year because it's July and still freezing in the house.

Perhaps the home is still owned by the ancient family that has always owned it. Despite the decline of the British Aristocracy, privations of war, onerous death taxes, and generations of inbreeding, they've managed to hang on to the place. Or perhaps they didn't, and it now belongs to the National Trust who try to maintain the house as it was in its long gone heyday. But the family still gets to live there, in a small apartment of twenty rooms at the back of the house. The house is in a perpetual state of shabbiness. That's the way the National Trust got the house, and that's the way they'll keep it. Or perhaps the charity that now runs the house will keep it that way. Either way, everyone is very well aware that the selling point of the house is that it never changes.

It was reluctantly opened to visitors on strange days of the year; as a consequence, it feels like it's always filled with too many people. There is no guided tour; you're trusted to wander around on a set path through the house. There's a docent in every room, perfectly willing to talk your ear off about some obscure element of the room. Sometimes, you let them because it's interesting. Sometimes, you can't wait to get out of the room because the person is slightly worrying you with a nervous tick or a bad smell. You wish that wasn't the case because there was something interesting in the room, but you couldn't find out anything about it.

Every room is filled to the brim with inexplicable treasures. The detritus of hundreds of years of materialism and hoarding - a complete unwillingness to throw anything away. It *could* be valuable, or not. Every little element adds to the feel of the place and mustn't be changed. Even when the house is closed, and the place is cleaned from top to bottom once a year, every item is cataloged, photographed and meticulously put back into place exactly where it was. Everything is just so.

The pathway leads you from grand room to grand room. Then, you go upstairs, and the rooms become smaller all of a sudden. This is where the family lived. And you get the joy of looking at their toilets and their closets. If you're very lucky, you might even get to see some vintage clothes that someone sourced from a local charity shop. The house has the most remarkable smell. It feels at first familiar, then foreign. It's a combination of dust, mold, and old leather books. It's marvelous.

Then you get to the part of the house that is less ready for visitors, the parts of the house they can't afford to restore because the family is too poor, or the National Trust doesn't deem it worthy. Here you see the real decay of long gone aristocracy, the echoes of a dead people. Then you find yourself on a staircase going down to the kitchens. The kitchens didn't use to be on the tour, but since the hits of several shows set in Stately Homes, everyone suddenly gained an interest. So, now you have the kitchens set up as they were *In The Past*. Even the kitchens were grand.

Wow, these people sure knew how to live.

That is until their economic burden became too much for the local and state economy, and the house had to be sold off. At least it was sold off. Other places like this were simply torn down or blown up in a farcical spectacle that would never be allowed today.

Still, the estate is a center for local employment. A landscaped garden still needs gardeners. The house still needs maintenance men. There's an army of volunteers too, but a large number of people are still employed to make sure this house doesn't change. Instead of working for an absentee lord with his own sense of entitlement, they work for managers who know how to maximize a Heritage Asset of National Importance.

You come out of the kitchens and back into the open; it's raining again. You make the soggy walk to the stables where the café and gift shop are conveniently located. You have another cuppa, but this time have a proper lunch because no grand day out to a Stately Home is complete without an ethically sourced local meal. You're tempted by the honesty secondhand bookshop at the back of the stables. You hope to find a moldy old book that perhaps might have once belonged to the house library, but most are just books nobody wanted anymore and didn't have the heart to throw away, and so they just =donated to the local charity shop.

As you survey the house and think about it, you imagine yourself living in it. Despite being a place of great wealth, it has a feeling about it that it could be just quite achievable, even if you're a middle-class American. It's easy to imagine yourself as William Waldorf Astor coming to rescue to the place from ruin. Of course, that idea is beyond silly. You'd have to be independently wealthy to own and maintain a house like this. And even if you could, it would be kind of wrong to have it all for yourself. You look around at all the families and couples having a grand day out. This house now belongs to all of them.

And that's beautiful - almost as beautiful as the house, and the gardens, and the landscape.

Even if you only got to experience it for a few hours, you inhabited the place for a time. You finish your cup of tea, eat the last piece of chocolate cake, make the muddy walk back to your car, and then go on to the next attraction on your list. A piece of you stays at that house. If you're in the area again, you know you're going to pay another visit because you can, from 10:00 a.m. to 4:00 p.m., weekends only, from March to October, and one week before Christmas. At least.

THE QUEEN AND ALL THAT

I saw the Queen once. This is not a hard thing for a British person to do. Well, maybe now that she's older. But when she was in her public events prime, you could count on seeing the Queen a few times in your life. I'm not British and for me, seeing the Queen was a once in a lifetime event. I'm happy to report I have actually seen her with my own two eyes.

I was standing on the Mall, the stately road that leads from Buckingham Palace to Whitehall and beyond during the royal wedding of Prince William and Kate Middleton. I'd woken up at 5:00 a.m. to get my spot on the Mall. I was lucky I'd had an interview with BBC Radio that morning; I was already within the media scrum area, so when I exited, all I had to do was sidle my way to a spot on the Mall. I was in the perfect spot to see everything happen.

It was a very long, boring morning until things started happening. Every slight movement that might have been interesting elicited excitement in the crowds. Even the street sweepers made the crowds cheer. Finally, the procession of fancy Rolls-Royces and Mercedes began as they all made their way to Westminster Abbey. I was close enough that I could clearly see the gates into the Buckingham Palace forecourt. As the ceremonies began and the loudspeakers boomed with preparations, the gates opened and a scarlet Rolls-Royce pulled out. The first thing I saw was the hat.

Then, I saw her.

Her Majesty in all her understated glory. HM, The Queen. I could see her smiling. I even took a picture. I almost teared up.

It's really strange, being an American and loving the head of state of another nation. But I do. Let's face it; elected presidents are nothing compared to a monarch. When we got rid of the British king, we decided to set up a system that was somewhat similar but instead of a king, we elected a president. As the years went on, despite the desire to not have a king, the presidency turned into a pseudo-monarchy. Our presidents don't inspire affection like a monarch does.

The Queen represents the entire nation of the United Kingdom (and her Commonwealth realms). Her government, which rules in her name, are the ones answerable to voters and they never have the same level of affection and popularity as the Queen has had - except maybe for Winston Churchill who basically had a king's funeral when he died. No, the Queen is Britain, and Britain is the Queen.

As I'm the same age as Prince William and a little older than Harry, my childhood mirrors their childhoods. Well, generationally, we literally could not have more in common than that! Princess Diana was a huge part of my childhood. My mother was an Anglophile, so she paid attention to all the Diana and Charles drama. Diana and the Royal Family just existed in the background of my life growing up. I saw the news stories about the marriage troubles, and I saw countless new stories about their kids. When I was very young, I would always watch CNN headline news right before school because I always loved to be informed about the day's news. The British Royal Family always seemed to be in the news.

It was a death that really began my fascination with the Royal Family.

When Diana died, I was just thirteen years old. I was in the phase of my life where my interest in Diana was merely, "She's hot," because I was getting quite tired of all the gossip at the time. But one night in August, I returned from an evening out at the local mall, when going to the mall was still a thing people did, and turned on the TV to see the news that Princess Diana had died in a car accident.

I was simultaneously devastated by the news and enthralled by it. It was the first real major royal event I remember witnessing via the media. I was glued to the TV for the next few weeks as all the details were revealed and pundits had endless debates about her death and what it meant for the Royal Family. The film *The Queen* starring Helen Mirren would later become one of my favorite films, but the interesting thing is that I had no idea what was really going on.

I just remember the Queen making a speech from Buckingham Palace and it being a really big deal. I just found it all really sad, and it made me sad.

I remember watching the funeral when it happened. It was broadcast on American TV. There was great interest here. I watched as Prince William and Harry walked behind the gun carriage that carried their mother's casket through central London. I was very sad for them. Prince William and I were close in age, and I couldn't imagine losing my mother and being practically alone to face that loss.

It was all a terrible tragedy, but from that tragedy came my great interest in the Royal Family and Britain itself as I became hungry to learn as much as I could about it all. I learned how Britain does great state events. I learned that the nation had changed from one proud of its stiff upper lip to one that was willing to mourn in public. I learned that maybe the Royal Family wasn't as great of an organization as I thought. My final memory of that terrible time was watching Diana's funeral hearse being followed through the green beautiful, rolling English countryside with golden sunlight overhead and roads lined with thousands of people just trying to pay their final respects.

Of course, now I know a lot more about what was really happening behind the scenes during that dark time. The Queen made a lot of mistakes. Despite what the Royal Family tries to get across, she is not a perfect, saintly woman. And that's okay. She's human. Still, she's a very good human. The best of us. She was never supposed to be Queen, but when it became clear she was going to be, she dedicated her life to being the best monarch she possibly could. The amount of affection she engenders in the average British person is astonishing.

I've never met a British person that hates the Queen or wants to get rid of the Royal Family. Oh, they'll take the piss out of them (they are quite weird). Prince Charles doesn't inspire nearly the same amount of affection as his mother does, and he never will. She represents the rock solid core of Britain and what it means to be British. She's permanence in an impermanent world. She's respect. She's deference. She's a symbol of an entire people. The monarch in Britain never technically dies. It literally continues immediately to the next person. She's in her 90s now, and the fact that she's still performing public duties is simply astonishing.

Every time there's a major royal event, the TV networks roll out the usual suspects from the Republican movement. Those are the folks who think the monarchy should be abolished, that they are a waste of money, and their existence fosters a culture based on class inequality. They're not completely wrong. Though, the Royal Family brings far more into Britain than it costs them. It's quite a bargain, actually. But even when you hear these people being interviewed, it's very clear that their hearts are not completely into the Republican movement. Britain having an elected president or head of state is such an out there concept, I don't think it's something that would ever happen.

Many Royal commentators say, "Well, just wait until Charles is king."

Yeah, no. That's not the way monarchies work. Look, he'll never be as popular as his mother, but I think Charles will be a decent enough king. The British Royal Family is so well respected and held in such high esteem that sixteen independent nations still choose to have her as their head of state. That's so bizarre. You have a country like Canada, our neighbors to the north and they still love their Queen. And that's the thing, all the countries think of her as their Queen. She's not just the British Queen. Even in the country of Australia, where Republicanism is much stronger, they still failed to abolish the monarchy when it was put to a referendum.

One day I hope to become a British citizen and part of that process will be that I'll have to swear an oath to the Queen. I will do it with all my heart and all my loyalty even if it's Charles by that point. God save the Queen (or King)!

FINDING MY ROOTS IN DURHAM

As I've embarked on this journey to understand why I love Britain so much, I've been searching and searching for a physical connection to the place that might explain why I felt such an affinity for it. It turns out, my British roots run rather deep. So, perhaps, I was genetically predisposed to like all things British. It has always been rather strange to feel like I was connected to a place, located 4,000 miles away, that my ancestors left long ago. It turns out, my ancestors were part of the fabric of British history. I just had to do a little digging to find out how.

When you look at me, it's not hard to imagine British roots. I have pale skin and red hair. Fill in the blanks there. My last name is Thomas, a very common name of Welsh origin. On my father's side, there are Taylors and Lambs. On my mother's side, there are the Roses. All very strong British names. This meant that my ancestors came from at least somewhere in the British Isles, but I simply had no idea. If I did have British ancestors, they were not near me in the family tree. Trust me, we looked so we could see if anyone was recent enough to get ancestry visa (to Britain or anywhere in the EU). No, it turns out my ancestors came to America long ago.

Last year for Christmas, we bought both my parents one of those ancestry DNA kits, something they had expressed an interest in doing. I will admit, it was the perfect gift for them because buying it for them was essentially buying it for myself. I probably wanted to know the results more than they did! After they'd filled their vials with spit and sent them away for testing, we waited patiently for the results. When they came back, it was a huge vindication for me.

My father's came back as over 50% British and Irish. My mother's came back as 37% from the British Isles (the less said about the 30% French & German bit, the better). This meant that, even by my remedial math skills that almost 90% of my ancestry comes from Britain. Sounds good to me. Now, I just wish it was close enough in the family tree to matter!

One day, when I was speaking with a relative, she told me she had begun digging into the family tree on her side of the family (my father's side) and had discovered that we had ancestors who came from Durham, England. The chap was named William Lamb, and he apparently lived at 10 Shincliffe Lane just outside of Durham. This was wonderful news to me and provided a great excuse for us to finally visit Durham, so we managed to fit in a visit when we were driving from Land's End to John O'Groats in 2018.

William Lamb was born in 1837 in Durham, England. I haven't dug up much about his life, but I know he died in 1872; in the intervening years he had four children, one of which was also named William Lamb, born in 1864, who is the one that emigrated to North America — settling in the USA before dying in 1928 in Chicago. This was the man who decided to seek better opportunities in North America. Born in a small village outside of Durham, he died in bustling Chicago, one of the largest cities in America.

I can only imagine the incredible journey he must have went on. He did it when he was just seventeen years old. Seventeen! I find it slightly ironic that I also visited Britain for the first time when I was seventeen years old. I can't imagine uprooting my entire life at that age and moving to a foreign country. What a brave man he must have been. He got married shortly after his arrival. His adulthood in America was filled with struggle. Each of the two times he married, both his wives died young.

We'd arrived in Durham the night before and planned to visit Shincliffe the next morning on our way out of town and into Scotland. The address we had was 10 Shincliffe Lane, but there was also a village called Shincliffe. We decided to start at the address and go from there. It took us only about ten minutes to drive there. When we arrived, it became a puzzle. We could not find 10 Shincliffe Lane. Google maps took us to a field. There was a 1, 2, 3, 4, Shincliffe Lane, but not a 10. Other than a cottage on the corner, all of the houses were too recent to be a house he was born in (they were Edwardian, or early 20th century).

We drove in circles and came across the postman. I didn't want to bother him, but Jackie insisted and literally hopped out of the car to ask him if he knew where 10 Shincliffe lane was. He said he has been working the route for forty years and there was no such address. So, after having a look around, we concluded that the address must have been a transcription error on the part of the 1920 US Census. It must have simply been 1 Shincliffe Lane, which was the only building on the street that could have been in existence when William Lamb was born. It's a charming old tumbledown cottage and the perfect place to imagine where my ancestors had come from.

The street was adjacent to a former manor house, so we can probably assume that that is where the family worked. Domestic staff was a very common profession in the mid-Victorian era. It would make sense with the story of the junior William Lamb that he would want to leave England for better opportunities in America. Durham was a very built up area, but most people either worked in service or in the coal mines. There were definitely more opportunities in America.

We sat for a few minutes and pondered what we found. I have spent my whole life looking for a physical connection to Britain, and there it was, right in front of me. A beautiful old cottage where my ancestors were born, lived, died, and left. I had, in a sense, come home. I got a little choked up. Sure, it wasn't Dorset, my favorite place in Britain, but I'd found the place where some of my ancestors started. Their blood was in the soil, which meant that my blood was in the soil. The connection is not strong - William Lamb Junior is my great-great-great-great-Grandfather. But it's there, and it's something.

We took the road to the village of Shincliffe, which was about a mile away. On the way, we saw that you could actually see Durham Cathedral from where we were; it was cool to see that my ancestors essentially lived in the shadow of one of the great cathedrals in Europe.

We parked in the village of Shincliffe, and for a weekday it was completely deserted. You could tell that it was once a place with everything you needed to live. There was a pub on the corner. There was an old post office, another old pub, an old forge, etc. - everything a village would need. The downside was all of these things were now gone and the village was now a "bedroom" village for Durham. We visited on a weekday, and there was nobody about, despite it being a thriving village. We walked around and took pictures, and I sat on a bench to admire the place. It was exactly the kind of place I fantasize about living if I ever get the chance to reside in Britain. It was quiet. It was beautiful. It was quintessentially English.

It felt good to come from a place like that. Anglotopia had come home.

I didn't want to leave.

Still, we had an adventure to continue, so we climbed back into our car and drove on. I left a little piece of me in Shincliffe, and I can't wait to go back one day.

WHY DON'T YOU JUST MOVE HERE?

It's a simple enough question, and I get it all the time. If you love Britain so much, why don't you just move there?

The short answer is this: I would love to, but I can't.

The long answer is this chapter. I have been trying to move to Britain since before I started Anglotopia. It's been a dream since I was in college. Every time I've visited, I've basically thought of it as a trainer trip to get me ready for the big show. When we spent five weeks there for one trip, it was an attempt to try and get a gauge of what it was like to live there. I have tried to move there several times, sometimes half-hearted. Several times the visa process was started. One time we were weeks away from moving our entire life to Britain.

Learning how difficult such a prospect it is has turned it into a lifelong lesson. Dreams take work, and some dreams require you to play the long game. When I graduated from college, I had no prospects. At first, at least. I visited England on spring break every year in college, and when I graduated, I wanted one thing: to move there immediately.

I learned quickly that such a thing was easier said than done.

Not knowing much about the world, I had no idea that to move to another country to work was a completely different thing than to visit there on vacation. To move to Britain, you needed a job. To get a job, you needed a visa. Worse yet, you couldn't just get any job; it had to be a job that was in demand in the economy and no one inside the entire European Union could do. You had to be special to move to the UK unless you were an EU citizen.

Surely, I had British ancestry and could use that to move to Britain somehow.

Nope.

I am both lucky and unfortunate in the sense that my ancestors have been in the USA since the mid-1800s. Even the ones who originally came over from Britain are so far removed, an ancestry visa is not possible. In fact, there isn't even an ancestry visa anymore. To move to Britain, the furthest you can go back is a grandparent, and even that has been phased out. Do you want a free pass to Britain? You need a British parent. Or be an EU citizen (until Brexit goes through). I looked into loopholes. Other EU countries like Ireland and Italy actually do have ancestry programs. If you can prove a grandparent had citizenship at birth, then you get a passport through descent. We searched both our family trees - I have ancestors from Ireland and Jackie has ancestors from Italy, but it was all too far back.

When I graduated from university, I had no work experience. So, no one in the UK was going to hire me for any job, let alone one they couldn't fill from within the EU. I needed work experience. I set out to get that and build a career. I found, though, that as time went on, even having several years of work experience didn't really help. The system, in the late 2000s, was designed to keep Americans out. When you apply for a British job online, most companies won't even look at your application unless you already have the right to work in the UK.

So, it was a catch-22. I need to get a job with a British company to be sponsored for a visa but to get a job with a British company I needed to already be in the UK. Over the years, I've applied for hundreds of job in Britain. Most never went beyond the interview phase. There was a special program called the Tier 1 visa. If you ticked enough boxes, made enough money, and could prove you wouldn't become a burden to the British taxpayer, you could move to Britain and search for a job on your own. I worked towards this visa as my career went on.

Then, in 2010, the political winds changed. The newly formed Conservative/Lib-Dem Coalition government took office on a very anti-immigration platform. They made it harder to move to the UK. They put a cap on work visas, raised requirements, and all around made it harder to move to the UK. They completely scrapped the Tier 1 visa. I'd lost the one way I could move to the UK.

By this point, Anglotopia was becoming a serious business, and I was slowly starting to make more money on the website than I was with my job. So, the goal became to figure out a way for Anglotopia to get us over to Britain. Options were thin. Since 2010, they instituted various entrepreneur visas; these looked like our way in, but those requirements were even more onerous. I would need two things, either £200,000 in cash to invest in a UK business or £50,000 from a licensed Angel investor. So, basically, I would have to win the lottery so that I could buy a visa. Anglotopia would never get me to Britain; it was too small.

No, if I was going to move to Britain, I would have to work for someone else.

Then one day, an opportunity arose.

Someone I followed on Twitter tweeted they had an opening for a digital marketing position at a London-based office. I replied right away and asked if they would sponsor for a visa for the right candidate. The CEO replied and said, in theory, yes. I applied immediately.

One week later, I found myself in London, being interviewed for the position. I worked in the office for a week, learning the ropes of the company and getting feel for the office to see if I would fit in. I was interviewed a few times. I did a couple of tests. I did a few odd jobs that needed doing. I had dinners with the staff, met the wives. I quickly became part of the team and made myself indispensable. I'll never forget the feeling of sitting in a pub next to the Thames with the owner and the CTO while they offered me the job. And the visa. And would cover the fees. And would pay me a salary that would allow me to live in London. And would help with the relocation costs. They really wanted me.

It felt like the whole country really wanted me.

They told me to think about it and make sure it was the right choice.

If you'd followed Anglotopia back in those days, you may recall me rhetorically asking the question to everyone, "If you were offered your dream, would you take it?" I was "vague booking." All the answers were, "Yes, do it!"

I accepted.

The visa process was started.

And then I stopped it. You see, it was the perfect job but at an imperfect time. Literally the day before the flight over for the interviews, we found out we were pregnant with our son. It was an exciting time already, but also a stressful one, and we'd had a lot of trouble getting and staying pregnant. So, to protect the baby and make sure it went full term, we decided that the stress of moving internationally was not the best the best course of action.

It was the right decision. The whole pregnancy was very difficult for Jackie and ended up being an emergency C-section. I can't imagine having gone through all that, just the two of us alone in Britain.

It gutted me to write the email to that company and tell them I had to turn the job down. I made Jackie hit the send button; I just couldn't bring myself to do it.

That was nine years ago as I write this. I haven't had another opportunity like that since. I refuse to believe that was our last chance to move to the UK. I'm always on the lookout for new opportunities. The problem now, though, is our comfort. We're settled now. We have two kids in school, one with special educational needs. We own a house. We have five pets that would have to be re-homed. I have 2,000 books that would have to be moved. But if an opportunity arose that allowed me to move to Britain, would I take it? In a heartbeat.

I'm in a different place now. I've had a career and left it behind. After I had to pass up the London job, I lost all passion for the corporate job I still had. It was a matter of time before I was let go from that job. Thankfully, Anglotopia had become much bigger than I'd ever imagined and was already making more than my salary. So, the day after I was fired, it was Day One at my new company, Anglotopia LLC. I've been running Anglotopia ever since. We've had our struggles. In fact, they never seem to end these days. Still, I've been very lucky since turning down that job. I've traveled to Britain several times a year, at least. It got to the point where I could go whenever I liked. In 2018, I went four times. If you had told that to 2010 Jon interviewing for that job, he would have laughed at you.

The pain of not being able to move there over the last fifteen years has been lessened by our frequent visits. But at the end of every trip, I'm always sad it's over. I'm always wondering when I can buy that one-way ticket and never have to leave.

The whole system has been made even more difficult since then as well. The work visa programs have been tightened. The requirements made on applicants increased - last time I checked, to even *get* a visa, not counting getting a company to sponsor it - I'd have to raise £10,000 (about $15,000) to pay a healthcare levy, and it's money you never see again. That's on top of the £1,000 visa fees for each of us. There are very few jobs I could even get in Britain that would justify those kinds of upfront costs.

But there is dawn on the horizon. I have not written about Brexit in this book and don't intend to write about it. I'm of two minds about Brexit. On the one hand, it's stupid and going to be a disaster for Britain. On the other hand, it may actually give us the opening we need to move to Britain. Once EU citizens can no longer freely work in the UK without visas, that will open up the job market to people outside the EU - specifically North America. Britain is already working to completely overhaul their immigration system, and, as of this writing, the official government policy is to make it easier for skilled migrants from North America to move to Britain for in-demand jobs. There's even talk of scrapping the healthcare levy. Britain also wants to negotiate a raft of new trade deals with countries around the world, and it's US government policy that migration between the two countries is a part of any trade discussions. The ideal solution would be for Britain to introduce a self-employed visa - if they did that I could continue to run Anglotopia, and that would be our source for living. I wouldn't even need a job. Either that, or some kind of special "Anglophile visa" geared toward people who have a genuine affinity for all things British (and I mean genuine) and can contribute to British society.

So, there's hope. Once Brexit actually happens, and as I'm writing this in early 2019, it's clear that nothing is going to stop the Brexit train, then the new UK immigration program may finally give us the opening we need to move to Britain. We certainly hope so; we're not getting any younger. I'm thirty-five years old now. Most countries start to discriminate the older you get for visas - they don't want people closer to retirement. But there's time.

There's still time for me to have my dream of living in an English cottage and writing about daily life in Britain. There's still plenty of time to get British citizenship and hold one of those scarlet passports (though by then they may be blue). I'm a big believer that the right opportunities will present themselves; you just have to take them. So, when you ask me why I haven't moved to Britain yet, the answer is: I've tried, and I'm still trying.

A LOVE OF ENGLISHNESS

Englishness. Britishness. Scottishness. Welshness. London-ness. It's easy to make up these words, but it's much harder to define them. I can only go on what I've watched, what I've seen, and where I've been. And after twenty years, my Anglophilia is like the layers of an onion and has evolved into a full-blown love of Englishness. It started from a desire to love something that was better than American-ness.

When you're young and impressionable, it's easy to have "grass is greener" ways of thinking. As I lived through the years of George W. Bush's wars, terror, and stupidity, I sought some solace in the outside world. I found it in England. It was easy to look at the way Britain does anything and go, "that's a better way to do it." For many years, a distaste for America is what drove my love for all things English, and it's not far out of the realm of possibility to say that many Anglophiles do this as well.

Over the years, as we've tried to move to Britain, there was a bit of a political protest as well. We wanted to show our disapproval for how America did things by leaving it. I've learned one key fact about this: *no one cares*. America is going to continue to America its way through history. It doesn't need my approval or anyone's approval. It will do as it wants. It will go through times of light and darkness. I learned that my desire to love Britain and move there didn't change when the political party in power changed. I found that after Bush left office and Obama came in, I still desired to move to Britain. I benefitted greatly under the Obama years - while I lost my job at the beginning, I grew a business to where it supported my family. I acquired health insurance. America felt like a better place.

As the pendulum swung the other way and He Who Must Not Be Named was elected, the first reflex was to research visas so we could get out. But almost three years into the man's term, we're still here. We're not particularly stuck. It's just that moving your entire family with two children (one with special needs) becomes harder when you own a house, have pets and cars, and all the accoutrement of life in America. Of course, I say all this from a position of enormous privilege. Moving abroad at this stage in our lives is not an easy proposition.

Disagreeing with the current president or political party in power is a pretty foolish reason to leave this country when there are much worse places in the world that people are desperate to flee. It will change in four or eight years. So, you have to really want to be somewhere to do it, to jump off that ledge and give up your good American life. Not liking the current occupant of the White House is a poor reason to make life changing decisions.

No, when we finally move to Britain, it will be because we really want to be there. Not because we're so dissatisfied with our life in America that the only option is to explore greener pastures somewhere else. If you apply logic to it, Britain is the last place we should consider going. They're in the throes of Brexit; there are uncertain days ahead for them (and Trump America and Post-Brexit Britain can hold hands together in turmoil). It would make more sense to move somewhere like New Zealand or Australia where they don't have these problems, where governments function, universal healthcare is a right, and there's a culture focused on enjoying life rather than work. And we've considered them all.

At the end of the day, my soul does not live in New Zealand, or Canada, or Australia. It lives in Britain, in the English countryside. Nothing else will do. When I do move there, it will be the culmination of a life's work and goals, not the desperation of someone wanting to flee a president they don't approve of.

So, what is Englishness to me? What is so attractive about English culture?

It's my culture. It's the culture of my ancestors. It's the basis of American culture, its legal history, and its philosophy. Americans tend to think our history only started in 1776 when we declared independence. But we were British long before that - for over 250 years, in fact. We were British longer than we have been American. Britain's Royal Family was our Royal Family until we chucked them out. Our grievances that lead to our independence were based on the tenant that we were being denied our rights as Englishmen. So, we did the only sensible thing, for which there was a precedent in British history - we rebelled.

Englishness to me is tea and biscuits on a cold day, or even a hot summer's day. It's a walk through the countryside. It's a visit to a Stately Home. It's laughing at your favorite dated British comedy. It's feeling inspired by my favorite Doctor Who, David Tennant. It's feeling the weight of history. It's learning about fascinating, obscure events in history. In America, there are few places where you can go *see* history. In England, you can't swing a cat without hitting some history. It's a place where even the smallest villages, like Castle Combe, can write an exhaustive history of their village that stretches back beyond the Romans.

It's reading a massive Sunday newspaper in the morning, then going out for a delicious Sunday Roast in the afternoon at a cozy, fire-warmed pub. It's reveling in the past but not living in it (just don't tell Brexiteers that). It's getting stuck in a British period film like *Master and Commander* or *Remains of the Day* and being more than entertained; it's enriching. It's binge-watching a British drama like *Inspector Morse, Foyle's War*, or *Brideshead Revisited* and being changed by the experience.

It's driving on the wrong side of the road. It's having a panic attack when you drive down a single track lane and someone comes from the opposite direction. It's being able to disagree with someone and not having to hate them or believe they're a part of some other tribe to which you don't have membership. It's a game of football on a weekend afternoon, or a genteel game of cricket on a warm summer's day. It's an education at Oxford or Cambridge (or, horror, the LSE).

A true love of Englishness is realizing it's not a utopia. It's not a perfect place. Just because somewhere is beautiful doesn't mean it's problem free. It's still inhabited by humans, trying their best to make the best of their lives and their world. They're bound together in a shared history and a shared monoculture that we just don't have here in Indiana. Here the vapid emptiness of Hollywood binds us together, and we don't like to admit that.

I think toast sums up perfectly what I love about English culture. Yes, toast! It's difficult to imagine a more mundane breakfast food. It's a food so basic to our diet that we don't think of it as something particularly special. Then again, we're not British, are we? In Britain, however, toast is a treat.

When I was interviewing with that British company for a job in 2010 and I spent a week in the offices, working with the team and getting a feel for things. I got to sit across from the CEO and connect with him. I also got an education in how a British office operates. It's very much different from an American office (so many cups of tea). One thing stood out to me the most.

His PA, personal assistant, offered to get him a sandwich or toast.

"Oh, yes, toast!" he said excitedly.

I should tell you, though, that his response took me quite by surprise. This CEO was a tough guy. He had a checkered past and rose above it to start one of Britain's leading software companies. He was impressive but intimidating; I wanted to impress him. It seemed strange to me that he would get so excited about toast.

He was a bloody CEO!

His PA came back a few minutes later with toast, and when he bit into it, I swear his eyes rolled into the back of his head.

"Oh, lovely toast, thank you."

The whole scene was rather strange to me.

Toast is the most unglamorous food you can imagine. But as I've traveled there and had toast plenty of times in Britain, I've realized why they think toast is such a treat. British toast is amazing. British bread is so much richer and fuller than our thin and sugary American bread. So, when you slather a piece of bread with good British butter and then slather some strawberry jam or marmalade on top, it is a truly wonderful dining experience. I get toast for breakfast whenever I can. It is amazing. If you don't believe me, watch British TV - you will see people enjoying toast all the time.

Toast!

Toast!

Of all things, toast!

Maybe it has its roots in the privations of World War II when bread and butter were scarce.

I have my own checkered history with British toast. When I make it myself, it's usually in Updown Cottage. The toaster there is a strange contraption. At home, I put toast in my toaster, push the lever down and a few minutes later toast pops up. This flummoxing British toaster doesn't automatically pop up. You set a timer and then pull the lever to lower the toast. When the timer goes off, you have to raise the toast yourself. I did not understand this the first few times I used this toaster.

I have burnt lots of toast in this toaster.

When it toasts it perfectly, it's amazing. We've actually looked into finding one of these toasters back home in America, but they just don't exist. We prefer our easy, thoughtless toasters.

The propensity for the British to love toast is a great example of the British enjoying the simple, unpretentious pleasures in life. Toast is to Englishness as patriotism is to Americaness. Like anyone or anything you love, though, you learn to love it for its flaws. Englishness is not a perfect culture, but it's endlessly fascinating, and I will be a student of it for the rest of my life. My only hope is that one day, the English will welcome me into the fold as one of them. I won't be a poser who just loves the idea of England but doesn't love the real England. I want my Anglophilia to mean something. I want it to have mattered.

MY BRITISH DREAM

I was supposed to be writing this final chapter this week from a desk in the sitting room at Updown Cottage in Shaftesbury, Dorset. But life had other plans. Running a business like Anglotopia has its ups and downs, and we've had more downs than ups lately, so that meant we had to take 2019 off from traveling to the UK (editing this in 2020 it looks like 2020 will be Britain free too). It's okay; I've had enough visits there in the last few years to keep me going until I'm able to go back. Still, it would have been special to write this final, most important chapter from the place that really started it all.

So, let's just pretend that I am, okay?

There are three true loves in my life.

My wife.

My children.

And England.

In that order. Jackie would disagree with that order and is convinced England will always be my first love. It was certainly at the top before I met her, and it was there before the kids. But my love of England has matured greatly, and most of that maturity came after I met her; she's such a big part of my happy memories of England. So, my dear, don't worry, I'll always choose you first.

As I pondered this book and thought about what I wanted to say, the biggest thing I wanted to get out of it was my own answer to the question I get asked so much. Not only that, but I want my love for Britain to mean something. What was it all for? I want Britannia to embrace me and tell me she understands and that I matter to her. I want Britannia to know how much I love her and I want her to love me back.

That will mean that, inevitably, I will have to live there. And I will live there.

I've spent my whole adult life wanting to be somewhere else. How do you have any amount of happiness like that? I'll admit, it's a challenge, but also the ultimate first world problem. It's not a real problem. No one really cares that I love a foreign country so much it hurts. But it matters to me.

Oh, you're commuting every day to Chicago? I'd rather be in London.

Oh, you're reading a mountain of English books to finish your degree? I'd rather be doing this at Oxford.

Oh, you're buying what is essentially a dream house? I'd rather it was a cottage in the English countryside. It will never be enough.

Oh, you have two lovely children? Yes, they're lovely. They'd be better with British accents.

So, I will only find true happiness simply by living there.

If you would have asked me twenty years ago how I would live in Britain, I would have said I wanted to live in London and be a Londoner. I've grown beyond that. I can't imagine anything worse than trying to live in London with its huge population, pollution, and high cost of living. Don't get me wrong, I love London, but as a place to visit for short periods of time. Living there would be terrible.

No, I want to live in the English countryside. It will be in Dorset. I'm not so foolish to think one day I'll live on Gold Hill. That would certainly be nice, but actually living on Gold Hill presents practical realities that don't really appeal to even the people who happen to live on Gold Hill. Gold Hill is lovely and perfect and my conception of what England is. It's critical to my soul. But I don't think I could endure tourists looking through my front window every day like an amusement park.

So, it will be somewhere in Dorset. It will have a view. I would like to live somewhere in the Blackmore Vale. With Jackie's love for the sea, I suspect I'll have to live by the sea, though. Which is fine, there are plenty of beautiful villages down by the Dorset coast.

That bit of information is most critical. It has to be a village.

I want a cottage in a village in the countryside, near the seaside. It will be at least 200 to 300 years old. A modern bungalow will just not do. It would be nice to have a thatched roof, but I'm aware of the upkeep and fire risk there. So, that's not a deal breaker. I want the cottage to ooze with history. I want it to be one of those places that you look at on the cover of a book and think, "That would be a lovely place to live." I think I'd like it to be Georgian, maybe even brick or stone. It will have a lovely garden that will change throughout the year (but I will have a gardener, because, let's be honest, I am not green-fingered). This cottage won't be in the center of the village, it will be on the outskirts, but not so far I can't walk into town.

The village itself will be like other English villages. Its high street will have long ago turned into homes. Perhaps there's still a village shop (probably community owned), a nice cozy pub with good food, and a picturesque church (that I'll never visit because I'm not religious) whose bells will ring out for important events. The village, despite long ago becoming a bedroom community, will still have a school and thriving social calendar of fetes and celebrations throughout the year - all of which I will gladly try to take part. By the time this actually happens, my children will probably be grown up, so I don't think they'll be going to the village school.

The cottage will need to be near several public footpaths so I can take an Ordnance Survey map out every day and learn the trails of my area. I want to learn it intimately to the point where I won't need the map anymore and will never get lost. I want to know all the secret places and ruins and castles and hill forts and trig points. As I wrote about previously, I can't walk outside my front door and go for a walk in the Hoosier countryside. Nearby public footpaths in my English cottage will be critical to this British dream being a success.

Ideally, by the time we go, a self-employed visa will be an option, and I'll be able to go over and continue to run Anglotopia as I do now. Instead of being 4,000 miles away, I'll be in England, and be able to write more than I can imagine from here in Indiana. I'll be able to write daily about life in England. Every observation will be an article one day. I'll take pictures every day. When I'm not wedded to the house writing, I'll go on adventures around Britain, near and far. I'll explore all the castles and ruins and Stately Homes I can handle. I'll venture out to remote Scottish Islands and distant Cornish coastal villages. I'll pop into London by train to go to a press preview of the latest exhibitions.

At my side through all of it will be Jackie. I won't be so presumptuous as to imagine her British life, that's for her to imagine. But I know she wants to do it. We just need the opportunity. What will happen to our life back in America? We don't know. I suspect we'll always own this house, so we have a place to stay when we visit family. I don't know if we'd cut ties completely. We worked so hard for what we have here. There's also the matter of my library of 2,000 books. There's no way I can bring that with us. I'll start a new library in the cottage. I'm sure the cottage will be small, so there won't be a dedicated room for it. There will be stacks of books everywhere, maddening Jackie to no end.

And we'll live there. We'll inhabit our place in the English countryside. We'll experience English winters and summers and springs and autumns. We'll see the rhythms of village life throughout the year. We'll make friends. Family will visit it. Parked outside of the cottage will be a late model Land Rover Defender (in British racing green of course). We'll have a couple rascally cats, rescued from the local shelter (unless we bring our cats with us from the US). We'll probably have a dog; I'll need someone to accompany me on my walks when Jackie has had enough. We'll become a part of the landscape. We'll tut-tut when the local council does something daft. We'll have to deal with the madness of waste and recycling.

And one day, after the requisite amount of time has passed, I will take the Life in the UK citizenship test (and hopefully pass it the first time), and then a year after that, I'll take an oath to the Queen (or King) and be given my own British passport. Whether this happens soon or when I'm old and grey, I want to be British one day. I know I'll never truly be British, but I want to get as close as I can. And one day, far in the future when I'm returning to Britain from abroad, instead of filing into the Non-UK citizen queue, I'll get to file into the queue for British citizens. I'll get to be cross with how long it takes with my fellow Brits. Then, I'll be welcomed home.

Why do I love Britain so much? Because it's wonderful. And I want everyone to know how wonderful it is.

ACKNOWLEDGEMENTS

Creation doesn't happen in a vacuum. This would book would not exist without the input from countless people. First, I would like to thank authors Kathryn Aalto and James Rebanks. Their decision to host the Rural Writer's Institute in 2018 was a life changing event for me, personally and creatively. Without what I experienced there, this book simply would not exist. Most of it was written after my time there. I hope this book is a good example of what can come about when writers gather together in beautiful, creative, open, and safe environment. James also deserves an extra thanks for support provided after the event, when during a dark time, when nothing was going right (with business, work, finances, and this book), he gave me the motivational kick in the arse that was needed to finish the first draft of this book.

I must also thank my mother, the first Anglophile I knew and who only ever encouraged my interest in Britain. It had to have been terrifying to travel alone with her teenage son to a completely foreign country. And then to be treated so poorly by that son. I have regretted it ever since.

Thank you to anyone who has read Anglotopia over the years, the fact that I can make a living from sharing my passion about Britain is an amazing thing, and I'm living the dream every day (even when it's a nightmare). The website has allowed us to meet so many wonderful people over the years who have shown us their bits of Britain, explained British culture to us, or have become friends. In all our years of travel in Britain, the most wonderful thing we have gotten out of it are the friends we made along the way. I will not name them as most would probably prefer to remain anonymous.

I cannot forget to make a special mention for those who have helped care for our children while we've traveled the length and breadth of Britain over the years - my parents, Lauren Schara, and Melissa Finan.

I must also single out Erin Moore, someone who has written for Anglotopia for many years, sharing her experiences about life in Britain. She graciously agreed to developmentally edit this book and her suggestions have turned this book into what you see now. Her unbiased advice proved invaluable in turning this into the book I set out to write two years ago.

And, finally, I must acknowledge the most important person in all of this, my wife Jackie. She had made everything possible. My wife is not an Anglophile. I don't hold it against her. Big of me, I know. If anything, she could be charitably described as a reluctant Anglophile. She loves me and understands how important England is to me, and so comes along for the ride. And we've been on lots of rides together. She has grown to love Britain in her own way, but not nearly as much as me. It turns out, though, that despite her general disinterest in all things British, she's the perfect travel partner.

We've been on so many great adventures together. We found Gold Hill together. We got lost walking in the English Countryside together. We laughed as we got stuck and fell into English mud together. We survived traveling to the Diamond Jubilee celebrations with our very young children together. We survived five weeks of Christmas holiday travel with our very young children. We found an abandoned village, explored grand Stately Homes, crossed miles-long bridges, rode through the Chunnel. We drove from Land's End in Cornwall to John O'Groats in Scotland.

Earnest Hemingway once said, "Never go on trips with anyone you do not love." In my opinion, that is the only way to travel. Trips without Jackie feel like trips that shouldn't have happened. I highly recommend everybody get a Jackie. You won't regret it.

ABOUT THE AUTHOR

Jonathan Thomas was born in the early 80s, and apart from a short stint in Texas, spent most of his childhood in Northern Indiana, just outside of Chicago. During high school, he found a poster of Gold Hill, in Shaftesbury, Dorset in a Hobby Lobby and instantly fell in love. That poster hung on his wall for years and motivated him to visit England for the first time in 2001 and finally to visit Shaftesbury in 2004. It was a life-changing experience for him.

Jonathan met his wife Jacqueline in remedial math class at Columbia College in Chicago. Both later attended Purdue University, where they completed their studies. Jonathan studied English literature and language. During their college years, they took their extra student aid money and financed yearly trips to England where they gained their first travel knowledge and eventually cemented their mutual love for all things British (well, Jonathan's anyway).

After college, Jonathan went to work in the internet marketing world, changing jobs every few years as he gained experience in digital marketing. He could not find a website that fed his Anglophilia, so he decided to start one. In 2007, in a closet in Chicago, he founded Anglotopia.net as a home online for Anglophiles around the world. It rode the blogging wave of the late 2000s and became the world's most trafficked website dedicated to all things British.

Anglotopia became Jonathan's full-time job in 2011, weeks before the Royal Wedding of William and Kate. Over the years, he's attended other major Royal events, appeared on the BBC and other media venues, and has been published in The Art of Manliness, The Independent and Dorset Life magazine. He publishes articles every day on Anglotopia.net and its sister website Londontopia. net, and puts out a quarterly print magazine.

Lightning Source UK Ltd.
Milton Keynes UK
UKHW041656030620
364279UK00002B/73/J